PEARL OF GREAT PRICE

A Literary Translation of the
Middle English *Pearl*

David Gould

University Press of America,® Inc.
Lanham · Boulder · New York · Toronto · Plymouth, UK

Library of Congress Control Number: 2012938250
ISBN: 978-0-7618-5924-6 (paperback : alk. paper)
eISBN: 978-0-7618-5925-3

Table of Contents

Preface
On Translating *Pearl*

Robert Frost, it is said, defined poetry as "what gets lost in translation." It is a simple matter to render the approximate meaning of a text written in one language into another language, although the systems of sounds and signs by which these meanings are conveyed may differ profoundly. However, poetry is a complex art employing language as its medium, which uses not only the meanings, but the sounds of language as well; poems are works of art whose aesthetic effects transcend mere meaning, even the "deeper meaning" beloved of English teachers. Thus a translation of a poem which renders only its meaning into the target language loses precisely those aspects of language which differentiate poetry from prose. This is true even if the poetry is to be translated not from a different language, but from an earlier version of the same language, to the extent that the original is unintelligible to modern speakers of the language, and its sounds and rhythms differ from those of the modern language.

The Middle English *Pearl* is one of the most intricate and beautiful poems ever written in the English language. In a tour de force of technical virtuosity, it combines the four-stress alliterative line of the native English tradition with the French poetic tradition of end-rhymed stanzas imported into England after the Norman Conquest. It also employs an elaborate system of concatenation, in which each group of five stanzas is linked together by the use of a key word or phrase in its first and last lines; the stanza groups, moreover, are linked together like a daisy chain by the repetition of the key word from the previous stanza group at the beginning of the first stanza of the following group. The last stanza of the poem is linked to the first in the same manner, so that the poem comes full circle: it is "round without end," and "fair without flaw," like the perfect pearl which it describes. Unfortunately for the reader ignorant of Middle English, however, this exquisite poem is written in a form of the English language which is, in the words of J.R.R. Tolkien, one of the poem's more successful translators, "practically unintelligible to the modern reader" (2). The present work is an attempt to make this "pearl of great price" accessible to a contemporary audience, and as far as possible, to recreate for that audience the aesthetic experience of reading the original poem.

To read great poetry in its original language would amply repay the effort of learning the language in which it is written, "had we but world enough, and time." Translation almost always results in an inferior substitute for the original poem in the target language; what is more, it is difficult for readers ignorant of the original language to judge the quality of a translation, as they cannot compare it with the original poem. Readers are often forced to choose between a literal and a literary translation, each of which has characteristic strengths and weaknesses.

In a literal translation, ideally each word in the translation corresponds to a word in the original; the focus is on accuracy in rendering the meaning of the original, with ornamental aspects of language such as rhythm and meter, and sound effects such as rhyme and alliteration, considered of secondary importance if considered at all. The ideal literal translation is word for word, scholarly, and accurate. The emphasis is on "letter" rather than "spirit"; to quote Matthew Arnold, on "matter" rather than "manner" (*On Translating Homer* 13-14). A literal translation is best at preserving the meaning of the original, but insofar as it does not preserve the rhyme scheme, alliteration, meter, and other prosodic features of the poem, it does not give us any impression of the poet's artistry. Many turns of phrase which in the original serve as essential components of the poetic form and thus contribute to the beauty of the poem may seem gratuitous and therefore ugly in a literal translation.

In a literary translation, on the other hand, the translator strives to recreate the poetic effects of the original poem, often at the expense of literal equivalency. The ideal literary translation is poetic, creative, and "true"; form is of first importance; the emphasis is on "spirit" rather than "letter"; "manner" rather than "matter." The problem with this approach is that the translator must substitute his own poetic skills for those of the original author. Imitation of the prosodic aspects of the poem in a translation, moreover, almost always necessitates straying from the meaning and diction of the original; most literary translations are actually imitations or paraphrases rather than true translations. Even when the translator is a talented poet, a literary translation often gives the reader a false impression of the original poem.

An expedient for minimizing the shortcomings of either a literal or a literary translation, which is useful when the reader has some knowledge of the original language, is the dual-language translation. This is especially useful in cases where poetry is being translated from an earlier version of the same language, as with the present translation. In college textbooks, Middle English poems are often presented in the original language, but with modernized spelling and with marginal glosses of words and phrases unfamiliar to the modern reader, so that instead of reading the poem entirely in translation, the reader is helped to puzzle out the meaning of the original. More helpful still, although it entails learning more of the original language, is the side-by-side or interlinear translation, where the translation acts as a "crib" or "pony" to the original; obviously, the more literal the translation in this case, the more helpful it will be to the reader in deciphering the meaning of the original. A unique feature of my translation of *Pearl* is that each stanza is illustrated on the facing page by a copy of the corresponding stanza of the poem in the original handwriting, prepared by tracing from photocopies of the facsimile of the manuscript published by the Early English Text Society. My intention in undertaking this time-consuming process was to provide a reading copy of the poem in its original language and orthography, free of the difficulties in deciphering the text of the manuscript facsimile, and to give the modern reader the opportunity to experience the aesthetic pleasures involved in reading a hand-written medieval manuscript, an opportunity which is normally available only to a few scholars. Modern translations or editions of *Pearl* usually leave the reader at several removes from the original; my translation intends to provide a text which is immediately comprehensible to the modern reader while at the same time forcibly reminding the reader of its original form and language. I welcome a close comparison between my translation and the original poem; my hope is that the juxtaposition of the translation with a reproduction of the handwritten original will draw readers into a comparison of the two in which each will throw light on the other. I hope this juxtaposition will also serve as an incentive to those who are approaching the poem for the first time to delve into the complexities of the Middle English language and medieval orthography. A transcription of the Middle English text, instructions on how to read the manuscript hand, and a glossary, are appended for those who wish to read the original poem; for those who are less ambitious, the illustrations have a beauty of their own as abstract designs.

Although my translation of *Pearl* is a literary translation insofar as it attempts to preserve the poetic form of the original poem, I have also attempted to make it as literal a translation as possible—far more literal than most literary translations. The ideal translation, in my opinion, would be one literal enough so that each word in the original would have its equivalent in the translation, and vice versa, while the meter, alliteration, rhyme scheme, and stanza pattern with its linking words and refrains would be preserved entire. In practice, no translation can attain this ideal; however, I have attempted to steer a middle course between imitating the prosodic aspects of the poem—its sound patterns—and rendering its exact meaning word for word. I have been enabled to do so by taking an approach that, insofar as it is novel, may be of some theoretical interest as well: quite simply, I have attempted to preserve as much as I could of the original language of the poem in my translation, substituting modern forms of words for their etymons in the poem wherever possible, and only replacing those words which are unintelligible or obsolete in Modern English. By this simple expedient, much of the poem is rendered intelligible, and at the same time, a good percentage of the original rhyme and alliteration is preserved. The problem of translation then becomes a matter of reconstructing in Modern English those portions of the original poem which cannot be rendered intelligible by this process, rather than a matter of constructing an entirely new poem, with new rhymes, alliterations, and link-words, alongside the original. This is in many ways a more difficult task than preparing either an entirely literal or an entirely literary translation. I conclude this preface with a short discussion of some of the practical problems involved in this approach in the hope that it may be of interest to the general reader, and of use to poets, scholars, and translators of Middle English.

In any language, words consist of two parts, sound and meaning. Preserving as much as possible of the wording of the original poem in Modern English leads to two different kinds of problems: problems with the sounds of words, and problems with their meanings. In a literal translation meaning is of most importance, and the sounds of words are unimportant, whereas in a literary translation sound may at times take precedence over meaning, when the sound of a word is important to the poetic form of the poem—for example, in words which rhyme or alliterate, or whose rhythm is essential to the metrical form of the poem.

One of the most difficult technical problems for a translator of *Pearl* is reproducing the rhyme scheme of the poem, due to the paucity of rhymes in Modern English. The stanzas rhyme ababababbcbc, thus requiring four rhyming words for the a-rhyme, six for the b-rhyme, and two for the c-rhyme. This is a rock on which many translators wreck. If one constructs an entirely new set of rhyme-words which conforms to the original rhyme scheme, one can hardly avoid straying from the meaning and diction of the original, or what is worse, resorting to far-fetched rhymes. On the other hand, if the original rhyme-words are replaced with modern equivalents, a good proportion of them will still rhyme, although the sounds of the words may be different in Modern English. This leaves the translator with the difficult task of filling in rhyme schemes in which some of the rhymes are in place, and others missing. For those rhyme words in the original which have no modern equivalents, or whose modern equivalents do not rhyme, it is obviously necessary to introduce new rhyme words into the rhyme scheme, whatever difficulties this may entail. For the class of rhyme words whose modern equivalents rhyme imperfectly, however, I have often found it expedient to relax the rules of rhyme in my translation, in order to conform more closely to the original in other respects. For example, in stanza XIII, 5, the b-rhymes are *ryf, vyf, lyf, stryf, dryf,* and *styf,* which rhyme perfectly in Middle English. If we translate them into their modern equivalents, we get "rife," "wife," "life," "strife," "drive," and "stiff." Four of these still rhyme perfectly in modern English (although the vowel sounds have shifted), but the other two have changed their pronunciation: the "f" in *dryf* has changed to a "v" in modern English, so that instead of rhyme we have assonance; the long vowel in *styf* has shortened so that instead of rhyme we have consonance. Nevertheless, it surely does less violence to the original to preserve these imperfect rhyme words intact in the translation than to seek to replace them with perfect rhymes, with the attendant neccesity of straying from the words (and meaning) of the original.

A good proportion of those rhyme-words in the original whose modern equivalents rhyme imperfectly consists of words which in Middle English are or can be accented on the final syllable, but which in modern English must be accented on the penultimate syllable. For example, in stanza VIII, 1, the b-rhyme words are *errour, honour, flour, fauour, dousour,* and *fasor,* all of which are accented on the last syllable. The last two of these words have no modern equivalents; the first four have modern equivalents which are accented on the first syllable: "error," "honor," "flower," and "favor." Again, it does less violence to the poem to commit the venial sin of rhyming unaccented syllables than it does to replace these four rhyme-words—which are placed in the emphatic position at the end of the line not only because of their sounds, but also because of their meanings—with perfect rhymes, with the attendant changes in meaning and diction which that would entail. The use of near-rhymes, and of assonance and consonance, in place of rhyme, does not greatly detract from the effect which the repetition of sounds at the line-ends has upon the reader, and it allows the translator to stick more closely to the diction and literal meaning of the original than would otherwise be possible in a verse translation.

How to deal with alliteration is another difficult problem for translators of *Pearl,* since alliteration is rarely used systematically in modern English poetry, and never as an essential element of poetic meter, as it was in Old and Middle English alliterative poetry—with the result that the modern reader's aesthetic appreciation of alliteration may not be as great as that of the poet's original audience, which would have been familiar with alliteration not as an ornamental sound-device for occasional use in poetry, but as an organizing principle as closely associated with poetry as rhyme is to readers of modern English poetry. The *Pearl*-poet does not stick as strictly to the alliterative pattern derived from the proto-Germanic alliterative verse-line in *Pearl* as he does in *Patience, Cleanness,* and *Sir Gawain and the Green Knight,* which make little or no use of rhyme. Between one-quarter and one-third of the lines in *Pearl* contain no alliteration at all, and about fifteen percent alliterate on all four stressed syllables, including the last, which in Old English alliterative poetry normally did not alliterate. Nevertheless, the amount of alliteration in the poem is far greater than in most modern poems, and what is more, the alliterative tradition has shaped the diction of the poem in many ways. For example, the expression *comly anvnnder cambe* (line 775) ["comely one under comb" in my translation] as a kenning for "woman," is a formulaic expression adapted to the needs of the alliterative line, thought it may seem far-fetched to modern readers. If the alliterative meter seems "harsh and stiff and rugged" (Tolkien 2) to those unaccustomed to it, it is probably because they are not used to so much alliteration. This leads many translators of Pearl to practice a sort of "alliterative avoidance," even those whose avowed object is an imitation of the alliterative form of the original, such as J.R.R. Tolkien, and Marie Borroff. For example, line 80 of the poem alliterates on each of the four stressed syllables in the line, as do many other lines in the poem: *Wyth schymeryng schene ful schrylle thay schynde* ["with shimmering sheen they shine so sheer" in my translation]. But translators are reluctant to reproduce this level of alliteration. Tolkien translates the line "They shone with a shimmer of dazzling hue" (126), which preserves two out of the original four alliterations in the line; Marie Boroff translates it "They shot forth light in shimmering play" (3), again with two out of the original four alliterations in the line. This aversion to alliteration extends even to expressions in the poem which translate directly into Modern English without any change of meaning; for example, line 136 of the poem reads as follows: *To the tenth dole of tho gladnes glade.* "Gladness glad" in Modern English means exactly the same thing as *gladnes glade* in Middle English; however, translators avoid the equivalent expression for some reason. Tolkien translates this line "For a tithe of the joyful joys displayed" (128), which at least imitates the repetition and alliteration of the original; Boroff translates it "To sustain one tenth of that pure joy" (4), with no alliteration at all. In line 938, the poet calls the pearl-maiden *specyal spyce*, again an expression which translates directly into Modern English as "special spice." In both Middle English and Modern English this is metaphorical language, but it is no more difficult for a modern reader to grasp the metaphor than it would have been for a medieval reader—in fact, this metaphor is part of the spice imagery which abounds in the poem, and which forms part of its aesthetic. Yet Tolkien translates the expression as "peerless maid" (120), dispensing with both the metaphor and the alliteration, and Boroff translates it as "spice heaven-sent" (24), preserving the imagery but losing the alliteration. Few modern translators share the *Pearl*-poet's exuberant delight in the richness of alliteration.

Another difficulty in translation is words in Middle English which are recognizable to the modern reader but whose meaning has changed in Modern English, either subtly or substantially. In a literal translation it would be important to substitute modern words exactly equivalent in meaning for these words, whereas in a literary translation the sound of a word is sometimes more important than its exact meaning. In the line just quoted, for example, *schymeryng* is a noun in Middle English, and *schene* an adjective, whereas in my translation, "shimmering" is an adjective and "sheen" a noun; in a literal translation, this difference would be significant, whereas in a literary translation, the distinction (not to say difference) between a shimmering which shines and a sheen which shimmers is insignificant: it is the sound of the words which matters most. Another example is the word *space* in, *Fro spot my spyryt þer sprang in space* (line 61) ["From that spot my spirit sprang up in space" in my translation]. E.V. Gordon argues that here the phrase "in space" means "not 'into space' (meaning 'into spatial distance'), which is a recent use, but 'after a time'" (49). I believe Gordon to be wrong as to the literal meaning of this word (as can be proven from a number of fourteenth century quotations in the OED), and agree with Morton W. Bloomfield, who argued that "In the fourteenth century it was believed that one's spirit did travel in space in a vision or even in sleep" (Vantuono 106). However, even were Gordon correct about the literal meaning of the phrase, it still would make sense to preserve the word "space" in a literary translation, as in this particular instance the sound of the word, which alliterates with *spot*, *spyryt*, and *sprang*, and which rhymes with *grace*, *face* and *wace* (Modern English "was"), is more important than its precise meaning. This is far better than to substitute another word or expression which would preserve the exact literal meaning of the original, at the cost of losing the rich alliteration and rhyme of the word *space*, and of having to substitute another word that although its precise equivalent in meaning, would necessitate either destroying the alliteration and rhyme scheme of the poem or substituting entirely different rhymes and alliterations throughout the stanza—a process which would surely lead to more wrenching of meaning than the preservation of the original word.

Another problem for the translator is imitation of the diction of the poem in Modern English. Imitation of the diction of *Pearl* is complicated by several factors. The first is that the poem is not written in the southern dialect of Middle English from which modern Standard English is derived, but from a dialect of the northwest Midlands which historically had little influence on modern literary English. Moreover, the diction is shaped by the metrical needs of the alliterative meter, which results in a number of expressions which may seem strange to a modern ear. While readers familiar with the history of English literature are comfortable with the wrenching of normal English syntax which results from the necessity of placing rhyme-words in the emphatic position at the ends of lines, because rhyme has been used as an organizing principle in English poetry for centuries, the artificial poetic diction which was created in response to the needs of the alliterative meter is not as familiar to most readers. Thus expressions which have been shaped by the needs of the alliterative meter, such as the kenning "comely one under comb" for "woman," which would have been instantly intelligible and perhaps even familiar to readers versed in the alliterative tradition, may appear strange and even distasteful to modern readers, who are not familiar with the use of alliteration as an organizing principle in versification. For these reasons, as Tolkien pointed out, the diction of *Pearl* may appear to be "at a superficial glance . . . archaic, queer, crabbed, and rustic" (Tolkien 3), rather than "courtly, wise, and well-bred–educated, indeed learned" (Tolkien 4), as it would have appeared to its original audience. However, a translation should not appear archaic, queer, crabbed and rustic simply because the original poem appears so to the reader unfamiliar with the alliterative tradition. Many translators deliberately choose archaic language in translating the poem, presumably to give an impression of its age. I have found that the process of preserving as much of the original language of the poem as possible, as explained above, by itself lends an archaic flavor to the diction of the poem, and so have not felt the need to resort to the use of deliberately archaic diction; I have used "thee" and "thou" sparingly, for example, most often in biblical quotations or to indicate moments of particular intimacy between the narrator and the pearl-maiden. I have tried at all times to imitate the smooth flow of the original poem, which in spite of its complexity is seldom forced or awkward. I have attempted throughout to employ diction which would seem natural to the modern reader; while at the same time I have not hesitated to use language which would be familiar to anyone well versed in the poetic tradition in Modern English, even if some of the words are archaic. Above all I have tried to translate the poet's characteristic figurative language literally even where the frame of reference might seem unusual to the modern reader, for example, "I stood as still as a dazed quail," "I stood as staid as a hawk in hall," "her hue more white than whale bone," "anger gains you not a cress," or "though you dance like a wounded doe." While the poet's choice of words may seem forced at times, due to the exigencies of rhyme or the requirements of the alliterative tradition, for the most part it is as fresh and original today as it was in the fourteenth century.

David Gould
Kingshill, VI
January 7, 2011

Acknowledgements

This book could not have been completed without the invaluable and in-defatigable assistance of Dr. Robin Sterns, who did the layout for me, helped me overcome technical problems with the graphic images, and patiently put up with my many changes and mid-course corrections.

Much of the work on this book was carried out during a sabbatical leave from the University of the Virgin Islands; thanks are due to (then) Provost Al Hassan Musah, for approving a "Margin for Excellence" grant which enabled me to travel to England and carry out research in the British Library. Thanks are due as well to the British Library for permission to use the cover image, to the staff of the Manuscript Reading Room for their assistance, and to Stephen and Melanie Peacock, who put me up, and put up with me (mostly) during my stay in London.

Thanks are also due to Lil Copan, who got me started on this project more than fifteen years ago, by asking me to translate selected stanzas of *Pearl* for a book she was editing. Several stanzas of my translation of the poem first appeared in *Images of Heaven: Reflections on Glory*, published by Harold Shaw Publishers in 1996; permission to reprint is gratefully acknowledged.

This book set in Bergamo with special characters in Cardo by David Perry.

Pearl

The kingdom of heaven is like unto a merchant man, seeking goodly pearls: who, when he had found one pearl of great price, went and sold all that he had, and bought it.

—Matthew 13: 45-6.

I, 1

Pearl, pleasant for a prince's play
To subtly set in gold so fair
Out of all the orient, I dare say
There never yet was a pearl her peer
So round, so perfect in every way   5
So small, so smooth her sides were
Wheresoever I judged of gems so gay
I set her apart as singular
Alas! She escaped from my tender care
In an herb garden, out of my hand it shot   10
I die, dejected, in deep despair
For that priceless pearl without a spot

Syþen í þat spote hit fro me sprange
ofte haf I wayted wyschande þat wele
þat wont watz whyle deuoyde my wrange
& heuen my happe & al my hele
þᵗ dotz bot þrych my hert þrange
my breste in bale bot bolne & bele
ȝet þoȝt me neuer so swete a sange
as stylle stounde let to me stele
for soþe þ fleten to me fele
to þenke hir color so clad í clot
O moul þ marrez a myry juele
my þuy perle wytouten spotte

I, 2

Since in that spot it from me sprang
Oft have I waited, wanting that wealth
That once was wont to right my wrong   15
Change my luck, and restore my health
And by its absence my heart is wrung
My soul in sorrow but burns and swells
Yet heard I never so sweet a song
As in quiet hours now to me steals   20
For in truth, many visions my spirit feels
To think of her beauty, buried in dirt
O Earth, you spoil the best of jewels
My own dear pearl without a spot

þat spot of spycez mot nedez sprede
þer such rychez to rot is runnen
blomez blayke & blwe & rede
þer schynez ful schyr agayn þe sunne
flor & fryte may not be fede
þer hit doun drof in moldez dunne
for vch gresse mot grow of graynez dede
no whete were elles to wonez wonne
of goud vche goude is ay bygonne
so semly a sede may no3t fayly not
þat spryngande spycez vp ne sponne
of þat precios perle wythouten spotte

1, 3

That spot with spices must needs be spread   25
Where such a richness to rot has run
Blossoms yellow and blue and red
There shine full sheer against the sun
Flower and fruit can never fade
Where it has down in the dark earth gone   30
Out of dead grain grows each grass blade
Else never would wheat to the barn be won
Each good is ever from good begun
So seemly a seed could fail not
So that flourishing spices should not be sprung   35
From that precious pearl without a spot

To þat spot þat I in speche expoun
I entred in þat erber grene
In Auguste in a hygh seysoun
Quen corne is coruen wyth crokeʒ kene
On huyle þer perle hit trendeled doun
Schadowed þis worteʒ ful schyre & schene
Gilofre gyngure & gromylyoun
& pyonys powdered ay by twene
ʒif hit watʒ semly on to sene
A fayr reflayr ʒet fro hit flot
Þer wonys þat worþyly I wot & wene
My precious perle wythouten spot

1, 4

To that spot upon which I in speech expound
I entered in to that garden green
When August's holy days came round
When corn is cut with sickles keen   40
On the hill that the pearl had trundled down
Bright flowers had fashioned a shady screen
Where gromwell, ginger, and cloves abound
With peonies scattered in between
If it was seemly to be seen   45
As fair a fragrance did from it float
Where abides, I believe, that worthy queen
My precious pearl without a spot

Bifore þat spot my honde I spend
for care ful colde þat to me caʒt
A deuely dele in my hert dened
þaʒ reson sette my seluen saʒt
I playned my perle þat þ þer gened
wyth fyrre styllez þat faste faʒt
þaʒ kynde of kryst me comfort kened
my wreched wylle I wo ny wraʒte
I felle vpon þat floury flaʒt
suche odor to my hernez ʃhot
I slode vpon a slepyng-slaʒte
on þat pcos perle wᵗ outen spot

1, 5

Before that spot I wrung my hands
For care full cold that had me caught   50
A doleful dolor in my heart denned
Though reason resignation taught
I mourned my pearl that there was pent
With arguments that fiercely fought
Though Christ's sweet nature comfort lent   55
My wretched will its own woe wrought
I fell upon that flowery plat
Such fragrance through my senses shot
I sank into a fainting fit
On that precious pearl without a spot   60

Fro spot my spyryt þer sprang in space
my body on balke þer bod in sweuen
my goste is gon in Godes grace
In auenture þer meruaylez meuen
I ne wyste in þis worlde quere þat hit wace
bot I knew me keste þer klyfez cleuen
Toward a foreste I bere þe face
Where rych rokkez wer to dyscreuen
þe lyʒt of hem myʒt no mon leuen
þe glemande glory þat of hem glent
For wern neuer webbez þat wyʒez weuen
Of half so dere adubbemente

II, 1

From that spot my spirit sprang up in space
My body lay sleeping upon the grave
But my soul was gone by God's grace
On a venture to where marvels live
I know not where in the world it was   65
But I know I alit where cliffs cleave
And toward a forest I turned my face
Where precious stones shone bright and brave
Their radiance might no man believe
The gleaming glory that from them glanced   70
For never were clothes that mortals weave
Of half so much magnificence

Dubbed wern alle þo downez sydez
Wyth crystal klyffez so cler of kynde
Holte wodez bryȝt aboute hem bydez
of bollez as blwe as ble of ynde
as bornyst syluer þe lef onslydez
þat þike con trylle on uch a tynde
quen glem of glodez agaynz hem glydez
wyth schymeryng schene ful schrylle þay schynde
þe grauayl þat on grounde con grynde
wern precious perlez of oryente
þe sunnebemez bot blo & blynde
In respecte of þat adubbement

II, 2

Those hillsides were magnificent
With cliffs of crystal bright and clear
Tall groves of trees upon them stand   75
With bright blue boles. With leaves as fair
As burnished silver the boughs are bent
That glitter when they shake and stir
When gleams of sunlight upon them glint
With shimmering sheen they shine so sheer   80
Strewing the ground like gravel there
Were precious pearls of orient
The sunbeams seemed but dark and drear
Compared with such magnificence

The adubbemente of þo downes dere
garten my goste al greffe forȝete
So frech flauores of frytes were
as fode hit con me fayre refete
Fowles þ flowen in fryth in fere
of flaūbande hwes bope smale & grete
bot sytole strȳg & gyternere
her reken myrpe moȝt not retrete
for quen pose bryddes her wynges bete
pay songen wyth a swete asent
So gracios gle coupe no mon gete
as here & se her adublement

II, 3

The magnificence of those hillsides dear   85
Made my sad soul all griefs forget
The fruits of such fresh fragrance were
They filled me like food with their savor sweet
Fowls flew in flocks in the forest there
Of flaming hues, both small and great   90
No troubadour, with lute or lyre
Their merry mirth could imitate
For when these birds their wings did beat
They sang with such sweet consonance
More graceful glee might no man meet   95
Than to see and hear their magnificence

To al watȝ dublet on dere Asyse
þat fryth þer fortime forth me ferez
þe derþe þerof for to deuyse
nis no wyȝ worþe þat tonge berez
I welke ay forth I wely wyse
no bonk so byg þ dio me derez
þe fyrre I þe fryth þe feier con ryse
þe playn þe plontez þe spyse þe perez
& rawez & randz & ryth reueres
as fyldor fyn her bnkez brent
I wan to a water by shore þat sherez
lorde dere watȝ hit adubbement

II, 4

Magnificent in glorious guise
That forest where fate my footsteps steers
To speak of the splendors that there arise
No tongue sufficient eloquence bears   100
I walked along right well at ease
No hill, though high, my pace impairs
The further in the forest, the fairer rise
The plain, the plants, the spice, the pears
Borders and banks and rich foreshores   105
Like fine gold thread were their steep strands
I came to a water by sheer shores
Lord, glorious its magnificence

The dubbement of þo derworth depe
Were bonkez bene of beryl bryȝt
Swangeande swete þe water con swepe
Wyth a rownande rourde raykande aryȝt
In þe founce þer stonden stonez stepe
As glente þurȝ glas þat glowed & glyȝt
A stremande sternez quen strope men slepe
Staren in welkyn in wynter nyȝt
For vcheon pobbel in pole þer pyȝt
Watȝ emerad saffer oþer gemme gente
Þat alle þe loȝe lemed of lyȝt
So dere watȝ hit adubbement

II, 5

Magnificent were those precious depths
With beauteous banks of beryl bright 110
Where sweetly swirling the waters swept
With a murmuring sound of pure delight
Bright stones stood in the waters deep
As if through a glass shone glimmering lights
As stars still staring while mortals sleep 115
Glow in the welkin on winter nights
For every pebble that came in sight
Seemed emerald or sapphire in opulence
And all the fountain gleamed with light
So glorious its magnificence 120

That dublemēt dere of doū & dales
Of wod & water & wlonk playnez
bylde in me blys abated my belez
fordiden my stresse dystryed my paynez
doū after astrein pat dryȝly hālez
I loūked in blys bred sul my braynez
pe fyrre I folȝed po se floūy valez
pe more strengppe of ioye myn herte straynez
As fortune farez þ as ip straynez
Whep solace ip sende oþ ellez sore
pe Syȝ to ſhmm her ſyne ip Saynez
hyttez to haue ay more & more

III, 1

The magnificence of downs and dales
Of wood and water and pleasant plains
Begot bliss in me, abated my ills
Dispelled my distress, and destroyed my pains
Down beside a stream that eternally rolls   125
I proceeded in bliss, brimful my brains
The further I followed those watery vales
The more strength of joy my heart constrains
As Fortune affords us whatever she deigns
Whether solace she send, or trials sore   130
The man who for once her goodwill gains
Is certain to have still more and more

More of wele in hert3 I pere doyle
þe I couþe telle þa3 I com hade
for vrþely herte my3t not suffyce
to þe tenþe dole of þo gladne3 glade
for þy I þo3t þat paradyce
was þer ouer gayn þo bonke3 brade
I hoped þe water were a deuyse
by tbene myrþe3 by mere3 made
byзonde þe broke by slente oþ slade
I hope þat more merked were
bot þe water was depe I dorst not wade
& euer me longed a more & more

III, 2

More of delight there was, in every wise
Than I could tell, though I leisure had
For an earthly heart would not suffice   135
For a tenth part of that gladness glad
Wherefore I thought that Paradise
Was there, beyond those banks so broad
I believed the stream was a quaint device
Between delights, a boundary made   140
Beyond the brook, by glen or glade
A city, I thought, was builded there
But the water was deep; I durst not wade
And ever I longed, still more and more

More ⁊ more ⁊ 3et welmare
melyste to se þe broke byzonde
for if hit watz fayr þ I con fare
wel loueloker watz þe fyrre londe
Aboute me con I stote ⁊ stare
to fynde a forþe faste con I fonde
bot woþez mo iwysse þ ware
þe fyrre I stalked by þe stronde
⁊ euer me þo3t I schulde not wonde
for wo þer welez so wynne wore
þene nwe note me com on honde
þat meued my mynde ay more ⁊ more

III, 3

More and more, and yet still more   145
I longed to see across the brook beyond
For if it was fair where I could fare
Far lovelier was the farther land
I stopped a while, to stand and stare
I strove steadfastly a ford to find   150
But greater dangers, indeed, were there
The further I strode beside the strand
I thought it wrong to be unmanned
By woes, where joys so winsome were
But now a new matter was near at hand   155
That moved my mind still more and more

Mor mervayle con my dom adaunt
I ses byzonde þat myry mere
a crystal clyffe ful relusaunt
mony ryal ray con fro hit rere
At þe fote þ of þ cete alaunt
anunden of menske ful debonere
blysnande whyt schal hyr blent
I kneu hyr wel I had sen hyr ere
as glysnande golde þat man con schere
So schon þat schene an under schore
on lenght I loked to hyr pere
þe lenger I kneu hyr more & more

III, 4

More marvels now my mind did daunt
I saw upon the farther shore
A crystal cliff, all resplendent
From which shone royal rays so rare   160
At the foot thereof was seated an infant
A courteous maiden, full debonair
Gleaming white was her outer garment
I knew her well, I had seen her before
As glistening gold that shines so sheer   165
So shone that shining one on the shore
The longer I looked upon her there
The better I knew her, more and more

To þe more I frayste hyr fayre face
her fygure fyn when I had fonne
Such gladande glory con to me glace
as lyttel by-fore þer-to was wonte
to calle hyr lyfte con me enchace
bot baysment gef myn hert a brunt
I seȝ hyr in so strange a place
Such a burre myȝt make myn herte blunt
þenne veres lp vp her fayre frount
hyr vysayge whyt as playn yuore
þat stonge myn hert ful stray atwunt
& euer þe lenger þe more & more

III, 5

The more I gazed upon her fair face
Her figure fine when I had found   170
Such a gladdening glory did my heart grace
As seldom before had been my wont
To call her, desire set me all ablaze
But by astonishment my heart was stunned
I saw her in so strange a place   175
Such a buffet well might my heart wound
Then lifts she up her lofty front
Her forehead white as ivory fair
That stung me, and did my heart astound
And ever the longer, more and more   180

IV, 1

More than desired, my dread arose
I stood full still and durst not call
With open eyes and mouth fast closed
I stood as staid as a hawk in hall
It seemed as though I had seen a ghost   185
I felt a dread of what might befall
Lest that beauteous vision should yet be lost
Ere I her for a parley could stop or stall
That gracious girl, so smooth, so small
So fair without flaw, so seemly, so slight   190
Arises arrayed in her royal apparel
A precious pearl with pearls bedight

Perleȝ pyȝte of ryal prys
pere moȝt mon by grace haf cene
auen peir frech as flor delys
wiþ þe bonke con þreue by cene
al blysnande whyt heeþ hir bellumps
vpon hir cpaȝ & wonden bene
wyth þe myryeste margarys at my denyce
peir on ycez ȝet wyth myn yȝen
wyth lappeȝ large I shor & schene
dubled wyth double ȝerle & dyȝte
her curtel of celf cuttu aene
wt preios ȝerleȝ al vmbe pyȝte

IV, 2

A set of pearls of royal price
A man might there by grace have seen
When that maiden fresh as fleur-de-lys   195
Down the bank descended then
Of bright white linen was her fair chemise
Open at the sides and broidered fine
With the fairest array of pearls of price
That ever yet mine eyes have seen   200
With ample sleeves, I saw it plain
With double pearls well decked and dight
Her kirtle fair, of like design
And all with precious pearls bedight

A pyʒt coronne ʒet wer pat gyrle
of marioys & non oþ con
hye pynakled of cler quyt perle
wyth flurted flowʒrez perfet vpon
to hed hade hy non oþ werle
her lere leke al hyr vmle gon
her semblaūt sade for doc oþ erle
her ble more blaʒt þen walles wyn
as schene golde schyr her faʒ þene schyn
on chylderez pat leʒth vilawd lyʒte
her ryte cold ʒet schoṙted non
of precios perle in wruful pyʒte

IV, 3

A crested crown yet wore that girl 205
Of margarets, and no other stone
With pointed pinnacles of clear white pearl
With florid flowers engraved thereon
She had on her head no other apparel
Her fair hair framed her face all round 210
Her air was grave as duke or earl
Her hue more white than whale bone
As shorn gold sheer her hair then shone
Which, loosened, lay on her shoulders, light
Her clear complexion far outshone 215
Her fine apparel with pearls bedight

Pyrt that pyned to verr alyme
At honde at syder at ouerture
Gyth whyte perle to non op geme
to bourysse mÿte that hyr nóture
bot a wonder perle w outen weme
in mÿdder hyr brette that sette so sure
amanez thin most dryrly deine
er mÿnde most matte that inesure
I hare notrng most endure
no carily carte say of þ cyrt
so that hit clene to cler to pure
þat þcios perle þ hit that pyrt

IV, 4

Bedight was wristband and every hem
At hands, at sides, at each aperture
With white pearl, and no other gem
And burnished white was all her vesture   220
But a wondrous pearl without any maim
Amidst her breast was set so sure
A man's wit would be put to shame
Who tried with words its worth to measure
I believe no tongue could ever utter   225
A suitable saying about that sight
So clean it was, so clear, so pure
That precious pearl that did her dight

Byȝt in perle þat precios pyle
on schyp half schaf comdun þe schyre
no gladder gunne hepen I to grete
þe j anen þo unbryme schore
þo schatȝ me nerre þen alice or nere
in y joy eur py schatȝ munch þe more
ho profered me speche þ special spyce
en dynande loꝛe I schon non loꝛe
cḻate of her coꝛoun of grete treluꝛe
ʒ hayl led me smych a loue lyȝte
wel schatȝ me þ en j schatȝ wꝛe
to schware þat schete I perleȝ pyȝte

IV, 5

With pearls bedight, that pearl of price
Across the stream came down the shore   230
No gladder man from here to Greece
Than I, to see the jewels she wore
She was nearer to me than aunt or niece
My joy therefore was much the more
She spoke me fair, that special spice   235
Bowed low, well learned in women's lore
Caught off her crown of treasure rare
And welcomed me with words polite
O well that me my mother bore
To greet that sweet with pearls bedight   240

O perle quod I in perlez py3t
Art þou my perle þat I haf playned
Regretted by myn one on ny3te
Much longeyng haf I for þe layned
Syþen into gresse þou me agly3te
Pensyf payred I am forpayned
& þou in a lyf of lykyng ly3te
In paradys erde of stryf vnstrayned
What wyrde hatz hyder my iuel vayned
& don me in þys del & gret daunger
Fro we in twynne wern towen & twayned
I haf ben a ioylez iuelere

V, I

O pearl, said I, with pearls bedight
Are you that pearl that caused me pain
That I have lamented alone at night?
For you in my heart have I longed in vain
Since you from my grasp into grass took flight   245
Pensive, perplexed, I am racked with pain
And did you in a life of joy alight
In Paradise, free from strife and strain?
What weird has hither my jewel ta'en
And left me dejected and in despair?   250
Since we two asunder were torn in twain
I have been a joyless jeweller

By hat inel pene in geinez geinte
vered up her vyce & pzen grayez
let on hyr cozon of perle vriet
& coverly after pene con hy say
Pze hat yo tale iny le teinte
to say yo perle is al abaye
pat is i cofer coroinly cleime
as i pis gardyn gracios graye
here she to lenge foreii & play
per mys ne mornyg coin neither
her shere afoater foz pe i taye
if p̃ shere a geintyl ineler

V, 2

That jewel in gems magnificent
Raised up her face with eyes of gray
Put on her crown of pearl of orient   255
And sighing, soberly did say
Sir, you the truth misrepresent
To say your pearl is gone away
That is in a coffer so comely pent
As is this gracious garden gay   260
To linger here forever, and play
Where grief or mourning comes never near
A treasure-casket indeed, you'd say
If you were a gentle jeweller

Bot jueler gentce if þ⁊ctpl luce
þy voy for agēin⁊ þat þe wurllef
ui⁊ þynk þe þat T auiad touple
z vul⁊e⁊ þe abou̇tė traycoū vref
For þat þ⁊letre⁊ Guat⁊ lot aroce
þat clod̄red z fayled as bynde hyt gef
nolx pur⁊ bynd⁊ of þe kyfte yt hyt con clofe
to a perle of pry6 hit is put T vref
z þ̊ lat⁊ called þy Gyrd⁊ apef
þat oft of nozt lat⁊ mad þe der
þ̊ blame⁊ þe wte of þy melthef
þ̊ art no bynd⁊ jueler

V, 3

But, gentle jeweller, if you would lose 265
Your joy for a gem that to you was lief
I think it madness that you should choose
To worry yourself for a cause so brief
For that which you lost was but a rose
That flowered and faded as nature gave 270
But by virtue of the chest which did it enclose
It now a pearl of price doth prove
And you have called your fate a thief
As if something for nothing had cost you dear
You blame the balm of all your grief 275
You are no genuine jeweller

a mel to me yen knatz vys grete
& mela hern hyr gentyl casses
I wyse ye I my blyssol leste
my grete dystresse ye al to drawes
to be excused I make requeste
I trawed my zerle don ont of asses
now he I fonce hyt scheal ma frere
& soury sit hyr Tohyr schod maches
I lone my lorde & al hys lawes
yet hatz me broz vys blys ner
now here I ett you byzond yice drawes
I here a ioyfol ineler

V, 4

A jewel to me then was this guest
And jewels were her sober saws
Indeed, said I, my blissful best
My great distress your tale undoes   280
To be excused I make request
I thought my pearl was forever lost
Now that I've found it, I'll be blessed
And dwell with it in shining shaws
And love the Lord and all his laws   285
Who brought me to this bliss so near
Now if I to you these waves could cross
I would be a joyful jeweller

Iueler sayde þat gemme clene
Sy lorde zemen comadde zte
þre wordez hatz þ spoken at ene
vn avyled forcope wer'n alle þre
þ ne swere in wordle quat   on dtz mene
py swere byfore py oyttte   conete
þ says þ tracwez me T pis aue
by acwce þ may sit þyen mere
Allos þ says T vys contre
py self wal shon of me ryzt lyre
þe prydde to palle pys wer' eve
vat may no loyful meuer

V, 5

Jeweller, then said that gem so clean
Why jest you men? What fools ye be!   290
For sooth, you spoke three words in one
And ill-considered were all three
You know not what in the world they mean
Your words before your wits did flee
You say you believe I am in this glen   295
Because you with your eyes my presence see
For another, you say, in this country
You'll live with me yourself right here
And third, you'd cross this water free
That may no joyful jeweller   300

Ihlde þat I neler lyttel to prayse
þeir loueȝ ... þ ir Cez Oryth yȝe
... nnch to blame & vn cortoyse
þat loueȝ oure lord wolde make a lyȝe
þat leily hyȝte yð lyf to rayse
þan fortune dyd yð flech to dyȝe
ȝe letten hys wordȝ En cheſſernays
þett loues ne pyk bot ȝe her lyȝe
& þat is a pryt oſorqnydryȝe
þet welp god non may euel byteme
to leue notale le fo to tryȝe
bot þat hys one ckyl mayden

VI, 1

I hold that jeweller worth little praise
Who believes that only which meets the eye
And greatly to blame, and devoid of grace
That believes our Lord would tell a lie
Who faithfully promised your life to raise   305
Though Fortune caused your flesh to die
You twist his words contrary ways
Who believe in nothing but what you see
And that is false pride, or surquidry
Which any good man would ill beseem   310
To believe no tale is trustworthy
But that which his own skill may deem

Deme now þy self if þ con dayly
as man to god ꝺꝛaꝛꝺꝭ ꞓ-ꜧꝛuꝺe ꝉene
þ ꞓꝺꝩtꝯ þ ꞓꞃꝺꝺ ꝺꞯuꝉ ꝩꞮꞅ kꝩꝓꝉꝩ
ꝳue pyꝺꝩ ꝙe ꝟuꝺꝺe ꝼꝩꞃꝺ ꝏꞓꝺe ꝉeꝳe
ꝭ ꞩet ꝏꞮ ꞡꞃꝺꞮꞁ þ ꝳuꝯꞇeꝯ ꝼꞇꝩꝉe
þ ꝺꝓuꝉꝳeꝯ ꝏꞮ pꝩꞅ ꞓꝙeꝺꝺꞮꞁ ꝏꞃꞯꝙꞯꝺe
eꞇ Ɪꝳuꝏꞇe þ ꞓꝓꞯeꞇ ꞯu ꝏꞅ ꞓꝏꞁꞓꝩꝩꝉ
ꝩy ꞓꝏꞇꞓeꞁ ꝺꝺꝏꞇ Ɪꞁꝏꞇ ꞇꝺꝺꝙeꞇ ꝟꝏꝳe
ꝼꞯꞃ ꝙꞮꞇ ꞯꞮꝏꞇꝯ ꝼꝏ꞊ ꞡꞃꝏꞇꝯe Ɪꞇꞇ ꝓꝏꞃꝏꝺyꞅ ꞡꞃꝏꞯꞮꝟ
ꝏꞮꞇꞯ ꝯ ꝏꞃꞯ ꞓꝏꝺꞯ ꝙꞮꞇꞇ ꞓꝏꞁ ꞮꞇꝩꞓꞇꞯꞯꞮꞇe
ꝓꞮꞇꝯ ꝏꞃ-ꞅꞃꝩ ꝯꞇꝙ ꝟꝯ ꞯꝙꞮ ꞮꞇꞮꝺ ꝺꞃꞯꞇꞮꞯe
eꞇ ꝏꞮ ꝩꝩꞅ ꝙꝺuꞮ ꝙꝩ ꞓꞯꞮyꞃꞇyꝺꞯuꞯe

VI, 2

Judge for yourself if you argued well
If a man with his words with God can strive
You say in this castle you wish to dwell   315
Methinks you ought first ask for leave
And yet to obtain it you still might fail
You desire to meet me across the wave
But first you must suffer another farewell
To clay must your corpse return in the grave   320
For it was corrupted in Eden's grove
Our ancient father did it condemn
Through dreary death must each man live
Ere God deem him worthy to cross this stream

Demeȝ þ me gy my ꝥete
to dol agayn pene j aꝩmyne
noꝥ laf j foitte pat j foꝛlete
Chal j efte tꝛ goꝛ litt oꝛ eñ jeyne
Why Chal j hit lope mycĩe ꝛ ... ete
my þcꝩs perle aꝛ me g.... ret pyne
Silæt lernez treſor lot graneȝ men grete
Wlen helit Chal efte Of terleȝ tyne
noꝥ redj meñ Faꝛꝩ aꝛlyne
ne lpⷰker of Eolde pæt mencꝥ me fleue
Wlen jan tartleȝ of perleȝ myne
Wt onꝛeicæ Coel Sⷰlæt may mæn deme

VI, 3

If you condemn me, said I, my sweet   325
To sorrow again, then indeed I pine
Now that which I lost at last I greet
Must I then forgo it, ere I life resign?
Why must I my jewel both miss and meet?
My precious pearl causes me great pain   330
What good is treasure, that seems so sweet
When a man must later its loss repine?
Now care I not how my days decline
Nor how far exiled I am from home
If I have no part in what is mine   335
Then enduring dolor must be my doom

Thow demez noȝt bot doel dystresse
þenne sayde þat wyȝt why dotz þou so
For dyne of doel of lurez lesse
ofte mony mon forgos þe mo
þe oȝte better þyseluen blesse
& loue ay god & wele & wo
For anger gaynez þe not a cresse
who nedez schal þole be not so þro
For þoȝ þou daunce as any do
braundysch & bray þy brabez breme
when þou no fyrre may to ne fro
þou moste abyde þat he schal deme

VI, 4

You deem life nothing but dire distress
Then said that child. Why dost thou so?
For loud lament over losses less
The greater grief men oft let go   340
You ought the rather yourself to bless
And love God always, in weal and woe
For anger gains you not a cress
Who needs must suffer should not fret so
For though you dance like a wounded doe   345
Writhing in anguish, or in anger scream
When you can prance no further, to nor fro
You must abide what God shall deem

Deme cryztyn euer hy hoyte
of þe þuay hfatt ne byllr bryppe
þy mendez moittez not auuyte
þer þ for cозэт te neu blyþe
fyst of pythvt ⁊ fyne tu flyte
⁊ leth þys blyþe ful swette ⁊ фryþe
þy prayer mau þys pyte byþe
þat mercy fhal þyr craftez þyþe
þys comfort may þy knuðð lyþe
⁊ þy lirez of lyzþly lerne
for marrv of madđ mæne ⁊ myþe
allys т hyin twdyзt ⁊ œme

VI, 5

Judge the Redeemer, and the Lord indict
He will not swerve out of his way   350
Your recompense mounts not a mite
Though you for sorrow be never gay
Stint of your strife and cease to fight
And seek his grace without delay
Your prayer his pity may excite   355
That mercy may her strength display
His comfort can your cares allay
And lightly all your loss redeem
For, mourn or rage, say yea or nay
What God shall deem will be your doom   360

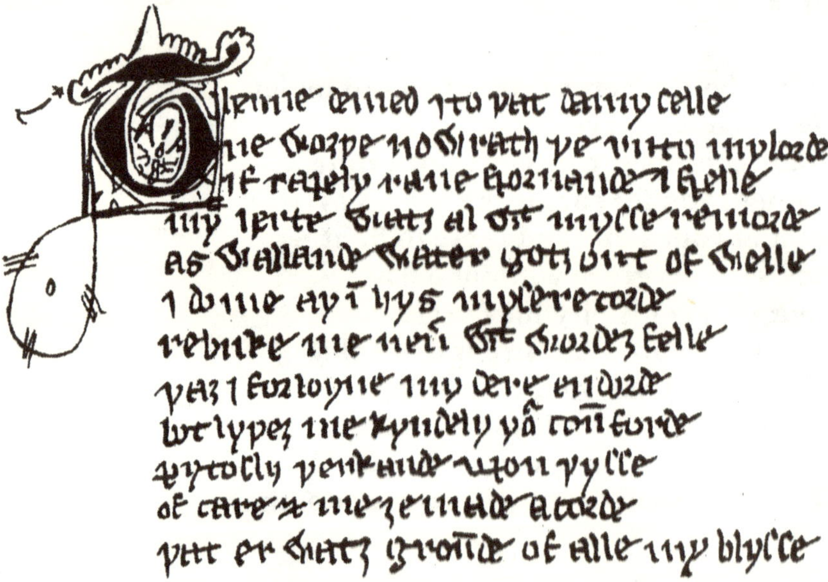

Thenne demed I to þat damyselle
Ne worþe no wrath vnto my lorde
If rapely I raue spornande in spelle
My herte watz al wyth mysse remorde
As wallande water gotz out of welle
I do me ay in hys myserecorde
Rebuke me neuer wyth wordez felle
Þaȝ I forloyne my dere endorde
Bot kyþez me kyndely your coumforde
Pytosly þenkande vpon þysse
Of care & me ȝe made acorde
Þat er watz grounde of alle my blysse

VII, 1

Then said I to that damosel
Let me not give offense unto my Lord
If I reckless rave, and rashly rebel
A grievous sorrow from my heart outpoured
As welling water spills out of a well   365
I commend myself ever to His tender heart
Rebuke me not with accents fell
Though I go astray, my dear adored
But kindly lend me your support
Piteously remembering this   370
You first made care and me consort
That erst were ground of all my bliss

In y blysse my tale zehan len hope
be much þe bygger zet ... my mon
fro þ ... broken fro ... a ...ope
I ... non quere my perle ... ...
... hit le ... lepez my love
... quen ... departed ... ...tt on
... ... le non ...rope
...eneten co ...den by ... ...
pay ...ayfly ze ... ...
I am be nol ...mareuez mylle
be crystes mercy ... mary ... on
pur arn ye ... of alle my blysse

VII, 2

My bliss, my bale, you have been both
But much the bigger has been my moan
Since you were delivered from every scathe   375
I knew not whither my pearl was gone
Now seeing it does my sadness soothe
And, when we departed, we were at one
God forbid we should now be wroth
We meet so seldom by stock or stone   380
Though you are courteous as any queen
I am but dust, and may manners miss
But Christ's mercy, and Mary and John
These are the ground of all my bliss

In blysse I se þe blyþely blent
& I a man al mornyf mate
ȝe take þeron ful lyttel tente
Þaȝ I hente ofte harmez hate
Bot now I am here in your presente
I wolde bysech wythouten debate
ȝe wolde me say in sobre asente
What lyf ȝe lede erly & late
For I am ful fayn þat your astate
Is worþen to worschyp & wele iwysse
Of alle my joy þe hyȝe gate
Hit is in grounde of alle my blysse

VII, 3

To bliss I see you now assigned 385
And I a man downcast and desolate
To my distress you pay little mind
Though often I suffer sorrows great
But now I myself in your presence find
I would beseech you, without debate 390
To tell me, if you would be so kind
What life you lead, early and late
For I am right glad that your estate
Has waxed unto weal and worthiness
Of all my joy the high street 395
It is, and ground of all my bliss

Rose blysse brynne not ye vrydw
yen cayde yett luffon of lyth & leve
& oielcu lyre to walk abydw
for now my herte is to me dwe
maytter til mod & hyze pryde
i lyte pe am leter ly lutted lyre
my lowdw ne lowez not gozto thydw
for meke am alle yt giowez up mere
& dulen Thys place yt whalagere
le dw denore T lyi mevenetic
my lowdw pelamb luney ay luch elgere
yett is ye gromdw of alle my blylle

VII, 4

Kind sir, may you all bliss betide
Said she of face and form most fair
And welcome here to walk and bide
For now your speech is to me dear   400
Masterful mood and haughty pride
I tell you, are bitterly hated here
My Lord the Lamb loves not to chide
And meek are all who dwell him near
And when in his presence you shall appear   405
Be deeply devout in humbleness
For well the Lord loves all such cheer
Who is the ground of all my bliss

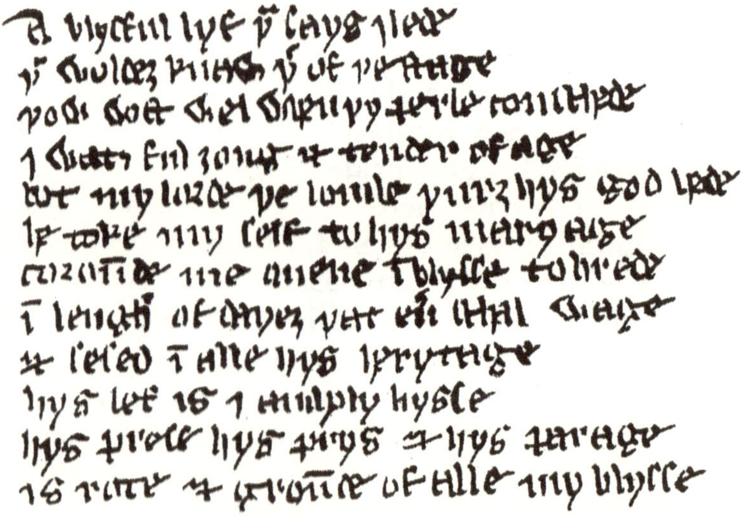
A blysful lyf þou says I lede
þou wolde3 knaw þerof þe stage
þow wost wel when þy perle con schede
I wat3 ful 3onge & tender of age
but my lorde þe lombe þur3 hys godhede
he toke my self to hys maryage
corounde me quene in blysse to brede
in lenghe of daye3 þat euer schal wage
& sesed in alle hys herytage
hys lef is I am holy hysse
hys pryse hys prys & hys parage
is rote & grounde of alle my blysse

VII, 5

A blissful life you say I lead
And of my estate you would know the stage   410
You know full well when your pearl died
I was very young and of tender age
But my Lord the Lamb through his godhead
He took me unto himself in marriage
And crowned me a queen in bliss, indeed   415
In a life that will last from age to age
And seized of all his heritage
His beloved is. I am wholly his
His place, his pride, and his lineage
Are root and ground of all my bliss   420

Blyssid y þ may vye þe tiske
oyeþlere nit iſ þ þeke ervō
þat þ þe quene of lenenes blsne
þ elvve Gorlor malor ynō
þe leuen an may þe þat place of greste
þat ler a lame of vyrgyn flō
þe crunne fro hyr þno mort rennte
lor ho hyr jaded T ſit emō
nō for cyngflerty olyr ōnilō
þe calle hyr ferye of arralny
þat eveles fleze of hyr fulor
luk to þe unen of cortylye

VIII, 1

Blissful one, said I, can this be true?
Be not displeased if I speak in error
Are you the queen of the heavens blue
To whom all the world shall do honor?
We believe in Mary, from whom grace grew   425
Who bore a child in her virgin flower
The crown from her who could withdraw
Unless she surpassed her in some favor?
Now, for uniqueness of her sweet nature
We call her the Phoenix of Araby   430
That flawless flew from its Creator
Like to the Queen of Courtesy

Cortayse quen þenne cþay þat gaye
knelande tv grounde enclose vy hyr face
makelez moder & myryeſt may
bleſſed bygynner of vch a grace
þenne ros þo vp & con reſtay
& ſpeke me tvwarde þ þat face
þ fele here toucþalez & fongez pray
lur ſupplantorez none oſ the þys place
þat erytage all enez haz
& vr þe & telle þ her laylo
of erytage zet non vigl w eþace
for þ is quen of cortayſye

VIII, 2

Courteous Queen, that fair one said
Kneeling to the ground, and covering her face
Matchless mother, and merriest maid   435
Blessed beginner of every grace
Then stood she up, her homage stayed
And spoke to me for a little space
Sir, crowns are won here and kings are made
But no usurpers are in this place   440
That empress all heaven has
And earth, and hell, within her sway
Yet from his estate will she no man chase
For she is the Queen of Courtesy

The cot of ye kyndom of god Alyne
hatz eqerty Tyyt Celf leyg
alle ye may per Tue Atyne
of alle ye reme is chere oy kyg
& nen oy zet hat ceyryne
we velputayn of over hat yg
& holde hy coun er chern corpe yo eyne
if tolyble here yer mendyg
we my lady of anon yesn con epyyg
ip halde ye enwyye on vg hil hyge
& yat dyglorez non of oure gyg
for w is chene of cortayoye

VIII, 3

The court of the kingdom of God Alive   445
Has a virtue inherent in its very being
So that any who may therein arrive
Of all the realm is queen or king
Yet never another shall he deprive
But each one rejoices in the others' having   450
And would wish that their crowns were each worth five
If indeed one could think of their bettering
But my Lady from whom the Christ did spring
Over us all holds sovereignty
Which displeases none of her following   455
For she is the Queen of Courtesy

VIII, 4

By courtesy, as says Saint Paul
We are all members of Jesus Christ
As head and feet, arms, legs and all
Are joined to the body with faith and trust   460
Just so is every Christian soul
A limb that belongs to the body of Christ
For look whether hatred or bitter gall
Between your limbs can indeed exist
The head will never the hand detest   465
Although on your finger you wear a ring
Each lives in love with all the rest
By courtesy, as queen and king

Þ ortayle þ ꝛ ı leue
& charyte grete leyoth amõg
bot my certe þat yow ne greue
þy calt ın leuen oft hyz þ leue
to make þe auen þat dıatz wꝛ outre
Vılat more lpnõ moꝛte ꝛþ achene
þat hade endured ı vioꝛldr ꝛ vı ıgꝛe
& lyued ı þenatice hys lyuez longe
Vıt lodyly hale hy blyʃʃe to hyye
Vılat more vioꝛtthyþ moꝛt lþ toıꝛte
þen to ro ñde be kÿg by coꝛthyʃe

VIII, 5

Courtesy, said I, I do believe
And charity great, unto you belong   470
Alas, that my speech should make you grieve
But it seems to me what you say is wrong
Too exalted a place to yourself you give
To call yourself queen that was so young
What higher honor might he achieve   475
That in the world had remained strong
And lived in penance his whole life long
With bodily bale heaven's bliss to buy?
Could a greater glory unto him belong
Than to be crowned king by courtesy?   480

That corthyle is to fre of dru
zyf hyt lecith par y cones cape
p lyfed not tho zer toure yere
y compez nen god nanp plere ne pruy
ne nen naw per pitter ne crede
t quen mad onpe fyrst day
I may not trasi to god me glear
par god chold surype to surange whay
of cuttres annycel tarinthay
Gen hapr Tignen tolplie a chrute
op elles alaay of lalle thay
lut a queue hit is to dere a late

IX, 1

That courtesy is too free, indeed
If all be true just as you say
Not two years in our land you stayed
You never learned how to please God, nor pray
Nor recite your Pater Noster, nor Creed   485
And made a queen on the first day!
I cannot believe, so God me aid
That the Lord could go so far astray
As a countess, damsel, by my fay
It were fair in heaven to hold estate   490
Or else as a lady of less degree
But queen! It is an end too great!

þer is no date of hys god nesse
þen laye to me þat siorpy dipyte
for al is trasspe þat he con dresse
& he may do no þynk bot ryȝt
he metheȝ meleȝ & ys mette
& vncþful þoȝel of god al myȝt
& cample þat can fil grappely grette
& lybneȝ hit to knen lyste
in my reynie he faythȝ is lyþ on hyȝt
to aluridy þat inde a nynie þ siatte
of tyme of ȝere þe terme siaþ tyȝt
to labe vyne siaþ are þe date

IX, 2

There is no end to his goodness
Then said to me that worthy wight
For all is truth he brings to pass   495
And he can nothing do but right
As Matthew tells you in your mass
In the true gospel of the Lord of light
A parable he sagely says
And likens it to heaven bright   500
My reign, he says, I liken might
To a lord who had a vineyard here
For vintage now the time was right
For season's end was drawing near

þat dcwe oƷevr Vielkmwe þys hyne
þe lowr fiderly vp leros
to hyre Vierkmen to hys vyne
& fyndeƷ þ̄ fitine to hy5 toaþos
into Aowre payvon cpdyne
for aƺene on Aday & Eoath payƷuƷ
durypen & dcoreþn & on grot þyne
kernen & caƷƷen & man hit clo6
Alcnne vncer þelowr to llderþed tutƷ
& yoI men ftancr Irty nceƷ þeratte
Vifty ttmcoƷe yoI le fay cr to po5
ne kmabreƷe of þi6 cay iw cetu

IX, 3

The season's end these farmers know	505
The lord full early up he rose	
To hire workers for his vineyard crew	
And there finds some that he can use	
A dollar a day shall be the wages due	
The bargain made, the crew forth goes	510
To harvest grapes the whole day through	
And earn their bread with the sweat of their brows	
At noon the lord to market goes	
And finds there some who idle stand	
Why stand you idle, he said to those	515
Do you think this day will never end?	

IX, 4

Ere the night was ended, and day begun
We arrived here—all the same answer brought
We've been standing here since arose the sun
And still no man has our service sought   520
Go to my vineyard, do what you can
So said the lord, and their aid besought
By night what wages your work has won
I will pay to you honestly, as I ought
Into the vineyard they went, and wrought   525
While the lord all day his way did wend
And new men into his vineyard brought
Till day was almost at its end

IX, 5

At the end of the day, at evensong
One hour before the sun went down   530
He saw there idle men full strong
And said to them in a solemn tone
Why stand you idle all day long?
They said that employment could not be found
Go to my vineyard, yeomen young   535
And work, do all that can be done
The world turned dim and dusky soon
The sun was down; it was getting late
To collect their wages he called them round
For day was at end; there was no more light   540

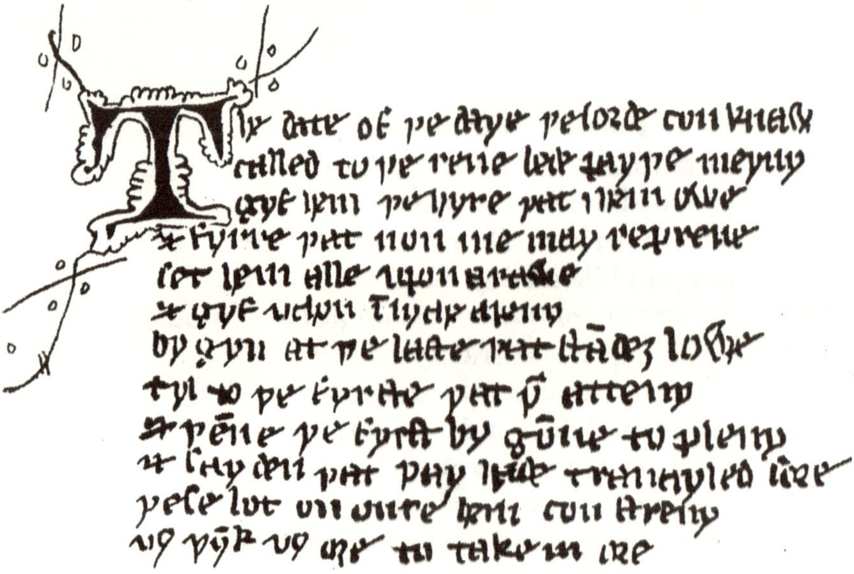
Þe date of þe daye þe lorde con knaw
called to þe reve lede pay þe meyny
gyf hem þe hyre þat I hem owe
& fyrre þat non me may reprene
set hem alle vpon a rawe
& gyf uchon inlych a peny
bygyn at þe laste þat standez lowe
tyl to þe fyrste þat þou atteny
& þenne þe fyrst bygonne to pleny
& sayden þat þay hade travayled sore
þese bot on oure hem con streny
vus þynk vus oȝe to take more

X, 1

That the day was ended the lord well knew
He called to his steward, Man, pay the men
Give them the wages that I them owe
And further, that none have cause to complain
Line them all up in a single row   545
And give a dollar to every man
Begin at the last, that stands most low
Until to the first you do attain
At that the first began to complain
And said that they had toiled sore   550
These but one hour have stood the strain
We think we ought to be given more

X, 2

More we deserve, if we do say so
That have suffered through the day's heat
Than these that worked not hours two   555
Whom yet you now as our equals treat
Said the lord to one who reproached him so
Friend, you and your fellows I will not cheat
Take what belongs to you, and go
You all for a dollar a day agreed   560
Why do you now begin to chide?
Was it not a dollar that you bargained for?
For more than his contract ought no man plead
Why then should you ask for more?

More þeſ Jonyly is me my gyfte
to cu ſnyth mnyn quett cu me lykez
uſ eller þun yʒe tulyſ is lyfte
for ʒein grade & nu by cſnykez
þy þhall gꝛ bꝛyfte þat cꝛyfte
velatte inene þe tyrא þat flꝛykez
& þe tyrꞛ þe latte be ir men cu ſnyt
for many ten calle vaʒ feſhe le ʒ uyꝛez
þy tore nten lꝛtꞛt ay þykez
þaʒ ꝛay conlatte & lyttel ſtore
& vaʒ lꝛt cſhenyꞛ ſnyth lyttel ar ſlykez
þe merciuf god is much þe more

X, 3

Moreover, is it not in my gift   565
To do with my own as I wish to do?
Or do you your eyes unto evil lift
Because I am good, and to none untrue?
So shall I, said Christ, the order shift
That the last shall be the first to go   570
And the first the last, be he never so swift
For the called are many, but the chosen, few
Thus poor men always will get their due
Though they come late, and lowly were
And although it's little that they can do   575
The mercy of God is much the more

Now Ihe̅ ꝗ of ioye ⁊ blyſſe lꝛetue
of lady Mꝫw gꝛet ⁊ hꝫeꝫ bloꝫ
þen alle þe gꝛyꝫeꝫ ⁊ þe dioude myꝫt viſꝫe
by þe day of ꝛyꝫt ꝛ̃ alꝛe dyme
vihꝑer Gieiuyall noſ̃ iꝛn by gꝛue
ꝯ euerity ꝯ ꝛutuþe vyꝛue iꝛme
tyꝛꝛ of my hyꝛe my luꝛe ꝯ̃ uꝑue
I Gieth iayed ꝯꝯ of ꝯl ꝛꝫꝯꝯ
ꝫeꝯ oꝫ þer ꝓeꝛue þᵗ tuꝛe uꝛꝫ̃uꝯ
þꝛꝛ ꝯ̃uꝛꝫe ⁊ ꝯ̃ꝫꝛ̃ fuꝫ loꝫe ꝫoꝫe
þꝛꝫeꝯ of hyꝛe noꝝyꝫk yꝫyꝫuꝯ
ꝫꝯꝯꝫ̃ noꝫt lꝛꝫl tuꝫ eꝛ̃ꝑ uꝛꝫe

X, 4

More have I of joy and bliss herein
Of ladyship great and of life's bloom
Than all the people on earth might win
Or claim by right, at God's just doom   580
And although I did only but just begin
And at eventide into the vineyard came
At the reckoning the Lord put me first in line
I was paid at once the entire sum
Yet others there were that spent more time   585
That labored longer, and sweated sore
That have not of their wages received one dime
And perhaps shall not for some years more

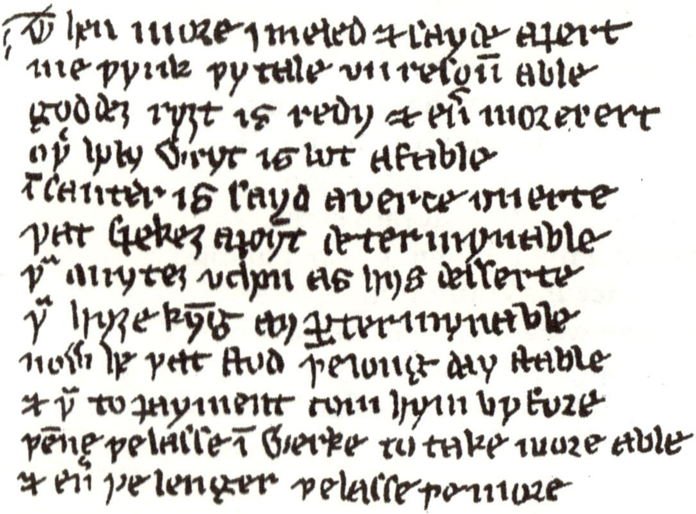

Then more I meled & sayde apert
me þynk þy tale vnresoñ able
goddez ryȝt is redy & eũ more rert
oþ holy wryt is bot a fable
I sauter is sayd a verce ouerte
þat spekez a poynt determynable
þu quytez vchon as hys desserte
þu hyȝe kyng ay p̄termynable
now he þat stod þe long day stable
& þu to payment com hym byfore
þenne þe lasse in werke to take more able
& eũ þe lenger þe lasse þe more

X, 5

Then more I spoke, in frank retort
Your tale to me seems unreasonable   590
God's justice is certain and ever assured
Or Holy Writ is but a fable
In the Psalter stands a verse overt
Which makes a point demonstrable
You give each man his just desert   595
You high king ever equitable
Take him that stood the long day stable
Now if you to payment come in before
Then he who worked less to take more would be able
And so it would follow: work less, get paid more   600

Of more & lasse in Godys ryche
þat gentyl layde hys no jowþrde
þe þer is uch mon payed inlyche
siþper lyttel of much be hys reþarde
for þe gentyl chenertayn is no dyche
quey to efi re wre nelþ of large
Iplanes hys gyftez as þat ofdyche
oþ grotez of gule þat neri charde
hys frauncyse is large þat eri dard
to hy þat meþz & cyne reþugh
iw blysse letz eru þem reþurde
for þe grace of god is gret j nowgh

XI, 1

Of more and less in God's estate
That damsel said, there is no hazard
For there each man is paid full rate
Whether little or much be his reward.
Our noble Chieftain is no cheapskate   605
Whatever he measures out, mild or hard
He lavishes gifts like a river in spate
Or streams from an ever-welling spring outpoured
Happy are those who serve the Lord
The One who gives from sin relief   610
No bliss or blessing on them is spared
For the grace of God is great enough

Bot noꝛp̄ꝺ mateʒ me foꝛ tu matte
pat j my ꝛeuy hat Graug tau lꝑe
p̄ ſayʒ pat j pat com̄ tuitte
ainuot ꝺꝛꝛpy ſoꝓꝛeeꝺeꝛe
ſulpꝛeꝺꝛyteʒ p̄ en̄ any wii me aute
euer ſolply Thiꝺ praꝛyere
pat þeneꝼuꝛſeteꝺ þn ſīꝛkyn ꝯatte
þe meꝺe ſm̄ tyme ofꝑuen es ꝺere
⁊ hy þeuꝺter þe alꝺeꝛpay ꝺiere
vhylaꝼꝛen ryʒt ⁊ ꝺiꝛuꝛꝛen Goghꝼ
mercy ⁊ ꝑꝛe muꝺke þm̄ þꝛ eꝛeꝛe
ꝼuꝛ þe ꝑꝛe uꝼ goꝺ iꝺ ꝗꝛet mo̅ꝛe

XI, 2

But now you argue, and me berate
That I have not been worth my hire
You maintain that I, who came too late   615
Am not worthy of a price so dear
When did God ever a man create
Ever so holy in his prayer
That he did not at some time forfeit
In some way, the meed of heaven clear?   620
And all the more often, the older they were
They left the right, and evil wrought
Then mercy and grace must see them clear
For the grace of God is great enough

Bot Þurgh of grace hatȝ Twcertt
As sone as Þay arn lune byhyue
T Þe Ƃatter of labrem Þay dycйente
Þ Erue Þay wrot T to Þe vyne
anon Þe day ꝰ avr enavtte
Þe nyȝt of deth Ðrȝ to en dyne
Þat Ƃiriȝt never Ƃirang er Þēne Þay Ƃiente
Þe ꝝentyle lurd Þēne ꝉayeȝ hyȝ hyne
Þay dyden hyȝ hyre Þay Ƃiern Þere me
Ƃihy cihilde lȝ not lȝ lalȝ alook
iyȝ ꝶ lav hym at pelyra eyne
for Þe grace of god iȝ ꝵvt Twgȝ

XI, 3

But enough of grace have the innocent   625
As soon as they are born in Adam's line
In the water of baptism they descend
They are brought to the vineyard, and enter in
Anon the day, its light soon spent
Does toward the night of death decline   630
They never wrought wrong ere thence they went
The gentle Lord then pays his hands
They obeyed his commandment, they were therein
Why should he not their labor approve
Indeed, and pay them, as first in line?   635
For the grace of God is great enough

Jnoʒe is knawen ꝼ mankyn grete
eyrꝛe ſiatʒ ſhroʒt to blylſe þareyt
onre ꝼoꝛme ꝼaꝺꝛ hit can ꝼoꝛꝼere
plrʒ an apple þat he wꝛon conbyte
al ſier ſhe ꝺampned ꝼoꝛ þett nere
tv oyʒe inꝺel ant oꝼ ꝺelyt
✝ ſv pen ſhenꝺe to ſelle hir
þ inefto ſion ſtotte ꝛeꝺyt
bit per on con abꝛte aſ tit
nyclp bloꝺ ꝛau on ꝛoꝺe co roꝛli
✝ ſiyne ſiat ve at þat þlyꝛ
pe gꝛce oꝼ goꝺ ſher gret inoꝛli

XI, 4

It is well enough known that mankind great
Was created to dwell in sweet delight
But our forefather did it forfeit
For an apple upon which he did bite   640
We all condemned were for that meat
To die in dole, without delight
And hence to wend to hell's heat
Therein to dwell without respite
But then came a remedy to set us right   645
Rich blood ran on the rood so rough
And winsome water; in that sad plight
The grace of God was great enough

In iwgh þer may oitt oitt of þat snelle
blod & fiint of broðe ffroiice
þe blod vp wit fro lale of lelle
& clifiied vp of þe deþ cetoiice
þe letter is lapterii þe lope to telle
þat folred þe glayne co gryly groiice
þat seiichþz away þe gyttz felle
þat adam bryeþ tue deþ vp droiice
noſ iſ þ noзt & þe ſworlde roiice
by tsiierie vp & biyclle lit þat lt ſit drez
& þat is rettozed ſleiy itoiice
& þe grace of god is gret ſnogh

XI, 5

Enough there flowed out of that well
Blood and water from that broad wound　　　　650
The blood us bought from the bale of hell
And man from the second death redeemed
The water is baptism, truth to tell
That followed the glaive, all grimly ground
And washes away the guilt so fell　　　　655
With which Adam had in death us drowned
No barriers now are there to bliss profound
That have not been abolished on our behalf
In a blessed hour was bliss regained
And the grace of God is great enough　　　　660

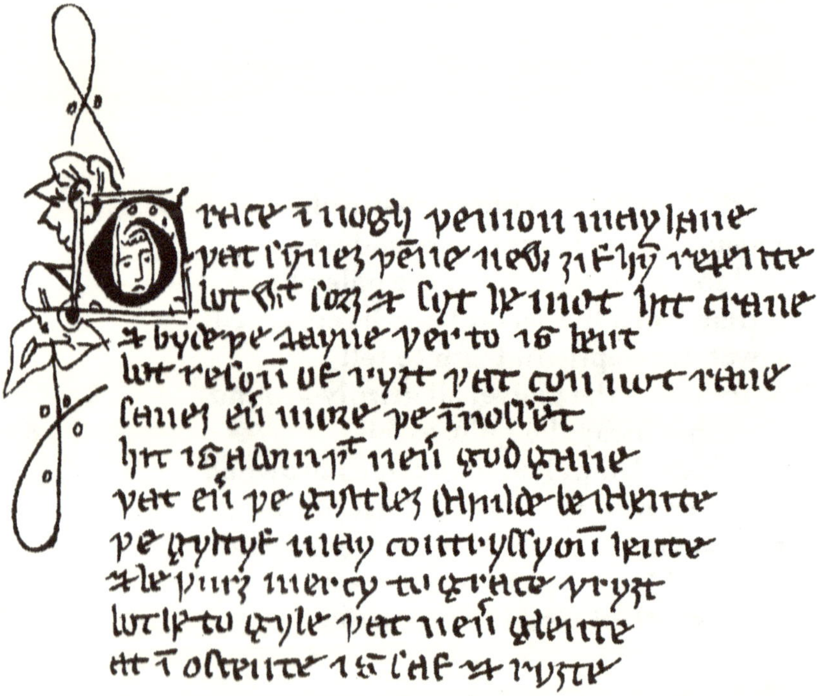
Grace innogh þe mon may haue
þat synnez þenne new, 3if hym repente
bot wyth sor3 & syt he mot hit craue
& byde þe payne þerto is bent
bot resoun of ry3t þat con not raue
saue3 euermore þe innossent
hit is a dom þat neuer god gaue
þat euer þe gyltle3 schulde be schente
þe gyltyf may contryssyoun hente
& be þur3 mercy to grace bry3t
bot he to gyle þat neuer glente
at inoscente is saf & ry3te

XII, 1

Grace enough the man may have
That sins anew, if he repent
But with sorrow and sighing he must it crave
And abide the pain that is consequent
But reason and right, that cannot rave   665
Save evermore the innocent
It is a judgment God never gave
That the guiltless are liable to punishment
The guilty man may become penitent
And be to grace through mercy brought   670
But he that to guile was never bent
That innocent is safe and right

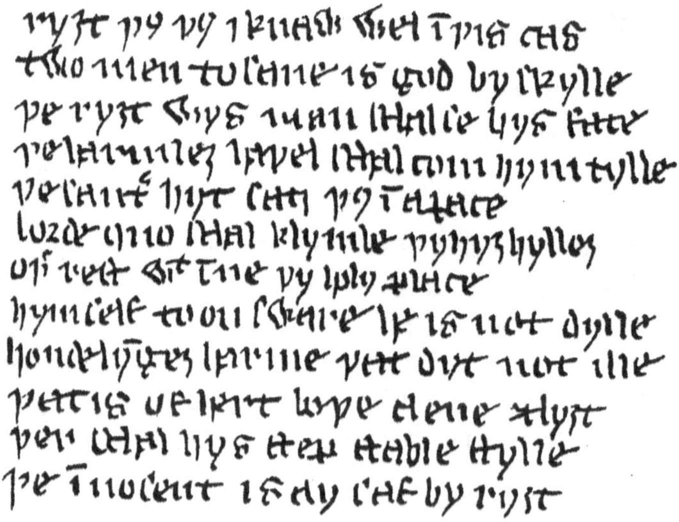
ryȝt þus I knaw wel ī þis cas
two men to saue is god by skylle
þe ryȝt wys man schal se hys face
þe harmles haþel schal com hym tylle
þe sauter hyt satȝ þus ī a pace
lorde quo schal klymbe þy hyȝ hylles
oþer rest wyt ine þy holy place
hymself to onsware he is not dylle
hondelyngeȝ harme þat dyt not ille
þat is of hert boþe clene & lyȝt
þer schal hys step stable stylle
þe īnocent is ay saf by ryȝt

XII, 2

Right thus I know well in this case
Two men are saved by God's good will
The righteous man shall see his face   675
The blameless come to him as well
The Psalmist says in a certain verse
Lord, who shall climb thy high hill
Or rest within thy holy place?
The answer he is not slow to tell   680
The harmless, with hands that did no ill
That is of heart both clean and light
There shall his steps be stable still
The innocent always is safe by right

XII, 3

The righteous man as well, 'tis plain   685
He shall approach that citadel
Who does not spend his life in vain
And cheats his neighbor not with guile
Of the righteous man says Solomon plain
How Wisdom did guide him in time of trial   690
In oppression did riches for him obtain
And showed him the kingdom of God awhile
As one who says, Lo, yon lovely isle
If you persevere, you may win it yet
But sure it is, that without fail   695
The innocent always is safe by right

An ende ryȝtwys men ȝet sayth euynne
Dauid in sauter if en ȝe seȝ lyt
lord py seruaunt aȝt neuer to dwne
for non lyuyende to pe is iustyfyet
for vy to corte men þ wyl com
per alle oure cauces shalle tryed
A leȝge peryst þ may be trowine
by pys ilke speech i haue aceuyed
wt le on rode þat blody dyed
delfully purȝ hondes pryȝt
gyue pe to salue þylen þ arte tryed
by innocens & not by ryȝte

XII, 4

About the righteous yet says a psalm
Of David, in the Psalter as you may read
Draw not thy servant, Lord, to doom
Before thee none living is justified   700
Therefore to court when you shall come
Where all our causes shall be tried
If you claim to be righteous, you may be undone
By this same speech I have espied
But he on the cross that bloody died   705
Grievously pierced through hands and side
Give thee to pass, when thou art tried
By innocence and not by right

XII, 5

Let him who the scripture can rightly read
Look in the book and be instructed   710
How Jesus in olden times walked abroad
And people did infants unto him lead
For the happiness and health that from him proceed
To touch their children they fair him prayed
Let be, his disciples with blame them bade   715
And many did with their words dissuade
Jesus to them then sweetly said
Keep still. Let children to me be brought
For such is the kingdom of God arrayed
The innocent ever is safe by right   720

Ʒe con calle to ĥy ĥys mylde
ꝛ cayde ĥys rycĥe noĥyȝ myȝt ѕ̃ĥ̃ne
ꝟ le con pryder ryȝt as acĥylde
oꝑ eꝉleȝ neꝛ moꝛe con ꝯ̃ꝟ̃ne
ĵanuleȝ trꝝe ꝛ vnde ѳylde
Ɋt oꝛꝛen mote oꝯ mallĥe ỡ ĥꝛꝉȝenꝺ ꝉĥ̃ne
ꝙ̃en cucĥ ꝑer en okzen oꝛ ꝟe bylde
tyt cĥꝓl ꝉꝛn meꝛ ꝑeȝate ꝟꝛꝓ̃ne
ꝑerıѕ ꝟebɦys ꝑꝛ coꝛꝛot ɦꝉ̃ñe
ꝑꝛt ꝟe meꝛer ꝉoꝛte ꝑꝛꝛȝ ȝeꝛꝛ̃e qꝛꝛѕ
ꝛ culde alꝛ ĥyѕ ꝙ̃ꝛo ꝛꝛ ѳꝛꝛꝛꝛ+ɦ̃ñe
ꝟꝛꝛĵe ĥ̃ñ aȝeꝛꝉe ꝙ̃ꝛ qꝛꝛꝛꝛeꝉꝉeȝ

XIII, 1

To him Jesus called his disciples mild
And said that his kingdom might no man win
Except he come thither like a little child
Or else nevermore might he come therein
Harmless, true, and undefiled   725
Without speck or spot of sullying sin
When such shall knock at the gate of the hold
Men will come quickly to let them in
There does the endless bliss begin
That the jeweller through precious gemstones sought   730
And sold all his goods, that he ever did win
To purchase a pearl immaculate

O þis makelles perle þat lyt is dere
þe ioueler gef fore alle hys god
is lyke þe reme of heuenesse clere
so sayde þe fader of folde & flode
for hyt is fieles clene & dere
& endeles rounde & blype of mode
& commune to alle þat ryȝtwys were
lo euen inmyddeȝ my breste hyt stode
my lorde þe lombe þat schede hys blode
he pyȝt hyt þere in token of pes
I rede þe forsake þe worlde wode
& porchace þy perle maskelles

XIII, 2

This matchless pearl, that is bought so dear
For which the jeweller gave all his goods
Is like the realm of the heavens clear   735
So said the Father of field and flood
For it is flawless, clean and clear
Round without end, and blithe of mood
And common to all who righteous were
Lo, here in the midst of my breast it stood   740
My lord the Lamb, that shed his blood
In token of peace he it there did set
I pray thee, forsake the mad world
And purchase your pearl immaculate

O markeles perle & perles pure
þat beres (þ) þe perle of prys
and fourmed þe vy fayre fygure
þat wrozt vy flesc is þat eui þys
þy lemine com nen of nature
þy mayhou paynted nen vy vys
ne aryþmel naþyp vy lys letture
of rare vekyna vele þuertez
vy cule talles þe Hs oeþys
vou angel hauyp to aene cutez
brene me bryt anete ryn oeþys
beres þe perle tomarkeles

XIII, 3

Immaculate pearl in pearls pure   745
That bears, said I, the pearl of price
Who formed for thee thy figure fair?
Who wrought thy raiment, was full wise
Thy beauty never came from nature
Pygmalion never painted your face   750
Nor Aristotle, for all his lore
Never discussed these properties
Thy color surpasses the fleur-de-lys
Thine angelic air is so delicate
Tell me, fair one, what high place   755
Is granted a pearl so immaculate?

My makelez lambe þat al may bete
ꝙ scho my dere destyne
me ches to hys make alþaȝ vnmete
Sū tyme semed þt assemble
When I wente fro yor worlde wete
he calde me to hys bonerte
Cū hyder to me my lemman swete
for mote ne spot is non in þe
he gef me myȝt & als bewte
In hys blod he wesch my wede on dese
& corounde clene in vergynte
& pyȝt me in perlez maskellez

XIII, 4

My matchless Lamb, that all may right
Said she, my precious destiny
Me chose for his mate, although unmeet
May once have seemed that assembly 760
When I went away from your world so wet
He called me to his felicity
Come hither to me, my love, my sweet
For mote nor spot is there none in thee
Beauty and might he gave to me 765
In his blood my garments he washed; in state
He crowned me clean in virginity
And clothed me in pearls immaculate

Why makelles þyd þat bryȝt con flambe
þat reiateȝ haþ to ryche a rye
Quat kyn þyng may be þat lambe
þat þe wolde wedde vnto hys vyf
on alle vp to hyȝ þ clambe
to lede wi þ hy colmdhly lyf
comony ronmly an vnder cmube
for bryȝt þan lyned ȝ much Stryf
ȝ þ con alle þo dere vnt aryȝ
ȝ Ero þeт marydǵ al vȝ depres
al only þylelf lostoιr ȝ aryf
a makeleȝ may ȝ maskelleȝ

XIII, 5

Immaculate bride, as bright as flame
Whose royalty reigns so rich and rife   770
What kind of thing must be that Lamb
That he would thee wed, and take to wife
Who over all others so high did climb
To lead with him such a ladylike life?
So many a comely one under comb   775
For Christ has lived in pain and strife
But you all his lovers away did drive
And deprived them all of that high estate
Save only yourself, so stout and stiff
A matchless maid and immaculate   780

XIV, 1

Immaculate, said that merry queen
Unblemished I am, without a blot
And that with honor may I maintain
But matchless queen: that said I not
We the Lamb's wives in bliss have been   785
A hundred and forty thousand odd
As in the Apocalypse it is seen
Saint John beheld them all in a knot
On the hill of Zion, that seemly spot
The apostle saw them in mystic dream   790
Arrayed for the wedding on that hill-top
The city of New Jerusalem

Of ihū i m gerlf gelle
ie þ̄ diyl kinᵹ wᵹt kyn le
my lomb my lᵫd my dere melle
my ioy my blyᵹ my lēmau ere
þe grete ylene of hᵹ con melle
prtouly of hyᵹ delonere
þat þlezyoᵹ gyltlez yᵗ mon con quelle
at oiten any cake of felonye
as allep to þe claᵹt þ̄ lad ᵹietᵹ le
ᵶ aᵹ lome þat ayþer ī land men
lo doled le hyᵹ monrth ere veh auery
quen meᵹ hᵹ mᵹᵹred ī ilhū

XIV, 2

Of Jerusalem I in speech shall tell
If you would know what kind is he
My Lamb, my Lord, my precious jewel   795
My joy, my bliss, my bridegroom free
The prophet Isaiah of him did tell
Of his gentleness, full piteously
That glorious innocent men did quell
Without any charge of felony   800
As a lamb to the slaughter led was he
And as a sheep before the shearer is dumb
He closed his mouth to each inquiry
When the Jews him judged in Jerusalem

XIV, 3

In Jerusalem was my true love slain   805
And rent on a rood with brigands bold
Willing to suffer all our pain
He took on himself our cares cold
With buffets they did his face profane
That was so lovely to behold   810
For sin he did his own life disdain
That never himself was by sin befouled
For our sins he let himself be sold
And broken upon a brutal beam
As meek as a lamb, no lament he told   815
When he died for us in Jerusalem

Intō jordan & galalye
per as baptyſed þe gode laſt jon
his charɣeꝫ acordꝺ to playe
biþen jſt con tulñ chara gou
lꝑayɒ of lñ pys atellye
lo gode tomlꝛ as treue as hou
pett dm achay þe lijnes oryȝe
ȝett alle pys charlde lꝑt̃ charoſt uþon
lñ cele ne charoſt neñ ȝet non
ſuꝑꝑor onhym cele le con al clem
hys generacyoñ dno roȝen con
þat dyȝed for uȝ ī ꝓrīn

XIV, 4

In Jerusalem, Jordan, and Galilee
Where was baptizing the good Saint John
His words with Isaiah's did well agree
When Jesus unto him had gone   820
He spoke about him this prophecy
Behold, God's Lamb steadfast as stone
From the grievous sins he sets us free
That all the world has ever done
Though he himself wrought never none   825
Yet for his own he them all did claim
His generation who reckon can
Who died for us in Jerusalem?

XIV, 5

In Jerusalem my true love sweet
Twice for a lamb was he taken there   830
By the true record of either prophet
For his meek manners and mild cheer
The third time does him as well befit
In Apocalypse is it written clear
In the midst of the throne, where the saints were set   835
How John the apostle saw him there
Opening the book with leaves foursquare
And the seven seals that were set thereon
And at that sight all quaked with fear
In hell, in earth, and Jerusalem   840

Thys jhesu lombe þad neu fethde
of op hnee brt anyt jolyt
þat not ne makille most on threde
for sholle anyte to ronk & rue
for þy velf seule þat lad neu teth
is to þer lomke A diorthyly dryt
I þen vel day afuze þ fethe
amoug vs cumes nonop þat ne hrye
brt vchon erle die diolde diere fyt
vena þe myryer to god me Wette
comyayny gret vnr lut con pryt
m lmd more & nen peiette

XV, 1

This Jerusalem Lamb had never blotch
Of any hue but purest white
Whom neither smear nor smut could smudge
For his white wool so rank and rife
Therefore each soul without reproach   845
Is to that Lamb a worthy wife
And though each day a host he fetch
Among us comes no stress nor strife
But every one we would were five
The more the merrier, so God me bless   850
In company great our love can thrive
In honor more and never the less

Lasse of blysse may non vus bryng
Þat beren þys perle vpon oure bereste
For þay of mote couþe neuer mynge
Of spotlez perlez þay beren þe creste
Alþaȝ oure corses in clottez clynge
& ȝe remen for rauþe wyth outen reste
We þurȝoutly hauen cnawyng
Of on dethe ful oure hope is drest
Þe lombe vus gladez oure care is kest
He myrþez vus alle at vch a mes
Vchonez blysse is breme & beste
& neuer onez honour ȝet neuer þe les

XV, 2

Unto less bliss may none us bring
Who bear this pearl upon our breast
For they of discord could never think 855
Who wear of spotless pearls the crest
And although to our corpses clods may cling
And you weep for ruth, and never rest
Yet we have perfect understanding
On one death all our hope is placed 860
The Lamb us gladdens; our cares offcast
He delights us all at every feast
And each one's bliss is brightest and best
Yet no one's honor is ever the less

leettes þ lene my talle taraude
ī ayꝛo callꝭꝩere ꝭs vꝛyten T Ⴎ꙾ꝛꙋ
ꝺ Ceꝺꝯ cay5 johū þe lomꝺ bꝩ ſtanꝺ
on þe moītt of ſyon eul yꝛymen ꝥ ꝛ꙾ꝛo
ꝥ Ⴎꝭyꝫ hyꝭn mayꝺꙟꝭꝫ all hūꝺrepe powſtanꝺ
ꝥ fo꙾ꝛe ꝥ forty po꙾ſtanꝺ mꝭꙋ
on alle lꝛꝭ forlꝛꝭꝫ ſvꝛyꝛꝭꝭu ꝭſtanꝺ
þe lomꝭlꝛꝫ nomꝭ hyꝫ faꝺꝛꝭꝫ allꙅ
alꝝnꝭ fro lꝛnꝭn ꝭ lꝛꝛ꙾ yꙋꙋ
lyꝝ florꝫ ꝼole laꝺꝭn ꝛmꝭ on vꝛllꝭ
ꝥ as pūꝺꝛ yꝛꙋvꝭꝫ T tuꝛꝛꝭꝫ blꙋ
vꝛtt loꝛꝭ ꝭlꝛꝭꝭ Ⴎꝭꝛꝫ neꝭꝭ vꝛlꝭꙅ

XV, 3

Lest less you believe my tale grand   865
In Apocalypse is written a verse
I saw, says John, where the Lamb did stand
On the mount of Zion, full fair of face
And with him maidens a hundred thousand
And forty-four thousand were in that place   870
The name of the Lamb and his Father, I found
On all their foreheads written was
And then from heaven I heard a noise
Like the roar of many rivers running in a rush
Or among blue hills the thunder's voice   875
That noise, I believe, was never the less

XV, 4

Nevertheless, though it was shouted sharp
With a loud clamor, which filled the air
A note full new I heard them shape
And lovely that melody was to hear   880
As harpers harping on their harps
That new song they sang so clear
In sonorous notes a psalm superb
In unison sang they the tune full fair
Right before God's heavenly chair   885
And the four beasts that his name confess
And the aldermen, so sad of cheer
They sang their song there, nevertheless

ffor þye lete non wraþ neñ co quoynt
for alle ye craftez þat eñ þay knethe
þat of þat conge myst siȝte aþoyt
wrþat meyny ye lomb þay chie
for þay am wt frope urþe aloyntte
as neuȝe kryt to god fuldne
& to ye geñtyl lomb lnt am amuȳt
as lyk to hym celf of lote & bhe
for neñ leþyȝ ne tole uñ trwe
ne twickd her tunge for no dystreffe
þat mateleȝ meyny may neñ remñe
fro þat mackelez mayþer neñ peleȝ

XV, 5

Nevertheless, none was ever so smart
For all the arts man ever knew   890
That of that song he could sing a note
Save those of the Lamb's own retinue
For they were redeemed from the earth, and brought
As the first fruits that to God are due
With the gentle Lamb do they consort   895
As like to himself in their look and hue
For never a lie, nor tale untrue
Was found in their mouths, for any distress
And never divorced is that spotless crew
From their immaculate master, nevertheless   900

Honer þe les let leuy pouc
ȝf I my perle þeȝ I aȝole
Ichulde not teruȝte þy ȝiȝt ca ȝloue
to kryȝteȝ chaubre þat art ȝclpce
I am wt mokke ȝ mul anuoȝ
ȝ þ co ryde areken rule
ȝ þyaȝ lere by þys blyfull truc
per luyuer lyſte may neu loſe
nowe hynur þat cyuȝenieſte cdeȝ enuoſe
I chode þe aſke apyȝre expreſie
ȝ þaȝ le budþys aȝ abloſe
let my tune vayl neu þe leſe

XV, 6

Pearl, never the less should you think my thanks
Said I, although I a question pose
I should not risk your censure frank
Whom Christ unto his chamber chose
For I am made of mud and muck   905
And you so fresh and fair a rose
Who abide here by this blissful bank
Where the joy of life you can never lose
Now, maid, whom simpleness imbues
I ask of you but one request   910
Though as any oaf I am obtuse
Let my prayer prevail, nevertheless

Neuer þe lese cler i you, by talle
If ʒe con se hyt le to dune
As þ art glorious wt outen galle
Vt nay þ neu my rueful tone
hat ʒe no stones i castel walle
ne man perʒe may mere & þou
þ telles me of þrin þe ryche ryalle
yer damd are wan dyʒt on trone
lot by þyse letter hit con not lyue
lot in quder hit is yt noble note
As ʒe ar makeles unor mone
ys stones shulde be wyth arten mote

XVI, 1

Nevertheless, I upon you call
If you can see how it can be done
As you are glorious without gall   915
Refuse me not my rueful boon
Have you no halls in castle walls
No mansions you can call your own?
Of Jerusalem's royal realm you tell
Where sat King David upon the throne   920
Yet by these woods it cannot be found
But in Judea is that place of note
As you are immaculate under the moon
Your dwelling should be without a spot

pys martelez meyny þ cunez of mele
of poulaudez pryst cagret aruirre
agret cete turze arni fele
pols by lps ипие ßt ourtеп dоитте
Cotily shabke of joly melg
ßer eilel dui ttbilde lyz þ uirte
zby pyle tunbez per jani gele
zije nobygoyc uashlpre аtuitte
ttrobie al one ze lenge z loirte
to lope onue glory of pys goop gute
1f þ hett uper lyryyez ttuitte
nols redi ие tu pett myry uote

XVI, 2

That immaculate company of which you tell 925
That throng of thousands, so great a rout
A city great, for you are innumerable
You needs must have, without a doubt
So comely a pack of jolly jewels
Were ill served, should they lodge without 930
Yet by these banks upon which I stroll
I see no buildings hereabouts
But to linger alone, and wander about
This beauteous stream, I believe, you sought
If you have other building stout 935
Now guide me to that specious spot

To þat mote þ meneȝ in ioy londe
þat gentyal gryce venturne þakk
þat is þe cyte þat þe lombe con founde
tu soffer þne for for menneȝ sake
þe olde ierin tu vnder stonde
for þere þe olde gultte ȝeth con slake
bot þe newe þat lyȝt of goðeȝ sonde
þe apostel in apocalyppe I henne contake
þe lompe þ ȝt oritten ȝotteȝ blake
htti seryed ȝyðer hys fayre flote
ȝtis hys flok is ȝt oritten flake
so is hys mote ȝt oritten indote

XVI, 3

That spot you mean in Judy land
That special spice then to me spake
Is the city in which the Lamb did stand
And suffer sorely for mankind's sake   940
The old Jerusalem, you understand
Where God the old guilt with blood did slake
But the new, the light that from God descends
The apostle in Apocalypse as his theme did take
The Lamb without a spot of black   945
Has carried thither his fair court
And as his flock is without a fleck
So is his city without a spot

Pearl of Great Price

Of motez twa to cẽ̃e clene
& min hyrt wye nawpetes
yat nys to yow no moze to mene
but rete of god of hyrt of ýes
& yat on oure ýes chen mad et ene
sit payne to suffer ye lowte hyt elpe
m̃ yat of is uoyt but ýes to clene
yat ny chal laffe sit arten reles
yat is ýe boz yat sie to pres
tros oure tresty be layd to rote
yer glozy & blycce chal ai entier
to ýe nieyny ýᵗ is ryᵗ oueten mote

XVI, 4

Of those two spots shall I speak plain
And both called Jerusalem, nevertheless   950
Which name to you can either mean
The City of God, or the Sight of Peace
In the one our peace did first begin
With pain to suffer, the Lamb it chose
In the other is nothing but peace to glean   955
That shall last forever, and never cease
That is the city toward which we press
As soon as our flesh is laid to rot
There glory and bliss shall ever increase
For that multitude without a spot   960

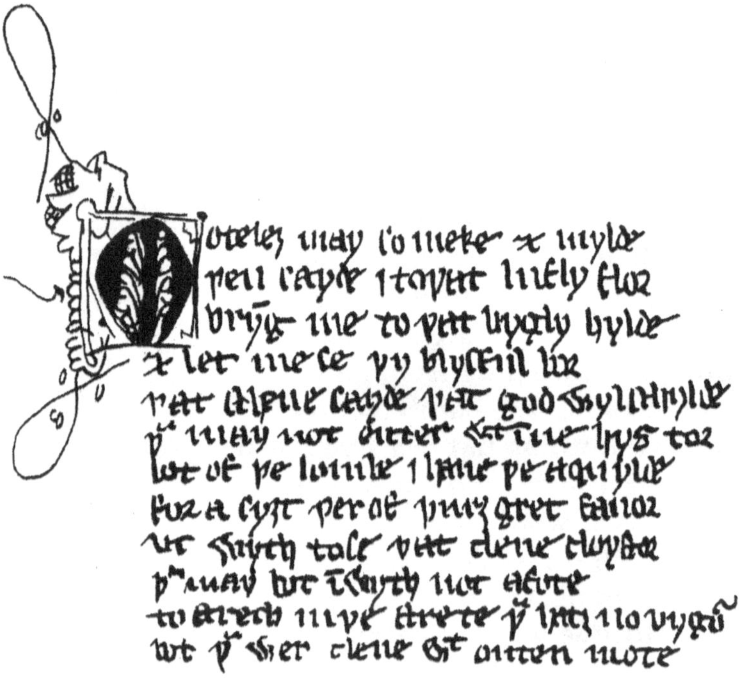

Motelez may so meke & mylde
þen sayde I to þat lufly flor
Bryng me to þat bygly bylde
& let me se þy blysful bor
þat schene sayde þat god wyl schylde
þou may not enter wyth-inne hys tor
Bot of þe lombe I haue þe aquylde
For a syȝt þer of þurȝ gret fauor
Vtwyth to se þat clene cloystor
þou may bot inwyth not a fote
To strech in þe strete þou hatz no vygour
Bot þou wer clene wyth outen mote

XVI, 5

Spotless maid so meek and mild
Then said I to that lovely flower
Bring me to that stout stronghold
And let me see your blissful bower
That fair one said, That God has foiled   965
You may not come within his tower
But to the Lamb have I appealed
That you might see that cloister pure
You may behold it from afar
But within those walls you cannot set foot   970
To walk that street you have no power
Unless you are clean, without a spot

Þis mote þe mytyl vn hyde
loke vp toward þys wonez herned
...j en endez þe on þis cyde
...þ... tylþ to ... be rened
þe douce no lenger byde
bot lurked by laticez co luetly lened
tyl on a hyl þat j asspyed
... blusched on þe burþ as j forth drened
byzonde þe bruk fro me ... keued
þat schyrrer þen sunne wyþ schaftez schyn
...þe apokalypce is þe fasoun ...ened
as deuysez hit þe apostel johan

XVII, 1

If I this spot for you shall bring to light
Walk up towards this water's head
And I shall follow upon this side   975
Until you have unto a hill been led
No longer then would I abide
But by lovely leafy limbs did tread
Till upon a hill I it espied
And gazed on the city while I forth sped   980
Beyond the brook was the burg outspread
That sheerer than shafts of sunshine shone
In Apocalypse you may about it read
As he describes it, the Apostle John

As Iohn þe apostel hit syʒ wit syʒt
I syʒe þat cyty of gret renoun
Ierusalem co nure & ryally dyʒt
As hit watz liʒt fro þe heuen adoun
þe borʒ watz al of brende golde bryʒt
As glemande glas burnist broun
Wit gentyl gemmez an under pyʒt
Wit bantelez twelue on basyng boun
þe foundementez twelue of riche tenoun
Vch tabelment watz a serlypez ston
As derely deuysez þis ilk toun
I herde calle þe apostel Iohn

XVII, 2

As John the apostle first saw that sight   985
I beheld that city of great renown
The New Jerusalem richly bedight
As it was descended from heaven down
The city was all of red gold bright
Clear and transparent as glass it shone   990
And garnished with jewels sparkling with light
Twelve were the pillars it was based upon
With twelve foundations from gemstones hewn
And every tier was a separate stone
As he so clearly describes this town   995
In Apocalypse, the apostle John

As þise ftonieȝ tonit con nemie
1 knewi þe name aff his tale
jaȝer llyft þe fyrft ȝreme
þat j on þe fyrft valle con ðiale
þe gleime ȝreue т þe loðiett iþine
lafter lþiðe þe leconðe ftale
þe tallydþyne þeme wтoimen ȝeime
т þe þryd table cmþirly tale
þe emerate þe furþe lo ȝreme of ftale
þe lardoþyle þe fyfþe ftoii
þe legte þe ryle þe coilþt ðiale
т þe eȝotalyþþce þe eȝoftel 1olþn

XVII, 3

As John these stones in scripture named
From his description I knew them all
Jasper was the foremost gem
That glittered green on the basement wall   1000
The lowest but not the least of them
Sapphire the second in order fell
The chalcedony all sublime
In the third tier shone clear and pale
The fourth was the emerald, greenest of all   1005
The sardonyx was the fifth stone
Ruby the sixth, as we hear him tell
In Apocalypse, the apostle John

Zet joyned john þe crysolyt
þe seuenþe gemme ī fundament
þe a3te þe beryl cler & quyt
þe tuuelye & þyne loʍ þe nőte endent
þe crysopase þe tenþe is ti3t
þ gacy3yh þe enleuenþe gent
þe twelfþe þe gentylette i vch a plyt
þe amatyzt purpre wt ynde blente
þe wal abof þe bantels bent
O Iasporye as glas þat glysnande ʃchon
I kneʍ hit by his deuyʃement
ī þe Apocalyppez þe Apostel john

XVII, 4

To these John added the chrysolite
The gem that stood on the foundation seventh   1010
The eighth was the beryl clear and white
The twin-hued topaz formed the ninth
On the tenth tier, chrysoprase was bright
The stately jacinth graced the eleventh
And the amethyst, noblest in all men's sight   1015
With purple and indigo adorned the twelfth
The wall well founded on the base beneath
Of jasper; like gleaming glass it shone
I recognized it as he set it forth
In the Apocalypse, the apostle John   1020

As john deuyſed yet ſa3 i þare
þiſe twelue degreſ wern brode + ſtayre
þe cyte ſtod abof ful ſware
as longe as brode as hy3e ful fayre
þe ſtretez of golde as glaſſe al bare
þe wal of Jaſper þat glent as glayre
þe wonez wythinne enurned ware
wyth alle kynnez perre þat mo3t repayre
þenne helde vch ſquare of þis manayre
twelue forlonge ſpace er euer hit fon
of he3t of brede of lenþe to cayre
for meten he mette þe a3oſtel john

XVII, 5

As John described it, I saw it there
Broad and steep was the twelve-step stair
The city stood above four square
As long as broad as high, full fair
The streets of gold like glass all clear   1025
The wall of jasper did gleam and glare
The rooms within adornéd were
With every kind of gem most rare
Of that domain each side was square
And each twelve thousand furlongs ran   1030
Height, breadth, and length were equal there
For he saw it measured, the Apostle John

XVIII, 1

As John writes, yet more did I there see
Each side of that place had three gates
So twelve all round did I espy   1035
The portals adorned with precious plates
And each gate made of a margery
A perfect pearl that never fades
On each the name, inscribed artfully
Of one of Israel's children, following their dates   1040
That is to say, by their birth-rights
The eldest was ever the first thereon
Such light there gleamed in all the streets
They needed neither sun nor moon

Of sunne ne mone had þay no nede
þe self god watz her lambe lyȝt
þe lombe her lantyrne wiþ outen drede
þurȝ hym blysned þe borȝ al bryȝt
þurȝ woȝe ʒ gron my lokyng ȝede
for sotyle cler noȝt lette no lyȝt
þe hyȝe trone þer moȝt ʒe hede
Wiþ alle þe apparaylmente vmbe pyȝte
As iohn þe apostel in termez tyȝte
þe hyȝe god self hit set vpone
A ren of þe trone þer ran out ryȝte
Watz bryȝter þen boþe þe sunne ʒ mone

XVIII, 2

Of sun or moon they had no need   1045
For God himself was their lamp-light
The Lamb their lantern, a sun indeed
Through him the city shone all bright
Through walls and rooms did my glance proceed
For all was transparent and clear to sight   1050
The high throne of glory was there displayed
With the elders around it, all dressed in white
As John the apostle described it aright
And the high God himself was seated thereon
A river ran out of the throne more bright   1055
By far than either the sun or moon

Sunne ne mone lþou non co chete
A þer euylon flode out of þat flet
Swyþe bit chewnge þurz vch a strete
Wf outen fylþe oþ galle oþ glet
Kyrk þer ine watz non zete
Chapel ne temple þat eu watz set
Þe Al myzty watz her mynyster mete
Þe Lombe þe saker fyse þer to re get
Þe zatez stoken watz neu zet
Bot eu more vpen att vche alone
Þer entrez non to take reset
Þat berez any spot an vndz mone

XVIII, 3

Sun nor moon never shone so sweet
As the copious flood that flows from that floor
Swiftly it swirled through every street
Without any filth, neither muck nor mire   1060
Church therein there was never yet
Chapel nor temple, nor house of prayer
The Almighty was their minster meet
The Lamb their sacrifice, there to restore
The gates bear neither bolt nor bar   1065
But always stand open at every lane
Yet no one ever takes refuge there
That bears any spot beneath the moon

Þe mone may per of her oþer no myȝte
to qwytty þ is of woy to grym
& al co þ ne is neṽ nyȝt
Whit whyle þe mone per conqas clym
& to even sẅyþ þer ȝozply lyȝt
þer wþhynez ẃon þe brokez bryn
þe planetez arn ī to wṅ aylyȝt
& þe self sīne fulfer to dym
alurtr þer Ṡẃ armtrez fulþhyn
þer twelue frytez of lyf conлere fulẃne
twelue cypez on ier þay wrṅ fulfrym
& renoẁlez n ṡe ī vẁe amone

XVIII, 4

The moon thereof cannot borrow light
Too spotty she is, of visage too grim   1070
And also there it is never night
Why should the moon in her compass climb
And try to vie with that glorious light
That shines upon the brook's brim?
The planets are in too poor a plight   1075
The sun itself is far too dim
There are trees so bright beside that stream
Twelve fruits of life they bear full soon
Twelve months a year crops load each limb
And renew themselves at every moon   1080

an vnder mone so gret in siayle
no erthly hert ne myʒt enduñe
as qñen j blushed vpon yat hily
so terly p of siʒth ye talure
j stod as stylle as dased cuayle
for terly of yat french figure
yat eñde j nasshp rette ne tñayle
so shen j tristy syth glisne ynñe
euñ j dar say hir conciens suñ
may bodyly burne abiden ye wñe
yeʒ alle clerkeʒ hñ had T care
his lyf ouer loke an vnder mone

XVIII, 5

Under the moon so great a miracle
No heart of flesh could well endure
As when I gazed upon that city wall
So rare and marvellous was its allure
I stood as still as a dazed quail　　　　　　1085
In amazement at that dream unsure
My limbs could feel neither rest nor toil
So was I ravished with its radiance pure
For I dare say with conviction sure
Had a bodily man endured that boon　　　　　1090
Though all physicians searched for a cure
His life would be forfeit under the moon

Ryȝt as þe mayncyul mone con rys
er þene þe day glem dryue aldou
lo codnly on a louder syce
Ȝ heen luar of a procellyou
þis noble cite of rych enprelle
Ȝuen codnly full Ȝt omen comou
of cuch vȝynuez Ȝ þe came gylle
þett Ȝuen my blyȝful an vnar crou
Ȝ corownd Ȝuernalle of þe came falou
degayır Ȝ þerlez Ȝ Ȝedez a Ȝyte
Ȝ velpnez breȝe Ȝuen woȝon wu
þe blyȝful þerle Ȝt omen delyt

XIX, 1

As when the mighty moon does rise
Before the day-gleam has sunken down
So all of a sudden, in wondrous wise   1095
That noble city of rich renown
Was instantly full; to my great surprise
I saw where a great procession wound
Of virgins in the self-same guise
As was my blissful one under her crown   1100
In the same fashion they all were crowned
And adorned with pearls, in garments white
On each one's breast was firmly bound
The blissful pearl, with great delight

Wt gret delyt þay glod Tchere
on golden gatez þat gleint as glasse
hundreth þowsandez] Wot þer were
& alle invirte her luirez schalle
wurto kuekz þe glaodeft dere
þelomle by ewe con proudly paffe
wyth hornez cemen ofred gloude cler
as prayfed perlez his siedz schalle
towarde þe throne þay trone ettras
þay þay dieru Gete no pres T plyt
wt mylde as may ørnez Ceme et mas
so oroz þay ferth Wt gret delyt

XIX, 2

With great delight they together fare 1105
On golden streets that gleam like glass
A hundred thousand I believe were there
Hard to know who had the happiest face
And all of one pattern the garments they wear
The Lamb in the forefront did proudly pace 1110
With seven horns of red gold clear
Like precious pearls his clothing was
As toward the throne they together pass
Though thick the throng, none quarrel nor fight
But mild as maidens meek at mass 1115
So fared they forth with great delight

Delyt þᵗ hys come enrroched
to much hit were of vrtu melle
þile alder men quen þe approched
croueþyg to hys fete þay felle
legyoñes of aungelez togeder worked
þer kesten enlens of swete smelle
þen glory⁊ gle sweti were abroched
allouge to loue þat gay in melle
þe heuen most stryke þurȝ þe vrþe to kelle
þat þe vtues of leuen of ioye endyte
to loue þe lomb his meyny in melle
I sigtte iugt agret delyt

XIX, 3

Delight that his arrival wrought
Was greater by far than tongue can tell
Those elders, on finding the one they sought
Grovelling at his feet they fell   1120
Myriads of angels together brought
There scattered incense of sweetest smell
To the angels the elders a new song taught
To praise that jewel that they love so well
That song could pierce through the earth to hell   1125
That the legions of heaven for joy recite
With his servants the worth of the Lamb to tell
Indeed I experienced great delight

Delit þe labe forto deuise
& much meruayle in mynde went
left þ: etz þ: þayeth & make twaryse
þat eu i kyde of gerly geint
to worply þ
his loþez ſyniple
lut
an ende þys
of his
Alas
anſ
or

XIX, 4

Delight upon the Lamb to gaze
Much mixed with marvel in my mind went   1130
Best was he, blithest, and most to praise
Of any on whom ever speech was spent
So gleaming white did his garments blaze
His looks so humble, himself so gent
But a wound full wide and wet there lies   1135
Close to his heart, where his hide was rent
His blood in torrents from his white side went
Alas, thought I, who did that spite?
With anguish should his breast have burnt
Ere in that deed he took delight   1140

To þe londe delyt nou lytte to wene
yat le diere hurt + õwtide hade
T his cemblant õatu neti cene
co diern his glentez gloryoy glade
J loked amõg his meyny õhene
luõ/ pay õyyti lye diern latte xlade
yt ceg j yer my lyttel quene
yat j õende had danden by me T hlade
luze much of nurye õiettz yat þ made
amõg her cewz yat õiett co cilyt
yat cyrt me gart to penk to õianr
foz luf longyg T gret delyt

XIX, 5

The Lamb's delight was plain to be seen
Though he was hurt, and a wide wound had
His countenance as the sun did shine
So glorious were his glances glad
I gazed upon that throng serene   1145
How fraught with life they were, indeed
Then saw I there my little queen
I had thought stood by me in the glade
Lord, much of mirth was that she made
Among her peers that was so white!   1150
That sight did move me the brook to wade
For love-longing, and great delight

Delyt me drof ⁊ pꝛeʒ ⁊ ere
my maneʒ mynde to maddyng matte
quen ſeʒ my frely I ſholde le yere
byʒonde þe ſꝛatter paꝛ lu þere ſualte
I poʒt þat noþyng myʒt me dere
to fech me bur ⁊ take me ſalte
⁊ to ſtart in þe ſtreiu þhuld non me ſtere
to witſine þe remnaſſe þaꝛ)ver þualte
luꝛ of þat miſt ſueʒ ln tait
ſiljen I whilde ſtart ⁊ þe ſtreiu aſtraye
out of þat cuſty ſueʒ by rait
hit ſueʒ not att my prynceʒ paye

XX, 1

Delight so drove me, in eye and ear
My mortal mind did to madness melt
When I saw my sweetheart, I would be there   1155
Beyond the water though she was walled
I thought that nothing could me deter
Fetch me a blow, or make me halt
Once I stood in the stream, none could me bar
From swimming the rest, though I there was killed   1160
But my firm purpose was soon forestalled
As I on the brink of the brook did poise
Out of that course I was recalled
It was not as my Prince would please

hit payed hym not þat I so flonc
ou meruelous merez so mad arayd
of raas þaȝ I were rach & ronk
ȝet rapely þer inne I watȝ restayed
for ryȝt as I sparred vnto þe bonc
þat brathþe out of my drem me brayde
þen wakned I þat erber wlonk
my hede vpon þat hylle watȝ layde
þer as my perle to grounde strayd
I raxled & fel in gret affray
& sykyng to my self I sayd
now al be to þat pryncez paye

XX, 2

It pleased him not that I headlong   1165
Over those wondrous waters, in madness strayed
In a reckless rush, to the stream I sprang
Yet suddenly my haste was stayed
For just as I bounded down the bank
That castle fair began to fade   1170
I woke within that arbor rank
My head upon that hill was laid
Where to the ground my pearl had strayed
I rubbed my eyes, with great unease
And sighing, to myself I said   1175
Now all be as that Prince would please

O e payed fin me tote out fleme
to sodenly of þat fayre region
fro alle yo syrtez to quykez & almeme
alonge þe keny me pruk t sdome
& resefully yfne q cumto reme
O perle qq of ryfy renou
to fiatz; hit me dere fy yy tun æme
T yys vay avy lyon
Te hit le ner ay & coch sermou
þet yy to frytez t garlande gay
tosielis me t yys del ongou
vet yy art to þtt pryntez þuye

XX, 3

It pleased me ill to be cast away
So suddenly, from that fair region
From all those sights so bright and gay
A heavy longing near made me swoon   1180
And ruefully I began to cry
O Pearl, said I, of rich renown
How dear to me what you did say
In this true and unerring vision
If all be sooth that you said in your sermon   1185
And in that gay garland you rest at ease
Delighted I am in this doleful dungeon
That you are as that Prince would please

To þat prynces paye hade I ay bente
& zerned no more þen watz me geuen
& halden me þer in trwe entent
As þe perle me prayed þat watz so þryuen
As helde drawen to goddez present
To mo of his mysterys I hade ben dryuen
Bot ay wolde man of happe more hente
Þen moзten by ryзt vpon hem clyuen
Þer fore my ioye watz sone to ruen
& I kaste of kythez þat lastez aye
Lorde mad hit arn þat arn agayn þe þryuen
Oþ proferen þe ozt agayn þy paye

XX, 4

To please that Prince had I been bent
And yearned for no more than to me was given   1190
And restrained myself, in that true intent
As my pearl prayed, that so well had thriven
Perhaps with God I would still be present
And know more of the mysteries of heaven
But man with good fortune is never content   1195
But covets the more what he is not given
Therefore from my joy I soon was riven
And expelled from a life of eternal ease
Lord, mad is the man who with thee has striven
Or offered thee aught that may displease   1200

And to say þe prince of lele coste
hit is ful eye to þe god krystyn
for j haf fonden hym boþe day & nazte
A god a lorde a frende ful fyn
on þis hyul þis late nazte
for pyty of my serle enchyn
& lypen to god þat by tazte
in krystes dere blessyng & myn
put in þe forme of bred & wyn
þe preste up hesies uch a day e
lp gret up to be his ipuyly hyue
And precios serles vnto his say amen · amen ·

XX, 5

To please that Prince, and set things right
For any good Christian, is easily done
For I have found him, both day and night
A God, a Lord, a friend full fine
And upon this hill have I found my fate   1205
As for pity of my pearl I lay prostrate
I into God's care did it at last resign
In Christ's dear blessing (as ever in mine)
That in the form of bread and wine
The priest here shows us every day   1210
Us all for his service he did design
As precious pearls to please him aye. Amen. Amen.

Transcription of the Manuscript

This transcription of that portion of Cotton Nero A. x. containing *Pearl* has been made from a high-resolution digital copy of the manuscript prepared by the British Library and available in the Manuscript Reading Room of the British Library in London, checked against the Early English Text Society facsimile of the manuscript, which was published in 1923, and which preserves many difficult or doubtful readings which are now more or less illegible in the digital copy and presumably in the manuscript itself. The transcription is letter for letter, except that abbreviations in the manuscript for which typographical representations do not exist are expanded and appear in italic type. The long "s" is represented by the character ſ, yogh by ȝ, and thorn by þ. The Tironian sign for "et" or "and," which in this manuscript is crossed with an oblique line, is represented by &. Majuscules in the manuscript are represented by capital letters in the transcription; illuminated capitals are represented by bold capitals. Where two oblique lines appear in the manuscript to indicate the beginning of a new stanza (Roberts 171-2), these are represented in the transcription by two virgules or forward slashes, thus: //. Where separate words are run together in the manuscript, they have been silently separated, and where parts of the same word have been separated in the manuscript, they have been silently joined, to facilitate use of the glossary. Letters which are conjecturally restored appear in square brackets; emendations for the most part have not been admitted in the transcription but are referred to and discussed in the textual notes.

F43
Perle pleſaunt to prynces paye
to clanly clos in golde ſo cler[e]
oute of oryent I hardyly ſaye
ne proued I neuer her precios pere
ſo rounde ſo reken in vche araye
ſo ſmal ſo ſmoþe her ſydeȝ were
quereſoeuer I Iugged gemmeȝ gaye
I ſette hyr ſengeley in ſynglure

5

allas I leſte hyr in on erbere
þurȝ greſſe to grounde hit fro me yot   10
I dewyne fordolked of luf daungere
of þat pryuy perle wᵗouten ſpot
Syþen in þat ſpote hit fro me ſprange
ofte haf I wayted wyſchande þat wele
þat wont watȝ whyle deuoyde my wrange   15
& heuen my happe & al my hele
þᵗ dotȝ bot þrych my hert þrange
my breſte in bale bot bolne & bele
ȝet þoȝt me neuer ſo ſwete a ſange
as ſtylle ſtounde let to me ſtele   20
forſoþe þer fleten to me fele
to þenke hir color ſo clad in clot
O moul þou marreȝ a myry iuele
my priuy perle wᵗouten ſpotte
þat ſpot of ſpyſeȝ [mo]t nedeȝ ſprede   25
þer ſuch rycheȝ to rot is runnen
blomeȝ blayke & blwe & rede
þer ſchyneȝ ful ſchyr agayn þe ſunne
flor & fryte may not be fede
þer hit doun drof in moldeȝ dunne   30
for vch greſſe mot grow of grayneȝ dede
no whete were elleȝ to woneȝ wonne
of goud vche goude is ay bygonne
ſo ſemly a ſede moȝt fayly not
þᵗ ſprygande ſpyceȝ vp ne ſponne   35
of þat precios perle wythouten ſpotte

F43v

To þat ſpot þat I in ſpeche expoun
I entred in þat erber grene
in augoſte in a hyȝ ſeyſoun
quen corne is coruen wyth crokeȝ kene   40
on huyle þer perle hit trendeled doun
ſchadowed þis worteȝ ful ſchyre & ſchene
gilofre gyngure & gromylyoun
& pyonys powdered ay bytwene
ȝif hit watȝ ſemly on to ſene   45
a fayr reflayr ȝet fro hit flot
þer wonys þat worþyly I wot & wene
my precious perle wythouten ſpot

Bifore þat ſpot my honde I ſpeɳnd
for care ful colde þat to me caȝt   50
a deuely dele in my hert deɳned
þaȝ reſouɳ ſette myſeluen ſaȝt
I playned my perle þᵗ þer watȝ ſpeɳned
wyth fyrte ſkylleȝ þat faſte faȝt
þaȝ kynde of kryſt me comfort keɳned   55
my wreched wylle iɳ wo ay wraȝte
I felle vpon þat floury flaȝt
ſuche odoᵘr to my herneȝ ſchot
I ſlode vpon a ſlepyɳg-ſlaȝte
on þat precos perle wᵗouten ſpot   60
Fro ſpot my ſpyryt þer ſprang iɳ ſpace
my body on balke þer bod iɳ ſweuen
my goſte is gon in godeȝ grace
in auenture þer meruayleȝ meuen
I ne wyſte in þis worlde quere þᵗ hit wace   65
bot I knew me keſte þer klyfeȝ cleuen
towarde a foreſte I bere þe face
where rych rokkeȝ wer to dyſcreuen
þe lyȝt of hem myȝt no mon leuen
þe glemande glory þat of hem glent   70
for wern neuᵉr webbeȝ þat wyȝeȝ weuen
of half ſo dere adubmente

F44
Dubbed wern alle þo downeȝ ſydeȝ
wᵗ cryſtal klyffeȝ ſo cler of kynde
holtewodeȝ bryȝt aboute hem bydeȝ   75
of bolleȝ as blwe as ble of ynde
as bornyſt ſyluer þe lef onſlydeȝ
þat þike con trylle on vch a tynde
quen glem of glodeȝ agaynȝ hem glydeȝ
wyth ſchymeryɳg ſchene ful ſchrylle þay ſchyndc   80
þe grauayl þat on grounde con grynde
wern precioᵘs perleȝ of oryente
þe ſuɳnebemeȝ bot blo & blynde
In reſpecte of þat adubbement
//The adubbemente of þo downeȝ dere   85
garten my goſte al greffe forȝete
ſo frech flauoreȝ of fryteȝ were
as fode hit con me fayre refete

fowleʒ þer flowen in fryth in fere
of flaumbande hweʒ boþe fmale & grete   90
bot fytole ftryng & gyternere
her reken myrþe moʒt not retrete
for quen þofe bryddeʒ her wyngeʒ bete
þay fongen wyth a fwete afent
fo gracos gle couþe no mon gete   95
as here & fe her adubbement
//So al watʒ dubbet on dere afyfe
þat fryth þer fortwne forth me fereʒ
þe derþe þerof for to deuyfe
nis no wyʒ worþe þat tonge bereʒ   100
I welke ay forth in wely wyfe
no bonk fo byg þᵗ did me dereʒ
þe fyrre in þe fryth þe feier con ryfe
þe playn þe plontteʒ þe fpyfe þe pereʒ
& raweʒ & randeʒ & rych reuereʒ   105
as fyldor fyn her b[o]nkes brent
I wan to a water by fchore þat fchereʒ
lorde dere watʒ hit adubbement

F44v
The dubbemente of þo derworth depe
wern bonkeʒ bene of beryl bryʒt   110
Swangeande fwete þe water con fwepe
wyth a rownande rourde raykande aryʒt
in þe founce þer ftonden ftoneʒ ftepe
as glente þurʒ glas þat glowed & glyʒt
a ftremande fterneʒ quen ftroþe-men flepe   115
ftaren in welkyn in wynter nyʒt
for vche a pobbel in pole þer pyʒt
watʒ Emerad faffer oþer gemme gente
þat alle þe loʒe lemed of lyʒt
fo dere watʒ hit adubbement   120
The dubbement dere of doun & daleʒ
of wod & water & wlonc playneʒ
bylde in me blys abated my baleʒ
fordidden my ftreffe dyftryed my payneʒ
doun after a ftrem þat dryʒly haleʒ   125
I bowed in blys bredful my brayneʒ
þe fyrre I folʒed þofe floty valeʒ
þe more ftrenghþe of ioye myn herte ftrayneʒ

as fortune fares þeras ho frayneȝ
wheþer folace ho fende oþer elleȝ fore 130
þe wyȝ to wham her wylle ho wayneȝ
hytteȝ to hauc ay more & more
//More of wele watȝ in þat wyfe
þen I cowþe telle þaȝ I tom hade
for vrþely herte myȝt not fuffyfe 135
to þe tenþe dole of þo gladneȝ glade
forþy I þoȝt þᵗ paradyfe
watȝ þer oþer gayn þo bonkeȝ brade
I hoped þe water were a deuyfe
bytwene myrþeȝ by mereȝ made 140
byȝonde þe broke by flente oþer flade
I hope þᵗ mote merked wore
bot þe water watȝ depe I dorft not wade
& euer me longed a more & more

F45

More & more & ȝet wel mare 145
me lyfte to fe þe broke byȝonde
for if hit watȝ fayr þer I con fare
wel loueloker watȝ þe fyrre londe
abowte me con I ftote & ftare
to fynde a forþe fafte con I fonde 150
bot woþeȝ mo Iwyffe þer ware
þe fyrre I ftalked by þe ftronde
& euer me þoȝt I fchulde not wonde
for wo þer weleȝ fo wynne wore
þenne nwe note me com on honde 155
þat meued my mynde ay more & more
//More meruayle con my dom adaunt
I feȝ byȝonde þat myry mere
a cryftal clyffe ful relufaunt
mony ryal ray con fro hit rere 160
at þe fote þerof þer fete a faunt
a mayden of menfke ful debonere
blyfnande whyt watȝ hyr bleaunt
I knew hyr wel I hade fen hyr ere
as glyfnande golde þat man con fchere 165
fo fchon þat fchene anvnder fchore
on lenghe I loked to hyr þere
þe lenger I knew hyr more & more

//The more I frayſte hyr fayre face
her ſygure ſyn quen I had fonte 170
ſuche gladande glory con to me glace
as lyttel byfore þerto watȝ wonte
to calle hyr lyſte con me enchace
bot bayſment geſ myn hert a brunt
I ſeȝ hyr in ſo ſtrange a place 175
ſuch a burre myȝt make myn herte blunt
þenne vereȝ ho vp her fayre frount
hyr vyſayge whyt as playn yuore
þat ſtonge myn hert ful ſtray atount
& euer þe lenger þe more & more 180

F45v
More þen me lyſte my drede aros
I ſtod ful ſtylle & dorſte not calle
wyth yȝen open & mouth ful clos
I ſtod as hende as hawk in halle
I hope þat goſtly watȝ þᵗ porpoſe 185
I dred onende quat ſchulde byfalle
leſt ho me eſchaped þat I þer chos
er I at ſteuen hir moȝt ſtalle
þat gracios gay wᵗouten galle
ſo ſmoþe ſo ſmal ſo ſeme ſlyȝt 190
ryſeȝ vp in hir araye ryalle
a precos pyece in perleȝ pyȝt
Perleȝ pyȝte of ryal prys
þere moȝt mon by grace haf ſene
quen þat frech as flor-de-lys 195
doun þe bonke con boȝe bydene
al blyſnande whyt watȝ hir beau mys
vpon at ſydeȝ & bounden bene
wyth þe myryeſte margarys at my deuyſe
þat euer I ſeȝ ȝet with myn yȝen 200
wyth lappeȝ large I wot & I wene
dubbed with double perle & dyȝte
her cortel of ſelf ſute ſchene
wᵗ precios perleȝ al vmbepyȝte
A pyȝt coroune ȝet wer þat gyrle 205
of mariorys & non oþer ſton
hiȝe pynakled of cler quyt perle
wyth flurted flowreȝ perfet vpon

to hed hade ho non oþer werle
her lere leke al hyr vmbegon 210
her femblaunt fade for doc oþer erle
her ble more bla3t þen whalle3 bon
as fchorne golde fchyr her fax þenne fchon
on fchyldere3 þat leghe vnlapped ly3te
her depe colour 3et wonted non 215
of precios perle in porfyl py3te

F46
Py3t wat3 poyned & vche a hemme
at honde at fyde3 at ouerture
wyth whyte perle & non oþer gemme
& bornyfte quyte wat3 hyr uefture 220
bot a wonder perle wᵗouten wemme
in mydde3 hyr brefte wat3 fette fo fure
a manne3 dom mo3t dry3ly demme
er mynde mo3t malte in hit mefure
I hope no tong mo3t endure 225
no fauerly faghe fay of þᵗ fy3t
fo wat3 hit clene & cler & pure
þat precios perle þer hit wat3 py3t
Py3t in perle þat precios pyfe
on wyþer half water com doun þe fchore 230
no gladder gome heþen into grece
þen I quen ho on brymme wore
ho wat3 me nerre þen aunte or nece
my Ioy forþy wat3 much þe more
ho profered me fpeche þᵗ fpecial fpyce 235
enclynande lowe in wommon lore
ca3te of her coroun of grete trefore
& haylfed me wyth a lote ly3te
wel wat3 me þᵗ euer I wat3 bore
to fware þat fwctc in perle3 py3te 240
O perle quod I in perle3 py3t
art þou my perle þat I haf playned
regretted by myn one on ny3te
much longey𝑛g haf I for þe layned
fyþen into greffe þou me agly3te 245
penfyf payred I am forpayned
& þou in a lyf of lykyng ly3te
in paradys erde of ftryf vnftrayned

what wyrd hatȝ hyder my iuel vayned
& don me in þys del & gret daunger   250
fro we in twynne wern towen & twayned
I haf ben a Ioyleȝ Iuelere

F46v
That Iuel þenne in gemmeȝ gente
vered vp her vyſe wᵗ yȝen graye
ſet on hyr coroun of perle orient   255
& ſoberly after þenne con ho ſay
ſir ȝe haf your tale myſetente
to ſay your perle is al awaye
þat is in cofer ſo comly clente
as in þis gardyn gracios gaye   260
hereinne to lenge foreuer & play
þer mys ne mornyng com neuer here
her were a forſer for þe in faye
if þou were a gentyl Iueler
Bot Iueler gente if þou ſchal loſe   265
þy ioy for a gemme þat þe watȝ lef
me þynk þe put in a mad porpoſe
& buſyeȝ þe aboute a rayſoun bref
for þat þou leſteȝ watȝ bot a roſe
þat flowred & fayled as kynde hyt gef   270
now þurȝ kynde of þe kyſte þᵗ hyt con cloſe
to a perle of prys hit is put in pref
& þou hatȝ called þy wyrde a þef
þat oȝt of noȝt hatȝ mad þe cler
þou blameȝ þe bote of þy meſchef   275
þou art no kynde Iueler
//A Iuel to me þen watȝ þys geſte
& iueleȝ wern hyr gentyl ſaweȝ
Iwyſe quod I my blyſſol beſte
my grete dyſtreſſe þou al todraweȝ   280
to be excuſed I make requeſte
I trawed my perle don out of daweȝ
now haf I fonde hyt I ſchal ma feſte
& wony wᵗ hyt in ſchyr wod-ſchaweȝ
& loue my lorde & al his laweȝ   285
þat hatȝ me broȝ þys blys ner
now were I at yow byȝonde þiſe waweȝ
I were a ioyfol Iueler

F47
Iueler fayde þat gemme clene
wy borde ȝe men fo madde ȝe be   290
þre wordeȝ hatȝ þou fpoken at ene
vnavyfed forfoþe wern alle þre
þou ne wofte in worlde quat on dotȝ mene
þy worde byfore þy wytte con fle
þou fays þou traweȝ me in þis dene   295
bycawfe þou may wᵗ yȝen me fe
anoþer þou fays in þys countre
þyfelf fchal won wᵗ me ryȝt here
þe þrydde to paffe þys water fre
þat may no ioyfol Iueler   300
I halde þat iueler lyttel to prayfe
þat loueȝ wel þᵗ he feȝ wyth yȝe
& much to blame & vncortoyfe
þat leueȝ oure lorde wolde make a lyȝe
þat lelly hyȝte your lyf to rayfe   305
þaȝ fortune dyd your flefch to dyȝe
ȝe fetten hys wordeȝ ful wefternays
þat loueȝ no þynk bot ȝe hit fyȝe
& þat ins a poynt o forquydryȝe
þat vche god mon may euel byfeme   310
to leue no tale be true to tryȝe
bot þat hys one fkyl may dem
//Deme now þyfelf if þou con dayly
as man to god wordeȝ fchulde heue
þou faytȝ þou fchal won in þis bayly   315
me þynk þe burde fyrft afke leue
& ȝet of graunt þou myȝteȝ fayle
þou wylneȝ ouer þys water to weue
er mofte þou ceuer to oþer counfayl
þy corfe in clot mot calder keue   320
for hit watȝ forgarte at paradys greue
oure ȝorefader hit con myffeȝeme
þurȝ drwry deth boȝ vch ma dreue
er ouer þys dam hym dryȝtyn deme

F47v
Demeȝ þou me quod I my fwete   325
to dol agayn þenne I dowyne

now haf I fonte þat I forlete
ſchal I efte forgo hit er euer I fyne
why ſchal I hit boþe myſſe & mete
my precios perle dotȝ me gret pyne   330
what ſerueȝ treſor bot gareȝ men grete
when he hit ſchal efte wᵗ teneȝ tyne
now rech I neuer for to declyne
ne how fer of folde þat man me fleme
when I am partleȝ of perleȝ myne   335
bot durande doel what may men deme
//Thow demeȝ noȝt bot doel-dyſtreſſe
þenne ſayde þat wyȝt why dotȝ þou ſo
for dyne of doel of lureȝ leſſe
ofte mony mon forgos þe mo   340
þe oȝte better þyſeluen bleſſe
& loue ay god & wele & woe
for anger gayneȝ þe not a creſſe
who nedeȝ ſchal þole be not ſo þro
for þoȝ þou daunce as any do   345
braundyſch & bray þy braþeȝ breme
when þou no fyrre may to ne fro
þou moſte abyde þat he ſchal deme
//Deme dryȝtyn euer hym adyte
of þe way a fote ne wyl he wryþe   350
by mendeȝ mounteȝ not a myte
þaȝ þou for ſorȝe be neuer blyþe
ſtynſt of þy ſtrot & fyne to flyte
& ſech hys blyþe ful ſwefte & ſwyþe
þy prayer may hys pyte byte   355
þat mercy ſchal hyr crafteȝ kyþe
hys comforte may þy langour lyþe
& þy lureȝ of lyȝtly leme
for marre oþer madde morne & myþe
al lys in hym to dyȝt & deme   360

F48
Thenne demed I to þat damyſelle
ne worþe no wrathþe vnto my lorde
if rapely raue ſpornande in ſpelle
my herte watȝ al wᵗ myſſe remorde
as wallande water gotȝ out of welle   365
I do me ay in hys myſerecorde

rebuke me neuer wᵗ wordeȝ felle
þaȝ I forloyne my dere endorde
bot lyþeȝ me kyndely your coumforde
pytoſly þenkande vpon þyſſe   370
of care & me ȝe made acorde
þat er watȝ grounde of alle my blyſſe
//My blyſſe my bale ȝe han ben boþe
bot much þe bygger ȝet watȝ my mon
fro þou watȝ wroken fro vch a woþe   375
I wyſte neuer quere my perle watȝ gon
now I hit ſe now leþeȝ my loþe
& quen we departed we wern at on
god forbede we be now wroþe
we meten ſo ſelden by ſtok oþer ſton   380
þaȝ cortayſly ȝe carp con
I am bot mol & marereȝ myſſe
bot cryſtes merſy & mary & Ion
þiſe arn þe grounde of alle my blyſſe
//In blyſſe I ſe þe blyþely blent   385
& I a man al mornyf mate
ȝe take þeron ful lyttel tente
þaȝ I hente ofte harmeȝ hate
bot now I am here in your preſente
I wolde byſech wythouten debate   390
ȝe wolde me ſay in ſobre aſente
what lyf ȝe lede erly & late
for I am ful fayn þat your aſtate
is worþen to worſchyp & wele Iwyſſe
of alle my Ioy þe hyȝe gate   395
hit is in grounde of alle my blyſſe

F48v
Now blyſſe burne mot þe bytyde
þen ſayde þat luſſoum of lyth & lere
& welcum here to walk & byde
for now þy ſpeche is to me dere   400
mayſterful mod & hyȝe pryde
I hete þe arn heterly hated here
my lorde ne loueȝ not for to chyde
for meke arn alle þᵗ woneȝ hym nere
& when in hys place þou ſchal apere   405
be dep deuote in hol mekeneſſe

my lorde þe lamb loueȝ ay ſuch chere
þat is þe grounde of alle my blyſſe
//A blyſful lyf þou ſays I lede
þou woldeȝ knaw þerof þe ſtage   410
þow woſt wel when þy perle con ſchede
I watȝ ful ȝong & tender of age
bot my lorde þe lombe þurȝ hys godhede
he toke myſelf to hys maryage
corounde me quene in blyſſe to brede   415
in lenghe of dayeȝ þat euer ſchal wage
& ſeſed in alle hys herytage
hys lef is I am holy hysſe
hys preſe hys prys & hys parage
is rote & grounde of alle my blyſſe   420
Blyſful quod I may þys be trwe
dyſpleſeȝ not if I ſpeke errour
art þou þe quene of heueneȝ blwe
þᵗ al þys worlde ſchal do honour
we leuen on marye þat grace of grewe   425
þat ber a barne of vyrgyn flour
þe croune fro hyr quo moȝt remwe
bot ho hir paſſed in ſum fauour
now for ſynglerty o hyr douſour
we calle hyr fenyx of arraby   430
þat freles fleȝe of hyr faſor
lyk to þe quen of cortayſye

F49
Cortayſe quen þenne ſyde þat gaye
knelande to grounde folde vp hyr face
makeleȝ moder & myryeſt may   435
bleſſed byngyner of vch a grace
þenne ros ho vp & con reſtay
& ſpeke me towarde in þat ſpace
ſir fele here porchaſeȝ & fongeȝ pray
bot ſupplantoreȝ none wᶜinne þys place   440
þat emperiſe al heuenȝ hatȝ
& vrþe & helle in her bayly
of erytage ȝet non wyl ho chace
for ho is quen of cortayſye
//The court of þe kyndom of god alyue   445
hatȝ a property in hytſelf beyng

alle þat may þerinne aryue
of alle þe reme is quen oþer kyng
& neuer oþer ȝet fchal depryue
bot vchon fayn of oþereȝ hafyng   450
& wolde her corouneȝ wern worþe þo fyue
if poffyble were her mendyng
bot my lady of quom Iefu con fpryng
ho haldeȝ þe empyre ouer vus ful hyȝe
& þat dyfplefeȝ non of oure gyng   455
for ho is quene of cortayfye
//Of courtayfye as faytȝ faynt poule
al arn we membreȝ of ihesu kryft
as heued & arme & legg & naule
temen to hys body ful trwe & tyfte   460
ryȝt fo is vch a kryften fawhe
a longande lym to þe mayfter of myfte
þenne loke what hate oþer any gawle
is tached oþer tyȝed þy lymmeȝ bytwyfte
þy heued hatȝ nauþer greme ne gryfte   465
on arme oþer fynger þaȝ þou ber byȝe
fo fare we alle wyth luf & lyfte
to kyng & quene by cortayfye

F49v
Cortayfe quod I I leue
& charyte grete be yow among   470
bot my fpeche þat yow ne greue
. . . .
þyfelf in heuen ouer hyȝ þou heue
to make þe quen þat watȝ fo ȝonge
what more honour moȝte he acheue   475
þat hade endured in worlde ftronge
& lyued in penaunce hys lyueȝ longe
wᵗ bodyly bale hym blyffe to byye
what more worfchyp moȝt ho fonge
þen corounde be kyng by cortayfe   480
That cortayfe is to fre of dede
ȝyf hyt be foth þat þou coneȝ faye
þou lyfed not two ȝer in oure þede
þou cowþeȝ neuer god nauþer plefe ne pray
ne neuer nawþer pater ne crede   485
& quen mad on þe fyrft day

I may not traw ſo god me ſpede
þat god wolde wryþe ſo wrange away
of countes damyſel par ma ſay
wer fayr in heuen to halde aſſtate   490
oþer elleȝ a lady of laſſe aray
bot a quene hit is to dere a date
//þer is no date of hys godneſſe
þen ſayde to me þat worþy wyȝte
for al is trawþe þat he con dreſſe   495
& he may do noþynk bot ryȝt
as mathew meleȝ in your meſſe
in ſothfol goſpel of god almyȝt
in ſample he can ful grayþely geſſe
& lykneȝ hit to heuen lyȝte   500
my regne he ſaytȝ is lyk on hyȝt
to a lorde þat hade a uyne I wate
of tyme of ȝere þe terme watȝ tyȝt
to labor vyne watȝ dere þe date

F50
//þat date of ȝere wel knawe þys hyne   505
þe lorde ful erly vp he ros
to hyre werkmen to hys vyne
& fyndeȝ þer ſumme to hys porpos
into acorde þay con declyne
for a pene on a day & forth þay gotȝ   510
wryþen & worchen & don gret pyne
keruen & caggen & man hit clos
aboute vnder þe lorde to marked totȝ
& ydel men ſtande he fyndeȝ þerate
why ſtande ȝe ydel he ſayde to þos   515
ne knawe ȝe of þis day no date
//Er date of daye hider arn we wonne
ſo watȝ al ſamen her anſwar ſoȝt
we haf ſtanden her ſyn ros þe ſunne
& no mon byddeȝ vus do ryȝt noȝt   520
gos into my vyne dotȝ þat ȝe conne
ſo ſayde þe lorde & made hit toȝt
what reſonabele hyre be naȝt be runne
I yow pray in dede & þoȝte
þay wente into þe vyne & wroȝte   525
& al day þe lorde þus ȝede his gate

& nw men to hys vyne he broȝte
wel neȝ wyl day watȝ paſſed date
//At þe day of date of euenſonge
on oure byfore þe ſonne go doun   530
he ſeȝ þer ydel men ful ſtronge
& ſade to hen wᵗ ſobre ſoun
wy ſtonde ȝe ydel þiſe dayeȝ longe
þay ſayden her hyre watȝ nawhere boun
gotȝ to my vyne ȝemen ȝonge   535
& wyrkeȝ & dotȝ þᵗ at ȝe moun
ſone þe worlde bycom wel broun
þe ſunne watȝ doun & & hit wex late
to take her hyre he mad ſumoun
þe day watȝ al apaſſed date   540

F50v
The date of þe daye þe lorde con knaw
called to þe reue lede pay þe meyny
gyf hem þe hyre þat I hem owe
& fyrre þat non me may reprene
ſet hem alle vpon a rawe   545
& gyf vchon inlyche a peny
bygyn at þe laſte þat ſtandeȝ lowe
tyl to þe fyrſte þat þou atteny
& þenne þe fyrſt bygonne to pleny
& ſayden þat þay hade trauayled ſore   550
þeſe bot on oure hem con ſtreny
vus þynk vus oȝe to take more
//More haf we ſerued vus þynk ſo
þat ſuffred han þe dayeȝ hete
þenn þyſe þat wroȝt not houreȝ two   555
& þou dotȝ hem vus to counterfete
þenne ſayde þe lorde to o[n] of þo
frende no wanig I wyl þe ȝete
take þat is þyn owne & go
& I hyred þe for a peny agrete   560
quy bygynneȝ þou now to þrete
watȝ not a pene þy couenaunt þore
fyrre þen couenaunde is noȝt to plete
wy ſchalte þou þenne ask more
//More weþer louyly is me my gyfte   565
to do wyth myn quatſo me lykeȝ

oþer elleȝ þyn yȝe to lyþer is lyfte
for I am goude & non byſwykeȝ
þus ſchal I quod kryſte hit ſkyfte
þe laſte ſchal be þe fyrſt þat ſtrykeȝ   570
& þe fyrſt þe laſte be he neuer ſo ſwyft
for mony ben calle þaȝ fewe be mykeȝ
þus pore men her part ay pykeȝ
þaȝ þay com late & lyttel wore
& þaȝ her ſweng wyth lyttel atſlykeȝ   575
þe merci of god is much þe more

F51
More haf I of Ioye & blyſſe hereinne
of ladyſchyp gret & lyueȝ blom
þen alle þe wyȝeȝ in þe worlde myȝt wynne
by þe way of ryȝt to aſke dome   580
wheþer welnygh now I con bygynne
in euentyde into þe vyne I come
fyrſt of my hyre my lorde con mynne
I watȝ payed anon of al & ſum
ȝet oþer þer werne þᵗ toke more tom   585
þat ſwange & ſwat for long ȝore
þat ȝet of hyre noþynk þay nom
paraunter noȝt ſchal to ȝere more
//Then more I meled & ſayde apert
me þynk þy tale vnreſounable   590
goddeȝ ryȝt is redy & euermor rert
oþer holy wryt is bot a fable
in ſauter is ſayd a verce ouerte
þat ſpekeȝ a poynt determynable
þou quyteȝ vchon as hys deſſerte   595
þou hyȝe kyng ay pertermynable
now he þat ſtod þe long day ſtable
& þou to payment com hym byfore
þenne þe laſſe in werke to take more able
& euer þe lenger þe laſſe þe more   600
Of more & laſſe in godeȝ ryche
þat gentyl ſayde lys no Ioparde
for þer is vch mon payed inlyche
wheþer lyttel oþer much be hys rewarde
for þe gentyl cheuentayn is no chyche   605
queþerſoeuer he dele neſch oþer harde

he laue₃ hys gyfte₃ as water of dyche
oþer gote₃ of golf þat neuer charde
hys fraunchyſe is large þᵗ euer dard
to hym þat mat₃ in ſynne reſcoghe   610
no blyſſe bet₃ fro hem reparde
for þe grace of god is gret Inoghe

F51v
Bot now þou mote₃ me for to mate
þat I my peny haf wrang tan here
þou ſay₃ þat I þat com to late   615
am not worþy ſo gret lere
where wyſte₃ þou euer any bourne abate
euer ſo holy in hys prayere
þat he ne forfeted by ſumkyn gate
þe mede ſumtyme of heuene₃ clere   620
& ay þe ofter þe alder þay were
þay laſten ry₃t & wro₃ten woghe
mercy & grace moſte hem þen ſtere
for þe grace of god is gret inno₃e
//bot innoghe of grace hat₃ innocent   625
as ſone as þay arn borne by lyne
in þe water of babtem þay dyſſente
þen arne þay boro₃t into þe vyne
anon þe day wᵗ derk endente
þe niy₃t of deth dot₃ to enclyne   630
þat wro₃t neuer wrang er þenne þay wente
þe gentyle lorde þenne paye₃ hys hyne
þay dyden hys heſte þay wern þere-ine
why ſchulde he not her labour alow
₃ys & pay hym at þe fyrſt fyne   635
for þe grace of god is gret innoghe
Ino₃e is knawen þᵗ mankyn grete
fyrſte wat₃ wro₃t to blyſſe parſyt
oure forme fader hit con forfete
þur₃ an apple þat he vpon con byte   640
al wer we dampned for þat mete
to dy₃e in doel out of delyt
& ſyþen wende to helle hete
þerinne to won wᵗoute reſpyt
bot þeron com a bote as tyt   645
ryche blod ran on rode ſo roghe

& wynne water þen at þat plyt
þe grace of god wex gret innoghe

F52

Innoghe þer wax out out of þat welle
blod & water of brode wounde   650
þe blod vus boȝt fro bale of helle
& delyuered vus of þe deth fecounde
þe water is baptem þe foþe to telle
þat folȝed þe glayue fo grymly grounde
þat wafcheȝ away þe gylteȝ felle   655
þat adam wyth inne deth vus drounde
now is þer noȝt in þe worlde rounde
bytwene vus & blyffe bot þat he w{t}droȝ
& þat is reftored in fely ftounde
& þe grace of god is gret innogh   660
Grace innogh þe mon may haue
þat fynneȝ þenne new ȝif hym repente
bot wt forȝ & fyt he mot hit craue
& byde þe payne þerto is bent
bot refoun of ryȝt þat con not raue   665
faueȝ euermore þe innoffent
hit is a dom þ{t} neuer god gaue
þat euer þe gyltleȝ fchulde be fchente
þe gyltyf may contryffyoun hente
& be þurȝ mercy to grace þryȝt   670
bot he to gyle þat neuer glente
at inofcente is faf & ryȝte
//ryȝt þus þus I knaw wel in þis cas
two men to faue is god by fkylle
þe ryȝtwys man fchal fe hys face   675
þe harmleȝ haþel fchal com hym tylle
þe fauter hyt fatȝ þus in a pace
lorde quo fchal klymbe þy hyȝ hylleȝ
oþer reft w{t}inne þy holy place
hymfelf to onfware he is not dylle   680
hondelyngeȝ harme þat dyt not ille
þat is of hert boþe clene & lyȝt
þer fchal hys ftep ftable ftylle
þe innofent is ay faf by ryȝt

F52v

The ryȝtwys man alſo ſertayn	685
aproche he ſchal þᵗ proper pyle	
þat takeȝ not her lyf in vayne	
ne glauereȝ her nieȝbor wyth no gyle	
of þys ryȝtwys ſaȝ ſalamon playn	
how kyntly oure con aquyle	690
by wayeȝ ful ſtreȝt he con hym ſtrayn	
& ſcheued hym þe rengne of god awhyle	
as quo ſays lo ȝon louely yle	
þou may hit wynne if þou be wyȝte	
bot hardyly wᵗoute peryle	695
þe innoſent is ay ſaue by ryȝte	
//Anende ryȝtwys men ȝet ſaytȝ a gome	
Dauid in ſauter if euer ȝe ſeȝ hit	
lorde þy ſeruaunt draȝ neuer to dome	
for non lyuyande to þe is Iuſtyfyet	700
forþy to corte quen þou ſchal com	
þer alle oure cauſeȝ ſchal be tryed	
alegge þe ryȝt þou may be innome	
by þys ilke ſpech I haue aſſpyed	
bot he on rode þat blody dyed	705
delfully þurȝ hondeȝ þryȝt	
gyue þe to paſſe when þou arte tryed	
by innocens & not by ryȝte	
//Ryȝtwyſly quo con rede	
he loke on bok & be awayed	710
how Ieſu hym welke in areþede	
& burneȝ her barneȝ vnto hym brayde	
for happe & hele þat fro hym ȝede	
to touch her chylder þay fayr hym prayed	
his deſſypeleȝ wᵗ blame let be hym bede	715
& wyth her reſouneȝ ful fele reſtayed	
Ieſu þenne hem ſwetely ſayde	
do way let chylder vnto me tyȝt	
to ſuche is heuenryche arayed	
þe innocent is ay ſaf by ryȝt	720

F53

Ieſu con calle to hym hys mylde
& ſayde hys ryche no wyȝ myȝt wynne
bot he com þyder ryȝt as a chylde

oþer elleȝ neuermore com þerinne
harmleȝ trwe & vndefylde   725
wᵗouten mote oþer mafcle of fulpande fynne
quen fuch þer cnoken on þe bylde
tyt fchal hem men þe ȝate vnpynne
þer is þe blys þat con not blynne
þat þe Iueler foȝte þurȝ perre pres   730
& folde alle hys goud boþe wolen & lynne
to bye hym a perle watȝ mafcelleȝ
//This makelleȝ perle þat boȝt is dere
þe Ioueler gef fore alle hys god
is lyke þe reme of heueneffe clere   735
fo fayde þe fader of folde & flode
for hit is wemleȝ clene & clere
& endeleȝ rounde & blyþe of mode
& commune to alle þat ryȝtywys were
lo euen in myddeȝ my brefte hit ftode   740
my lorde þe lombe þat fchede hys blode
he pyȝt hit þere in token of pes
I rede þe forfake þe worlde wode
& porchace þy perle mafkelles
//O mafkeleȝ perle in perleȝ pure   745
þat bereȝ quod I þe perle of prys
quo formed þe þy fayre fygure
þat wroȝt þy wede he watȝ ful wys
þy beaute com neuer of nature
pymalyon paynted neuer þy vys   750
ne aryftotel nawþer by hys lettrure
of carpe þe kynde þefe properteȝ
þy colour paffeȝ þe flour-de-lys
þyn angel-hauyng fo clene corteȝ
breue me bryȝt quat kyn offys   755
bereȝ þe perle fo mafkelleȝ

F53v
My makeleȝ lambe þat al may bete
quod fcho my dere deftyne
me ches to hys make alþaȝ vnmete
fumtyme femed þᵗ affemble   760
when I wente fro yor worlde wete
he calde me to hys bonerte
cum hyder to me my lemman fwete

for mote ne ſpot is non in þe
he gef me my3t & als bewte 765
in hys blod he weſch my wede on deſe
& coronde clene in vergynte
& py3t me in perle3 maſkelle3
Why maſkelle3 bryd þat bry3t con flambe
þat reiate3 hat3 ſo ryche & ryf 770
quat kyn þyng may be þat lambe
þat þe wolde wedde vnto hys vyf
ouer alle oþer ſo hy3 þou clambe
to lede wᵗ hym ſo ladyly lyf
ſo mony a cumly anvnnder cambe 775
for kryſt han lyued in much ſtryf
& þou con alle þo dere out dryf
& fro þat maryag al oþer depres
al-only þyſelf ſo ſtout & ſtyf
a makele3 may & maſkelle3 780
Maſkelles quod þat myry quene
vnblemyſt I am wythouten blot
& þat may I wᵗ menſk menteene
bot makele3 quene þenne ſade I not
þe lambes vyue3 in blyſſe we bene 785
a hondred & forty þowſande flot
as in þe apocalyppe3 hit is ſene
ſant Iohan hem ſy3 al in a knot
on þe hyl of ſyon þat ſemly clot
þe apoſtel hem ſegh in goſtly drem 790
arayed to þe weddyng in þᵗ hyl-coppe
þe nwe cyte o Ieruſalem

F54
Of Ieruſalem I in ſpeche ſpelle
If þou wyl knaw what kyn he be
my lombe my lorde my dere Iuelle 795
my ioy my blys my lemman fre
þe profete yſaye of hym con melle
pitouſly of hys debonerte
þat gloryous gyltle3 þᵗ mon con quelle
wᵗouten any ſake of felonye 800
as a ſchep to þe ſla3t þer lad wat3 he
& as lombe þat clypper in lande men
ſo cloſed he hys mouth fro vch query

quen Iue3 hym iugged in Iherusalem
//In Ierusalem wat3 my lemman flayn 805
& rent on rode wᵗ boye3 bolde
al oure bale3 to bere ful bayn
he toke on hymfelf oure care3 colde
wᵗ boffete3 wat3 hys face flayn
þat wat3 fo fayr on to byholde 810
for fynne he fet hymfelf in vayn
þat neuer hade non hymfelf to wolde
for vus he lette hym fly3e & folde
& brede vpon a boftwys bem
as meke as lomp þat no playnt tolde 815
for vus he fwalt in Ierusalem
Ierusalem Iordan & galalye
þeras baptyfed þe goude faynt Ion
his worde3 acorded to yfaye
when Iesu con to hym warde gon 820
he fayde of hym þys profeffye
lo gode3 lombe as trwe as fton
þat dot3 away þe fynne3 dry3e
þat alle þys worlde hat3 wro3t vpon
hymfelf ne wro3t neuer 3et non 825
wheþer on hymfelf he con al clem
hys generacyoun quo recen con
þat dy3ed for vus in Ierusalem

F54v

In ierusalem þus my lemman fwatte
twye3 for lombe wat3 taken þare 830
by trw recorde of ayþer prophete
for mode fo meke & al hys fare
þe þryde tyme is þerto ful mete
in apokalype3 wryten ful 3are
in myde3 þe trone þere faynte3 fete 835
þe apoftel iohan hym fayt3 as bare
lefande þe boke with leue3 fware
þere feuen fyngnette3 wern fette in feme
& at þᵗ fy3t vche douth con dare
in helle in erþe & Ierusalem 840
Thys Ierusalem lombe hade neuer pechche
of oþer huee bot quyt Iolyf
þat mot ne mafklle mo3t on ftreche

for wolle quyte ſo ronk & ryf
forþy vche ſaule þat hade neuer teche 845
is to þat lombe a worthyly wyf
& þaȝ vch day a ſtore he feche
among vus commeȝ no noþer ſtrot ne ſtryf
bot vchon enle we wolde were fyf
þe mo þe myryer ſo god me bleſſe 850
in compayny gret our luf con þryf
in honour more & neuer þe leſſe
Laſſe of blyſſe may non vus bryng
þat beren þys perle vpon oure bereſte
for þay of mote couþe neuer mynge 855
of ſpotleȝ perleȝ þa beren þe creſte
alþaȝ oure corſes in clotteȝ clynge
& ȝe remen for rauþe wythouten reſte
we þurȝoutly hauen cnawyng
of [o]n dethe ful oure hope is dreſt 860
þe lou[m]be vus gladeȝ oure care is keſt
he myrþeȝ vus alle at vch a mes
vchoneȝ blyſſe is breme & beſte
& neuer oneȝ honour ȝet neuer þe les

F55
leſt les þou leue my talle farande 865
in appocalyppece is wryten in wro
I ſeghe ſays Iohan þe loumbe hym ſtande
on þe mount of ſyon ful þryuen & þro
& wyth hym maydenneȝ an hundreþe þowſande
& fowre & forty þowſande mo 870
on alle her forhedeȝ wryten I fande
þe lombeȝ nome hys fadereȝ alſo
a hue fro heuen I herde þoo
lyk flodeȝ fele laden runnen on reſſe
& as þunder þroweȝ in torreȝ blo 875
þat lote I leue watȝ neuer þe les
Nauþeles þaȝ hit ſchowted ſcharpe
& ledden loude alþaȝ hit were
a note ful nwe I herde hem warpe
to lyſten þat watȝ ful lufly dere 880
as harporeȝ harpen in her harpe
þat nwe ſonge þay ſongen ful cler
in ſounande noteȝ a gentyl carpe

ful fayre þe modeȝ þay fonge in fere
ryȝt byfore godeȝ chayere   885
& þe fowre besteȝ þat hym obes
& þe aldermen so sadde of chere
her songe þay songen neuer þe les
//Nowþelese non watȝ neuer so quoynt
for alle þe crafteȝ þat euer þay knewe   890
þat of þat songe myȝt synge a poynt
bot þat meyny þe lombe þay swe
for þay arn boȝt fro þe vrþe aloynte
as newe fryt to god ful due
& to þe gentyl lombe hit arn anioynt   895
as lyk to hymself of lote & hwe
for neuer lesyng ne tale vntrwe
ne towched her tonge for no dysstresse
þat moteles meyny may neuer remwe
fro þat maskeleȝ mayster neuerþeles   900

F55v
Neuer þe les let be my þonc
quod I my perle þaȝ I appose
I schulde not tempte þy wyt so wlonc
to krysteȝ chambre þat art Ichose
I am bot mokke & mul among   905
& þou so ryche a reken rose
& bydeȝ here by þys blysful bonc
þer lyueȝ lyste may neuer lose
now hynde þat sympelnesse coneȝ enclose
I wolde þe aske a þynge expresse   910
& þaȝ I be bustwys as a blose
let my bone vayl neuerþelese
Neuerþelese cler I yow bycalle
if ȝe con se hyt be to done
as þou art gloryous wᵗouten galle   915
wᵗnay þou neuer my ruful bone
haf ȝe no woneȝ in castel walle
ne maner þer ȝe may mete & won
þou telleȝ me of Ierusalem þe ryche ryalle
þer dauid dere watȝ dyȝt on trone   920
bot by þyse holteȝ hit con not hone
bot in Iudee hit is þᵗ noble note
as ȝe ar maskeleȝ vnder mone

your wone3 fchulde be wythouten mote
//þys motele3 meyny þou cone3 of mele 925
of þoufande3 þry3t fo gret a route
a gret cete for 3e arn fele
yow byhod haue wᵗouten doute
fo cumly a pakke of Ioly Iuele
wer euel don fchulde ly3 þeroute 930
& by þyfe bonke3 þer I con gele
& I fe no bygyng nawhere aboute
I trowe alone 3e lenge & loute
to loke on þe glory of þys gracous gote
If þou hat3 oþer lygynge3 ftoute 935
now tech me to þat myry mote

F56
That mote þou mene3 in Iudy londe
þat fpecyal fpyce þen to me fpakk
þat is þe cyte þat þe lombe con fonde
to foffer inne for for mane3 fake 940
þe olde Ierusalem to vnderftonde
for þere þe olde gulte wat3 don to flake
bot þe nwe þat ly3t of gode3 fonde
þe apoftel in apocalyppce in theme con take
þe lompe þer wᵗouten fpotte3 blake 945
hat3 feryed þyder hys fayre flote
& as hys flok is wᵗouten flake
fo is hys mote wᵗouten moote
//Of mote3 two to carpe clene
& Ierusalem hy3t boþe nawþeles 950
þat nys to yow no more to mene
bot cete of god oþer fy3t of pes
in þat on oure pes wat3 mad at ene
wᵗ payne to fuffer þe lombe hit chefe
in þat oþer is no3t bot pes to glene 955
þat ay fchal lafte wᵗouten reles
þat is þe bor3 þat we to pres
fro þᵗ oure frefch be layd to rote
þer glory & blyffe fchal euer encref
to þe meyny þᵗ is wᵗouten mote 960
Motele3 may fo meke & mylde
þen fayde I to þat lufly flor
bryng me to þat bygly bylde

& let me ſe þy blyſful bor
þat ſchene ſayde þat god wyl ſchylde   965
þou may not enter wᶦinne hys tor
bot of þe lombe I haue þe aquylde
for a ſyȝt þerof þurȝ gret fauor
vtwyth to ſe þat clene cloyſtor
þou may bot inwyth not a fote   970
to ſtrech in þe ſtrete þou hatȝ no vygour
bot þou wer clene wᶜouten mote

F56v
If I þis mote þe ſchal vnhyde
bow vp towarde þys borneȝ heued
& I anendeȝ þe on þis ſyde   975
ſchal ſve tyl þou to a hil be veued
þen wolde no lenger byde
bot lurked by launceȝ ſo luſly leued
tyl on a hyl þat I aſſpyed
& bluſched on þe burghe as I forth dreued   980
byȝonde þe brok fro me warde keued
þat ſchyrrer þen ſunne wᵗ ſchafteȝ ſchon
in þe apokalypce is þe faſoun preued
as deuyſeȝ hit þe apoſtel Ihoan
//As Iohan þe apoſtel hit ſyȝ wᵗ ſyȝt   985
I ſyȝe þat cyty of gret renoun
Ieruſalem ſo nwe & ryally dyȝt
as hit watȝ lyȝt fro þe heuen adoun
þe borȝ watȝ al of brende golde bryȝt
as glemande glas burniſt broun   990
wᵗ gentyl gemmeȝ anvnder pyȝt
wᵗ banteleȝ twelue on baſyng boun
þe foundementeȝ twelue of riche tenoun
vch tabelment watȝ a ſerlypeȝ ſton
as derely deuyſeȝ þis ilk toun   995
in apocalyppeȝ þe apoſtel Iohan
As þiſe ſtoneȝ in writ con nemme
I knew þe name after his tale
Iaſper hyȝt þe fyrſt gemme
þat I on þe fyrſt baſſe con wale   1000
he glente grene in þe loweſt hemme
ſaffer helde þe ſecounde ſtale
þe calſydoyne þenne wᶜouten wemme

in þe þryd table con purly pale
þe emerade þe furþe ſo grene of ſcale   1005
þe ſardonyſe þe fyfþe ſton
þe ſexte þe rybe he con hit wale
in þe apocalyppce þe apoſtel Iohan

F57
//Ʒet Ioyned Iohan þe cryſolyt
þe ſeuenþe gemme in fundament   1010
þe aʒtþe þe beryl cler & quyt
þe topaſye twynne-how þe nente endent
þe cryſopaſe þe tenþe is tyʒt
þe Iacyngh þe enleuenþe gent
þe twelfþe þe gentyleſte in vch a plyt   1015
þe amatyſt purpre wᵗ ynde blente
þe wal abof þe bantels bent
o[ſ] Iaſporye as glas þat glyſnande ſchon
I knew hit by his deuyſement
in þe apocalyppeʒ þe apoſtel Ihan   1020
//As Iohan deuyſed ʒet ſaʒ I þare
þiſe twelue degres wern brode & ſtayre
þe cyte ſtod abof ful ſware
as longe as brode as hyʒe ful fayre
þe ſtreteʒ of golde as glaſſe al bare   1025
þe wal of Iaſper þat glent as glayre
þe woneʒ wᵗinne enurned ware
wyth alle kynnes perre þat moʒt repayre
þenne helde vch ſware of þis manayre
twelue forlonge ſpace er euer hit ſon   1030
of heʒt of brede of lenþe to cayre
for meten hit ſyʒ þe apoſtel Iohan
As Iohan hym wryteʒ ʒet more I ſyʒe
vch pane of þat place had þre ʒateʒ
ſo twelue in pourſent I con aſſpye   1035
þe portaleʒ pyked of rych plateʒ
& vch ʒate of a margyrye
a parfyt perle þat neuer fateʒ
vchon in ſcrypture a name con plye
of iſrael barneʒ folewande her dateʒ   1040
þat is to ſay as her byrþ whateʒ
þe aldeſt ay fyrſt þeron watʒ done
ſuch lyʒt þer lemed in alle þe ſtrateʒ

hem nedde nawþer sunne ne mone

F57v
Of sunne ne mone had þay no nede   1045
þe self god watȝ her lambe lyȝt
þe lombe her lantyrne wᵗouten drede
þurȝ hym blyfned þe borȝ al bryȝt
þurȝ woȝe & won my lokyng ȝede
for sotyle cler noȝt lette no lyȝt   1050
þe hyȝe trone þer moȝt ȝe hede
wᵗ alle þe apparaylmente vmbepyȝte
as Iohan þe appostel in termeȝ tyȝte
þe hyȝe godeȝ self hit set vpone
a reuer of þe trone þer ran outryȝte   1055
watȝ bryȝter þen boþe þe sunne & mone
//Sunne ne mone schon neuer so swete
a þat foysoun flode out of þat flet
swyþe hit swange þurȝ vch a strete
wᵗouten fylþe oþer galle oþer glet   1060
kyrk þerinne watȝ non ȝete
chapel ne temple þat euer watȝ set
þe almyȝty watȝ her mynyster mete
þe lombe þe saker:fyse þer to reget
þe ȝateȝ stoken watȝ neuer ȝet   1065
bot euermore vpen at vche a lone
þer entreȝ non to take reset
þat bereȝ any spot anvndeȝ mone
The mone may þerof acroche no myȝte
to spotty ho is of body to grym   1070
& also þer ne is neuer nyȝt
what schulde þe mone þer compas clym
& to euen wyth þat worþly lyȝt
þat schyneȝ vpon þe brokeȝ brym
þe planeteȝ arn in to pouer a plyȝt   1075
& þe self sunne ful fer to dym
aboute þat water arn tres ful schym
þat twelue fryteȝ of lyf con bere ful sone
twelue syþeȝ on ȝer þay beren ful frym
& renowleȝ nwe in vche a mone   1080

F58
Anvnder mone so gret merwayle

no fleſchly hert ne myȝt endeure
as quen I bluſched vpon þat baly
ſo ferly þerof watȝ þe faſure
I ſtod as ſtylle as daſed quayle   1085
for ferly of þat freuch fygure
þat felde I nawþer reſte ne trauayle
ſo watȝ I rauyſte wyth glymme pure
for I dar ſay wᵗ conciens ſure
hade bodyly burne abiden þat bone   1090
þaȝ alle clerkeȝ hym hade in cure
his lyf wer loſte anvnder mone
Ryȝt as þe maynful mone con rys
er þenne þe day-glem dryue al doun
ſo ſodanly on a wonder wyſe   1095
I watȝ war of a profeſſyoun
þis noble cite of ryche enpreſſe
watȝ ſodanly ful wᶜouten ſommoun
of ſuch vergyneȝ in þe ſame gyſe
þat watȝ my blyſful anvnder croun   1100
& coronde wern alle of þe ſame faſoun
depaynt in perleȝ & wedeȝ qwyte
in vchoneȝ breſte watȝ bounden boun
þe blyſful perle wᶜouten delyt
//wᵗ gret delyt þay glod in fere   1105
on golden gateȝ þat glent as glaſſe
hundreth þowſandeȝ I wot þer were
& alle in ſute her liureȝ waſſe
tor to knaw þe gladdeſt chere
þe lombe byfore con proudly paſſe   1110
wyth horneȝ ſeuen of red glode cler
as prayſed perleȝ his wedeȝ waſſe
towarde þe throne þay trone a tras
þaȝ þay wern fele no pres in plyt
bot mylde as maydeneȝ ſeme at mas   1115
ſo droȝ þay forth wᵗ gret delyt

F58v
Delyt þᵗ hys come encroched
to much hit were of for to melle
þiſe aldermen quen he aproched
grouelyng to his fete þay felle   1120
legyounes of aungeleȝ togeder uoched

þer keſten enſens of ſwete ſmelle
þen glory & gle watȝ nwe abroched
al ſonge to loue þat gay Iuelle
þe ſteuen moȝt ſtryke þurȝ þe vrþe to helle   1125
þat þe vertues of heuen of Ioye endyte
to loue þe lombe his meyny in melle
Iwyſſe I laȝt a gret delyt
Delit þe lombe for to deuiſe
wᵗ much meruayle in mynde went   1130
beſt watȝ he blyþeſt & moſte to pryſe
þat euer I herde of ſpeche ſpent
ſo worþly whyt wern wedeȝ hys
his lokeȝ ſymple hymſelf ſo gent
bot a wounde ful wyde & weete con wyſe   1135
anende hys hert þurȝ hyde torente
of his quyte ſyde his blod out ſprent
alas þoȝt I who did þat ſpyt
ani breſte for bale aȝt haf forbrent
er he þerto hade had delyt   1140
//The lombe delyt non lyſte to wene
þaȝ he were hurt & wounde hade
in his ſembelaunt watȝ neuer ſene
ſo wern his glenteȝ gloryous glade
I loked amonge his meyny ſchene   1145
how þay wyth lyf wern laſte & lade
þen ſaȝ I þer my lyttel quene
þat I wende had ſtanden by me in ſclade
lorde much of mirþe watȝ þat ho made
among her fereȝ þat watȝ ſo quyt   1150
þat ſyȝt me gart to þenk to wade
for luf longyng in gret delyt

F59
Delyt me drof in yȝe & ere
my maneȝ mynde to maddyng malte
quen I ſeȝ my frely I wolde be þere   1155
byȝonde þe water þaȝ ho were walte
I þoȝt þat noþyng myȝt me dere
to fech me bur & take me halte
& to ſtart in þe ſtrem ſchulde non me ſtere
to ſwymme þe remnaunt þaȝ I þer ſwalte   1160
bot of þat munt I watȝ bitalt

when I fchulde ftart in þe ftrem aftraye
out of þat cafte I watȝ bycalt
hit watȝ not at my prynceȝ paye
//hit payed hym not þat I fo flonc   1165
ouer meruelous mereȝ fo mad arayde
of raas þaȝ I were rafch & ronk
ȝet rapely þerinne I watȝ reftayed
for ryȝt as I fparred vnto þe bonc
þat brathe out of my drem me brayde   1170
þen wakned I in þat erber wlonk
my hede vpon þat hylle watȝ layde
þeras my perle to grounde ftrayd
I raxled & fel in gret affray
& fykyng to myfelf I fayd   1175
now al be to þat prynceȝ paye
//Me payed ful ille to be out fleme
fo fodenly of þat fayre regioun
fro alle þo fyȝteȝ fo quykeȝ & queme
a longeyng heuy me ftrok in fwone   1180
& rewfully þenne I con to reme
O perle quod I of rych renoun
fo watȝ hit me dere þᵗ þou con deme
in þys veray avyfyoun
inf hit be ueray & foth fermoun   1185
þat þou fo ftykeȝ in garlande gay
fo wel is me in þys doel-doungoun
þat þou art to þat prynfeȝ paye

F59v
To þat prynceȝ paye hade I ay bente
& ȝerned no more þen watȝ me geuen   1190
& halden me þer in trwe entent
as þe perle me prayed þat watȝ fo þryuen
as helde drawen to goddeȝ prefent
to mo of his myfterys I hade ben dryuen
bot ay wolde man of happe more hente   1195
þen moȝten by ryȝt vpon hem clyuen
þerfor my ioye watȝ fone toriuen
& I kafte of kytheȝ þat lafteȝ aye
lorde mad hit arn þat agayn þe ftryuen
oþer proferen þe oȝt agayn þy paye   1200
To paye þe prince oþer fete faȝte

hit is ful eþe to þe god kryſtyin
for I haf founden hym boþe day & naȝte
a god a lorde a frende ful fyin
ouer þis hyul þis lote I laȝte   1205
for pyty of my perle enclyin
& ſyþen to god I hit bytaȝte
in kryſteȝ dere bleſſyng & myn
þat in þe forme of bred & wyn
þe preſte vus ſcheweȝ vch a daye   1210
he gef vus to be his homly hyne
Ande precious perleȝ vnto his pay Amen. Amen.

Textual Notes

2 *cler[e]* Although editors uniformly read a final "e" on this word, the letter is not legible on the high-resolution digital copy of the manuscript; on the facsimile there are traces of what might be an "e," but the letter is blotted and almost entirely illegible.

23 *iuele* Morris (1864) reads *mele*, "discourse," which alliterates; Gordon (1953) *iuele*, which makes better sense in context. As the letter(s) in question consist(s) of three minims, the textual evidence seems ambiguous; however, Vantuono (1995) points out that "the mark over the first minim denotes *i* equalling *j* in *juele*" (101-2). Dotted 'i's are also found in lines 245, 249, 558, 1104, 1139, 1202, and 1206; see the Cotton Nero A.x. Project's miniscule alphabet for a description of this letter-form, which seems to be used when the "i" is preceded or followed by a letter consisting of minims, which might otherwise cause confusion. The form of this letter clearly establishes *iuele* as the correct reading.

29 *fede* A number of editors gloss *fede* as "faded" or "withered," deriving it from OF *fade;* Gollancz glosses it as a past participle derived from ON *feyja,* "decay"; Vantuono suggests "wasted," derived from OF *fade* (Vantuono 101).

35 *fprygande fpyce3* Most editors emend to *fpryngande fpyce3,* "springing spices"; Vantuono, following Hillmann and DeFord, reads *fpryg ande fpyce3,* "shrubs and spices."

51 *deuely* Morris reads *denely,* "loud," and interprets *denned* in the same line as "resounded." Gordon read *deuely,* "desolating," and glosses the line as "A desolating grief lay deep in my heart." As both "n" and "u" consist of two minims, the textual evidence is ambiguous.

54 *fyrte* Morris reads *fyrte,* "fearful, trembling"; Gordon emends to *fyrce,* "vehement." The form of the "t" is such that it could be a carelessly written "c," although the top of the vertical stroke clearly extends above the horizontal stroke of the letter.

77 *onflyde3* Gordon reads this as two words, *on slyde3,* which he glosses "slides on (the trees)" (153). In his note to the line he mentions the reading of C. G. Osgood and I. Gollancz, of *onflyde3* as "slip open, unfold" or "sway"

(50), adopted by the OED, which glosses the word "to slide open; open, unfold." Vantuono glosses *onflyde3* "hang" (240).

78 *trylle* Gordon glosses this word "quiver," comparing it to MDu *trillen*, "vibrate" (157). Vantuono glosses it "trail," comparing it to "Swed. and Norw. *trilla*, Dan. *trille*, & EFris. *trullen*" (249).

79 *glode3* Hillman glosses *glode3* as "glades"; Gordon "clear patches of sky"; Vantuono suggests "open spaces (clearings) in trees" (Vantuono 106-7).

89 *flowen* The "w" is corrected from "y" in the manuscript.

106 *b[o]nkes* There is no trace of an "o" in the manuscript; Vantuono argues for the reading *bukes*, ". . . as a variant reading of *MED bek* n. 1, 'small stream'" (108).

192 *pyece* The "c" looks like a "t" because of the upstroke of the preceding "e."

197 *beau mys* The manuscript has five minims in a row following the "a," which could be interpreted as a number of combinations of the letters "i," "n," "m," and "u," none of which results in an obvious reading. Gordon reads *beau uiys* and emends to *beau biys*, "fair fine linen," citing Rev. 19:8 and its reference to the *byssinum* or fine linen garment of the bride of the Lamb (54). Vantuono argues for Gollancz's reading of *beau mys*, and interprets *mys* as "a shortening of *MED amit* n., (variant *amis*)" (113), meaning "cloak."

209 *werle* Gordon glosses this word as "circlet, circular ornament" (161), explaining it as "probably a form of ME. *wherl* "whorl"" (54). The OED glosses it (s.v.) as "covering, attire," deriving it from "wear *v.* + -le."

210 *lere leke* Morris emends to *here heke*, "hair also"; Gordon reads *here leke*, and glosses *leke* as "past tense of *louke* 'to enclose,'" rendering the line "Her hair, lying all about her, enclosed her countenance." The *MED* tentatively renders *lere leke* as "face linen, wimple," interpreting *leke* as a variant of *lake*, "fine linen, cambric" (Vantuono 114).

262 *ne* Most editions read *nee*; however, Gollancz reads "*nu* (altered to *ne*)." There is an upright stroke following the first "e," which does not, however, resemble an "e" in form. It could be the second minim of an original "u," but is curved more than is usual for a minim.

285 *loue* In this line, as in lines 342, 1124, and 1127, the word could be read either as "love," from OE *lufian*, or as "honor," from OE *lofian*. The reader will have to try to decide from context which word is meant.

302 *loue3* In this line, as in line 308, the word could be read either as "loves," from OE *lufian*, or as "honors," from OE *lofian*. The reader will have to try to decide from context which word is meant.

304 *leue3* The word in the manuscript looks like *loue3* or *lyue3*; under much magnification the letter between "l" and "u" appears to be an "e," perhaps altered from "y." Many editors emend *loue3* in 304 and 308 to *leue3* as well.

307 *westernays* Most editors gloss this word "reversed," or "awry," either emending to *besternays* or taking the manuscript reading as an altered form of that

word. Others, following M. V. Hillman, read *west ernays,* "empty pledge" (Vantuono 119). The OED takes it as an adverb, "wrongfully, perversely," deriving it from OF *bestorneis.*

309 *ins* The scribe has apparently put a macron above the "i" of the word "is" by mistake.

313 *dayly* Gordon glosses *dayly* as "contend, dispute," deriving it from ON *deila;* various other editors gloss it as "speak," "speak lightly," and "speak courteously," deriving it from OF *dalier* (Vantuono 120).

353 *fyne* The word looks like *fone* in the manuscript, but under magnification a very faint and short tail is visible on the "y."

354 *fwefte* The "ft" in the manuscript is run together and looks very much like a combined "long s" and "t."

358 *leme* Gordon emends to *fleme,* "drive," from OE *flēman* (as in line 334), and translates *of fleme* "banish" (131). Vantuono retains the manuscript reading *leme,* "shine," from OE *lēoma* (235) and translates the line "And among misfortunes gently gleam" (33). However, in his note on the line (121), he also mentions E. G. Stanley's analysis of *of lyȝtly leme* as a tmesis in which the word *lyȝtly* intervenes between the two elements of the verb *offleme*—giving the same meaning as Gordon's emendation, while retaining the manuscript reading.

359 *myþe* Gordon glosses this word "conceal (one's feelings)," deriving it from OE *mīþan* (143). Vantuono glosses it "mutter," deriving it from OE *mūþ, mūþa,* "mouth" (239).

362 *worþe* The word looks like *woȝþe* in the manuscript, as the combining form of "r" is detached from the "o."

372 *my* A peculiar form of the letter "y" may be the result of a scribal error; it appears the scribe initially miscounted the minims in the "m" and wrote *ny,* then corrected the error by adding another stroke to the "y." A similar correction appears in lines 395 and 565.

382 *marereȝ* Morris suggests reading *marreȝ,* "mars"; Gordon, following earlier editors, emends to *manereȝ,* "manners." The *MED* follows Osgood, who retains the manuscript reading and translates *marereȝ mysse* as "a botcher's blunder" (Vantuono 122), which makes sense, but is inconsistent with Christian theology. Vantuono gives a complete list of other suggestions and interpretations, none of which has found general acceptance. Although the manuscript reading is clear, the emendation to *manereȝ* is plausible, as the substitution of the first "r" for an "n" in the exemplar could easily have resulted from an eye skip by the scribe.

416 *wage* Morris glosses this word "endure" (208). Gordon suggests either "guarantee; pay (hire); *intr. or absol.* continue securely *or* bring reward" (160).

419 *prefe* Morris glosses this word "praise, honour," deriving it from Sp. *prez,*

"honour, glory" (181). Gordon glosses it "great worth," deriving it from OF *pris*, "infl. by AFr *preser*, to value" (147).Vantuono reads *pyese*, which he glosses "maiden" (124).

436 *byngyner* It appears that the scribe mistakenly put a macron above the first "y" rather than the second.

460 *tyste* Morris, Gordon, and others emend to *tryste*, "faithfully"; Vantuono argues for retaining the manuscript reading, which he glosses as "joined" or "woven together" (128).

461 *fawhe* The scribe has mistakenly written an "h" for an "l" here, but it is clear from the rhyme scheme that the word should be *fawle*.

524 *pray* Most editors emend to *pay*. Vantuono retains the manuscript reading and interprets *hyre* in the previous line as "service" (130).

532 *fade* The "d" appears to be altered from an original "y."

533 *longe* The "l" appears to be altered from an original "ʒ."

538 *& &* Most editors delete the second "and"; Vantuono retains it, taking the second "and" as "when," and translates "and when it became late" (47).

544 *reprene* Morris reads *repreue*, which makes sense and is a valid reading of the two minims in the manuscript; however, the rhyme scheme calls for an "n" rather than a "u." *Reprene*, "find fault with" (Gordon) or "censure" (Vantuono), from the stem of OFr *reprendre*, "reprove," makes equal sense and preserves the rhyme.

557 *o[n]* The manuscript has "om" with the last minim of the "m" crossed out but still legible.

558 *wanig* Morris emends to *wrang*, "*wrong;*" other editors emend to *wani[n]g*. "diminution, loss." The manuscript has a "dotted i" in *wanig* (see note to line 23 above); it is possible that the scribe mistakenly wrote the mark above the "i" instead of a macron to designate an omitted "n." Gordon glosses *ʒete* "grant," derived from "Late OE *ge(a)tan*, *after* ON *játa*," and translates the expression *no waning ʒete* as "propose to make no curtailment (of what is due)" (135). Vantuono, following Emerson, glosses *ʒete* "do," derived from ON *geta*, WS *gietan*, and reads *wani[n]g* as rendering Latin *iniúriam* in Matthew 20:13, "Amice, non fácio tibi iniúriam," "Friend, I do thee no wrong" (132).

616 *lere* Morris suggests emending to *here*, "reward" (166). Gordon emends to *fere*, "fortune, rank, dignity" (130). Vantuono retains the manuscript reading and translates "abode," from OE *leger*, but in his note on the line (136) also mentions M. V. Hillman's reading of *lere* as "recompense," from MED *lūre*, *n.* 1.

630 *niyʒt* Morris and others read *myʒt*, which is consistent with the textual evidence and makes sense; Gordon argues convincingly for *niyʒt* as an equally valid reading of the three minims which begin the word, which moreover "completes the metaphor of the day in the vineyard representing the life of

man: death is, naturally, the night at the end of the day" (69). He also points out two examples of the same spelling of the word *niyȝt* in the manuscript.

649 *out out* The repetition of the word *out* seems to be a scribal error.

673 *þus þus* The repetition of the word *þus* appears to be a scribal error, and is omitted by Gordon and other editors. However, Vantuono glosses the second occurrence of the word "therefore" (251).

675 *face* The "c" in this word looks like a "t," and the word "fate" would make sense here, but the rhyme scheme shows the letter to be a carelessly-written "c."

678 *hylleȝ* The rhyme scheme calls for the singular *hylle,* as does the passage from Psalm 24 which the poet is paraphrasing.

690 *oure* Most editors emend this line more or less drastically, in an attempt to make it correspond roughly to the language of what is believed to be the passage alluded to, *Wisdom of Solomon* 10:10. Vantuono suggests a reading which avoids emendation, reading *kyntly* as "kindly, as a variant of MED *kīndelī,*" *oure* as "mercy, from MED *ōr(e n.* 2, sense 1a," and *aquyle* as "prevail," giving a reading of the line as "how kindly Mercy did prevail" (139).

700 *for* The "ſ" is clearly a scribal error for an "f" which the scribe carelessly neglected to cross.

734 *Ioueler* The "r" at the end of the word is a "round r," which is normally used only after "o" and very occasionally after other rounded letters, but not after "e," and appears to be corrected from an original "ȝ."

739 *ryȝtywys* The second "y" is partially covered by the following "w," as if the scribe was attempting to correct an error in spelling.

751 *aryſtotel* The "ſ" appears to have been corrected from an original "ȝ."

775 *anvnnder* The "a" has an uncharacteristic shape and appears to have been altered from an original "o" by the addition of two legs which extend below the line; Morris reads *cumly on vunder cambe,* "comely one under comb," which is another valid reading of the ambiguous textual evidence.

799 *gyltleȝ* The first "l" has been altered from an original "ſ," and the "t" is written as a separate letter, which probably indicates an immediate correction, as the scribe normally joins "ſ" and "t."

802 *in lande men* Gordon reads *hande* rather than *lande* here, and emends *men* to *nem,* "seize," along with several other editors. Vantuono argues for retaining the manuscript reading *men* as "an aphetic form of MED āmen v., sense 2, 'appraise' (OF *aesmer)*" (84). The poet in this and the following line is obviously paraphrasing Isaiah 53:7, "he is brought as a lamb to the slaughter, and as a sheep before her shearers is dumb, so he openeth not his mouth"; none of the proposed readings or emendations gives a satisfactory rendering of the verse being paraphrased, which should at this point refer to the silence of the lamb before the shearer.

830 *þare* The "a" appears to have been altered from an original "e" in order to

match the other b-rhymes in the stanza.

848 *no noþer* The manuscript reading is *nonoþer;* Morris reads *non oþer;* Gollancz emends to *noþer;* Gordon to *nouþer;* Vantuono reads *no noþer,* which gives an emphatic double negative.

860 *[o]n* The first letter of the word is blotted and illegible.

861 *lou[m]be* The manuscript reads either *lonbe* or *loube,* which could indicate either that the scribe intended to write *lombe* and miscounted the minims, or that he intended to write *loube* with a macron over the "u," as in line 867, but neglected to add the sign of abbreviation which would stand for the missing "m."

865 *left les þou leue my talle farande* Catch words at the bottom of the previous page read *lefte les þow leue my tale fara,* with a macron over the final "a."

894 *fryt* The "r" appears to be corrected from "y."

911 *bloſe* Morris reads this word as "blaze, flame," comparing OI *blossi;* Gollancz (1891) emends to *woſe,* "wild man"; Andrew and Waldron emend to *boſe,* "peasant"; Vantuono suggests that *bloſe* is "a variant spelling of MED *blǎs* n., sense a, 'blowing (of wind), a gust' "(Vantuono 150).

933 *loute* Morris glosses this "abide, sit," (168), but gives no derivation. Gordon glosses it "make one's way, go," from OE *lūtan* (141); Vantuono glosses it "stroll," giving the same derivation as Gordon. However, the word may be derived from OED *lout v.* 2, "lurk, lie hid": although the connotations of "lurk" may seem inappropriate to the context, *lenge & loute* seems to be an alliterative formula, "linger and lurk." Such formulas are often adopted even when not precisely adapted to the particular context.

935 *lygyngeȝ* Some editors read or emend to *bygyngeȝ,* "buildings." The first letter could in fact be the form of "b" used in combination with other letters, but this combination form of the letter is not normally used with "y."

958 *freſch* Most editors read *freſth* and emend to *fleſch;* Vantuono argues that the emendation is unnecessary and glosses *freſch* as a substantive adjective meaning "young bodies."

961 *Moteleȝ* The initial "M" is an illuminated capital, although this stanza does not begin a stanza group, and the link-words in the first and last lines show it belongs with the preceding group.

985 *Iohan* The "o" is squeezed in between the "I" and the "h" and appears to have been added after those letters were written.

997 *nemme* This verb is normally transitive and active, but there is no subject in the sentence as written; many editors insert "John" or "Johan" in this line after the word "as."

1018 *o[f]* A miniature "f" appears to have been squeezed in between the "o" and the "I" of *Iasporye* and repeated above the line.

1058 *a* Morris reads "a" as an interjection, followed by an exclamation point; Gordon emends to "as"; Vantuono retains the manuscript reading, ex-

plaining it as "a shortened form of *as*," and noting "the omission of the
final letter of monosyllabic words in 144, 309, 429, 792, and 1058" (109).

1064 *faker:fyfe* The colon or two dots seem to indicate a compound word,
where a hyphen would be used today.

1073 *ly3t* The "l" hooks to the right at the top and could also be read as an "f";
either *ly3t* or *fy3t* makes good sense.

1084 *fafure* Morris reads *falure*, but does not define the word in his "glossarial
index"; Gollancz notes "s *altered from* l." Later editors read *fafure* without
comment.

1086 *freuch* Morris reads *french*, which is a possible reading as both "u" and "n"
consist of two minims and cannot be distinguished by textual evidence
alone. In the margin, he proposes *fresch* as a possible emendation, with a
question mark in parentheses, and in his "glossarial index," glosses *french* as
"an error for *frech* (*fresh*) or *frelich*." Gordon reads *freuch*, but adopts Morris's
suggested emendation to *frelich*, "noble." Vantuono cites the MED definition of *freuch* under the word *frough*, as "delicate; ? delightful," but argues
that *freuch* "may be a variant spelling of *frech* 195 and *fresch* 958" (157).

1104 *w'outen delyt* Morris, Gollancz, and Gordon emend to *wyth gret delyt*, as in
the first line of the following stanza; Vantuono retains the manuscript reading and argues for Hillman's interpretation of *wythouten delyt* as "beyond
delight" (158).

1108 *liure3* The "i" is a "dotted i" (see note to line 23 above).

1111 *glode* Evidently a scribal error for *golde*, perhaps influenced by *glod* in line
1105 above. Most editors emend to *golde* without comment.

1119 *aldermen* The "r" appears to have been altered from "3."

1139 *ani* The "i" is a "dotted i."

1158 *halte* Gordon glosses *halte* as an adjective, "lame," from OE *halt*, and translates the expression *take me halte* "stop my advance" (135). Vantuono glosses *halte* as a verb, "waver," from OE *haltian, healtian* (231), and translates
"Make me halt" (89).

1166 *arayde* The "d" is blotted or corrected and only parts of the "e" are legible
or visible.

1170 *brathe* The "h" appears to be corrected from some other letter, perhaps
"þ" (Gollancz) or "3."

1174 *raxled* There is a space between the "e" and the "d," with a faint mark,
perhaps an erasure.

1185 *inf* The scribe apparently placed a macron over the "i" in *if* by mistake.

1197 *perfor* The "r" is irregularly shaped and placed above the line, with a space
between it and the "o."

1201 *prince* The manuscript has *pnce* with a blotted abbreviation sign above the "p."

1202 *krystyin* The "i" is a "dotted i."

1206 *enclyin* The "i" is a "dotted i."

Glossary

This glossary is based on the transcription of the manuscript beginning on page 205; all words in the poem appear in the glossary along with the line number in which they appear, except that for words which appear many times over in the same meaning the line number entries are truncated after the third entry. The Middle English letters "ȝ" (yogh) and "þ" (thorn) are alphabetized following "g" and "t" respectively; "ſ" ("long s") and "s" are alphabetized together; the letters "i," "u," "v," "w," and "y" are alphabetized according to the order of the Modern English alphabet, regardless of their function. All words are listed in the glossary as they are spelled in the poem, with manuscript abbreviations silently expanded (except for the superscript abbreviations for *wyth* and *þat*), and with cross-references where necessary. Inflected forms of verbs are identified by person, tense, and number.

For the meanings and derivations of words I have relied mainly on the *Middle English Dictionary,* the *Oxford English Dictionary,* and the glossaries in the editions of *Pearl* of Morris, Gollancz, Gordon, and Vantuono, as well as Bosworth's and Toller's *Anglo-Saxon Dictionary* and *Supplement.* A question mark preceding a definition or etymology indicates that it is doubtful; where the etymology of a word is unknown a question mark appears in brackets following the entry for the word. An asterisk preceding an etymology indicates a word-form that is theoretically reconstructed but not found in literature; following a line number an asterisk indicates a textual note. A key to abbreviations used may be found immediately following the glossary.

A

a (1) *indef. art.* a, an 19, 23, 34, etc. **an** 640, 869 **on** 9, 1079; **vch a, vche a**: *see* **vch** [OE ān]

a (2) (shortened form of **as**) *prep.* like 115

a (3) *conj.* as (?) or *interj.* ah (?) 1058*

a (4) *adv.* 144. *See* **ay**

abate 617. *See* **abyde**

abated *pret. 3 plur.* put an end to 123 [OF abatre]

abiden. *See* **abyde**

able *adj.* able 599 [OF able]

abof *prep.* above 1017 *adv.* 1023 [OE abufan]

aboute *prep.* around, about 75, 1077

abowte 149 concerning 268 near 513 *adv.* nearby 932 [OE onbūtan]

abroched *pp.* let loose 1123 [OF abrochier]

abyde *vt.* bear patiently, endure 348 **abiden** *pp.* endured 1090 **abate** *vi. pret. 3 sing.* remained stable 617 [OE abīdan]

acheue *v.* attain 475 [OF achever]

acorde *n.* consistency 371 agreement 509 [OF acorde]

acorded *pret. 3 plur.* accorded, were consistent 819 [OF acorder]

acroche *v.* acquire 1069 [OF accrocher]

adam *n.* Adam 656

adaunt *v.* daunt 157 [OF adanter]

adoun *adv.* down 988 [OE of dūne]

adubbement *n.* adornment 84, 96, 108, 120 **adubbemente** 85 **adubmente** 72 [OF adoubement] Cf. **dubbement**

adyte *imp. sing.* accuse, indict 349 [OF aditer]

affray *n.* apprehension, dismay 1174 [OF effrei]

after *prep.* along 125 according to 998 **after þenne** *adv.* afterwards 256 [OE æfter]

agayn *prep.* against 28, 1199, 1200 **agaynʒ** 79 [OE ongægn]

agayn *adv.* again 326 [OE ongægn]

age *n.* age 412 [OF aäge, eäge]

aglyʒte *pret. 2 sing.* slipped away 245 [?]

agrete *adv.* in all, all told 560 [OE an + grēat; cf. OF en gros]

aʒt. *See* **oʒe**

aʒtþe *adj.* eighth 1011 [OE eahtoða]

al *adj.* all, the whole 16, 86, 119, etc. **alle** 73, 292, 372, etc. [OE eal]

al *pron.* all, everything, everyone 360, 458, 495, etc. **alle** 404, 447, 467, etc. **of al & fum** in full 584 [OE eal]

al *adv.* wholly, entirely 97, 197, 204, etc. **alle** 1108 [OE eal]

alas *interj.* alas 1138 **allas** 9 [OF ha las]

alder, aldeſt. *See* **old**

aldermen *n. plur.* elders 1119* [OE ealdorman]

allas. *See* **alas**

alegge *pres. 2 sing. subj.* allege, claim 703 [OF aligier, alegier]

almyʒt *adj.* almighty 498 [OE ælmihtne, ælmeahtig]

almyʒty *n.* 1063 [OE ælmihtne, ælmeahtig]

alone *adv.* alone 933 [OE eal + ān]

al-only *adv.* solely, exclusively 779 [OE eal + ǣnlīce]

alow *v.* recognize 634 [OF alouer]

aloynte *pp.* removed, distant 893 [OF aloigner]

als *adv.* also 765 **alfo** 685, 872, 1071 [OE al-swa]

alþaʒ *conj.* although 759, 857, 878 [OE eal þēah]

alyue *adj.* alive, living 445 [OE on līfe]

am *pres. 1 sing.* am 246, 335, 382, etc. [OE am]

amen *interj.* amen 1212 [L āmēn]

amatyſt *n.* amethyst 1016 [OF ametiste]

among *prep.* among 470, 848, 1145, 1150 *adv.* together, mingled 905 [OE on gemang]

[and] (&) *conj.* and 16, 18, 27, 29, 538,* etc. **ande** 1212 [OE and]

anende *prep.* about, concerning 697 opposite 1136 **anendeʒ**

across from 975 **onende** about, concerning 186 [OE on efen]

angel-hauyng *n.* angelic air 754 [OF angele + ME hauyng]

anger *n.* grief, anger 343 [ON angr]

ani. *See* **any**

anioynt *pp.* joined, united 895 [OF ajoint]

anon *adv.* immediately, at once 584, 629 [OE on ān]

anoþer *adj.* another 297 [OE ān ōðer]

anſwar *n.* answer 518 [OE andswaru]

anunder *prep.* at the foot of 166 under 1092 **anvnnder** 775★ **anvndeʒ** 1068 **anvnder** 1081, 1100 [OE on under]

any *adj.* any 345, 463, 617, 800, 1068 **ani** 1139★ [OE ǣnig]

apere *v.* appear 405 [OF apareir]

apert *adv.* openly, plainly 589 [OF apert]

apocalyppce *n.* Apocalypse, Revelation 944, 1008 **apocalyppeʒ** 787, 996, 1020 **apokalypce** 983 **apokalypeʒ** 834 **appocalyppece** 866 [L apocalypsis]

apoſtel *n.* apostle 790, 836, 944, etc. **appoſtel** 1053 [OE apostol]

apparaylmente *n.* array 1052 [OF apareillement]

apple *n.* apple 640 [OE æppel]

appoſe *pres. 1 sing. subj.* pose questions 892 [OF aposer]

aproche *vt.* approach 686 **aproched** *vi. pret. 1 sing.* drew nearer 1119 [OF aprochier]

aquyle *v.* obtain 690 **aquylde** *pp.* obtained (permission) 967 [OF acueillir]

ar *pres. 2 plur.* are 923 **arn** *pres. 3 plur.* 402, 404, 626, etc. *pres. 1 plur.* 458 *pres. perf. 1 plur.* 517 *pres. perf. 3 plur.* 893, 895 **arne** *pres. 3 plur.* 628 **art** *pres. 2 sing.* 242, 423, 904, etc. **arte** 707 [OE eart, aren]

aray *n.* rank 491 **araye** array 5, 191 [OF arei]

arayed *pp.* prepared 719 arrayed 791 **arayde** disposed 1166★ [OF areyer]

arme *n.* arm 459, 466 [OE earm]

arn, arne. *See* **ar**

aros *pret. 3 sing.* arose, increased 181 [OE arīsen]

arraby *n.* Arabia 430 [OF arrabi]

aryʒt *adv.* swiftly 112 [OE ariht]

aryſtotel *n.* Aristotle 751★

aryue *v.* arrive 447 [OF ariver]

as *conj.* as 20, 96, 172, etc. according to 595 since 915, 923 while 980 [OE all-swā]

as *prep.* like 77, 88, 106, etc. according to 1041 [OE all-swā]

as *adv.* as 836, 911, 1024, etc.; **as...as** *correl. adv.* 76, 184, 626, etc. [OE all-swā]

aſent *n.* concord, harmony 94 agreement 391 [OF a(s)sent]

aſk *v.* ask for 564 **aſke** 316, 580, 910 [OE āscian]

aſſemble *n.* union 760 [OF a(s)semblee]

aſſpye *v.* observe 1035 **aſſpyed** *pp.* observed 704 *pret. 1 sing.* 979 [OF espier]

aſtate *n.* rank, social standing 393 **aſſtate** 490 [OF estat]

aſtraye *adv.* astray 1162 [OF estraié]

aſyſe *n.* fashion, style 97 [OF assise]

at[1] *prep.* at 161, 198, 218, etc. for 188

in 199 with 287 as 672 to 1164
at ene at once 291 once and for
all 953 [OE æt]

at² *rel. pron.* which 536 [ON at]

atount *pp.* astounded 179 [Cf. ME
astoned, F étonné]

atflyke3 *pres. 3 sing.* slip away, are
spent 575 [ME at + MLG slīken]

atteny *pres. 2 sing.* attain, reach 548
[OF ateindre]

augofte *n.* August 39 [L augustus]

aungele3 *n. plur.* angels 1121 [OF
angele, L angelus]

aunte *n.* aunt 233 [OF aunte]

auenture *n.* adventure 64 [OF
aventure]

avyfyoun *n.* vision 1184 [OF
avision]

away *adv.* away 488, 655, 823 **awaye**
gone 258 [OE on weg, aweg]

awayed *pp.* informed, instructed 710
[OF avier]

awhyle *adv.* for a while 692 [OE ān
hwīle]

ay *adv.* always 33, 44, 56, etc. **a** 144
ever 101, 366 still 156 forever
956 **aye** 1198 [ON ei]

ayþer *adj.* each of the two, both 831
[OE ǣgðer]

B

babtem. *See* **baptem**

bale *n.* woe, sorrow 18, 373, 478,
651, 1139 **bale3** *plur.* 123, 807
[OE balu, bealu]

balke *n.* mound 62 [OE balca]

baly *n.* castle wall 1083 [OF bail,
bail(l)e]

bantele3 *n. plur.* tiers 992 **bantels**
1017 [OF *bantel]

baptem *n.* baptism 653 **babtem** 627
[OF baptême]

baptyfed *pret. 3 sing.* baptized 818
[OF baptiser]

bare *adv.* plainly, clearly 836 *adj.*
clear 1025 [OE bær]

barne *n.* child 426 **barne3** *plur.* 712,
1040 [OE bearn]

baffe *n.* base, foundation 1000 [OF
base]

bafyng *n.* base, foundation 992 [OF
base + ME –yng]

bayly *n.* domain 315 dominion 442
[OF baillie]

bayn *adj.* ready, willing 807 [ON
beinn]

bayfment *n.* astonishment,
confusion 174 [OF abaïssement]

be *v.* be 29, 281, 421, etc. *pres. 1 sing.*
subj. should be 344 may be 710,
911 *pres. 2 sing.* 976 *pres. 2 sing.*
subj. be 352, 694 *pres. 3 sing subj.*
be 482, 571, 572, etc., is 311,
794, 914 *pres. 1 plur. subj.* should
be 379 *pres. 2 plur.* are 290 *pres. 3*
plur. 958 *imper. sing.* be 406 **ben**
pp. been 252, 373, 1194 *pres. 3*
plur. are 572 **bene** *pres. 1 plur.* are
785 **bet3** *fut. 3 sing.* will be 611
[OE bēon]

be *prep.* See **by**

beau *adj.* beautiful 197★ [Late OF
beau]

beaute *n.* beauty 749 **bewte** 765
[OF beaute]

bede *pret. 3 plur.* bade, ordered 715
[OE bēodan]

bele *v.* burn 18 [Cf. OI bǣla]

bem *n.* beam 814 [OE bēam]

bene *adj.* beautiful 110 *adv.*
beautifully 198 [?AF ben (CF
bien)]

bent *pp.* attached, tied 664 *pret. 3*
sing. tended, rose 1017 **bente**

pp. yielded, inclined 1189 [OE bendan]

ber *pres. 2 sing. subj.* wear 466 *pret. 3 sing.* bore 426 **bere** *inf.* bear 807, 1078 *pret. 1 sing.* turned 67 **beren** *pret. 1 plur.* 854 *pret. 3 plur.* 856, 1079 **bereʒ** *pres. 3 sing* bears 100, 746, 756, 1068 **bore** *pp.* born 239 **borne** 626 [OE beran]

berefte. *See* **brefte**

beryl *n.* beryl 110, 1011 [OF beryl]

beft *adj.* best 1131 **befte** 279, 863 [OE betst]

befteʒ *n. plur.* beasts 886 [OF beste]

bete *pret. 3 plur.* beat 93 [OE bēatan]

bete *v.* amend, restore 757 [OE bētan]

better *adv.* better, to greater advantage 341 [OE betera]

bewte. *See* **beaute**

beyng *n.* being, nature 446 [OE bēon]

bifore. *See* **byfore**

bitalt *pp.* shaken, aroused 1161 [OE be- + tealtian]

blaʒt *pp. adj.* bleached, white 212 [OE blǣc(e)an]

blake *adj.* black 945 [OE blæc]

blame *v.* blame 303 **blameʒ** *pres. 2 sing.* 275 [OF blâme]

blame *n.* censure 715 [OF blâmer]

blayke *adj.* pale, light-colored 27 [ON bleikr]

ble *n.* color, hue 76 complexion 212 [OE blēo]

bleaunt *n.* cloak, mantle 163 [OF bliaut]

blent *adj.* incorporated 385 **blente** blended 1016 [OE blendan, blandan]

bleffe *v.* bless, cross oneself 341 *pres. 3 sing. subj.* bless 850 **bleffed** *pp.*

blessed 436 [OE blētsian]

bleffyng *n.* blessing 1208 [OE blētsung]

blo *adj.* dark 83, 875 [ON blā]

blod *n.* blood 646, 650, 651, etc. **blode** 741 [OE blōd]

blody *adj.* bloody 705 [OE blōdig]

blom *n.* bloom 578 **blomeʒ** *plur.* blossoms, flowers 27 [ON blōm]

blofe *n.* blaze (?) (Morris); uncouth person (?) (MED); gust of wind (?) (Vantuono) 911★

blot *n.* blot, stain 782 [? Cf. OF blo(s)tre]

blunt *adj.* dull, stunned 176 [? Cf. OE blinnan]

blufched *pret. 1 sing* gazed 980, 1083 [OE blyscan, a)blysian]

blwe *adj.* blue 27, 76, 423 [OF bleu]

blynde *adj.* dull, dark 83 [OE blind]

blynne *v.* end, cease 729 [OE blinnan]

blys *n.* bliss 123, 126, 286, etc. **blyffe** 372, 373, 384, etc. [OE blīðs]

blyffol *adj.* blissful 279 **blyfful** 409, 907, 964, 1104 *subst.* blissful one 421, 1100 [OE blīðs + full]

blyfnande *pres. p.* gleaming, shining 163, 197 **blyfned** *pret. 3 sing.* gleamed, shone 1048 [OE blysian]

blyþe *adj.* blithe, happy 352, 738 **blyþeft** *superl.* most gracious 1131 [OE blīðe]

blyþe *n.* mercy, grace 354 [OE blīðe]

blyþely *adv.* happily 385 [OE blīþelīce]

bod. *See* **byde**

body *n.* body 62, 460, 1070 [OE bodig]

bodyly *adj.* bodily 478 in the flesh 1090 [OE bodig]

boffete3 *n. plur.* buffets, blows 809 [OF buffet]

bo3 *pres. 3 sing. impers.* it behooves, it is necessary 323 **byhod** *pret. 3 sing.* it was necessary 928 [OE behōfian]

bo3e *v.* turn, go 196 **bow** *imper. sing.* turn, go 972 **bowed** *pret. 1 sing.* went 126 [OE būgan]

bo3t. *See* **bye**

bok *n.* book 710 **boke** 837 [OE bōc]

bolde *adj.* bold 806 [OE bald]

bolle3 *n. plur.* boles, tree-trunks 76 [ON bolr]

bolne *v.* swell 18 [ON bolgna]

bon *n.* bone 212 [OE bān]

bonc. *See* **bonk**

bone *n.* "boon"; request 912, 916; favor 1090 [ON bōn]

bonerte *n.* happiness 762 [OF bonerte]

bonk *n.* bank, slope 102 **bonke** 196 **bonc** 907, 1169 **bonkes** *plur.* banks 106★ **bonke3** 110, 138, 931 [Cf. OI bakki]

bor *n.* "bower," dwelling 964 [OE būr]

borde *pres. 2 plur.* talk nonsense 290 [OF bourder]

bore. *See* **ber**

bor3 *n.* city 957, 989, 1048 **burghe** 980 [OE burg, burh]

borne. *See* **ber**

borne3 *n. gen. sing.* stream's 974 [OE burna]

bornyſt *adj.* burnished 77 **burniſt** 990 **bornyſte** shining 220 [OF burnir]

boro3t. *See* **bryng**

boſtwys *adj.* rough, rude 814

buſtwys rude, wild, "boisterous" 911 [OF boisteus]

bot *conj.* but 66, 91, 143, etc. *adv.* only, merely 17, 18, 83, etc. *prep.* other than, barring 312, 336, 337, etc. [OE be-ūtan]

bote *n.* remedy 275, 645 [OE bōt]

boþe *pron.* 373, 950; *correl. conj.* (with **and**) 90, 329, 682, 731, 1056, 1203 [OE bā þā]

boun *adj.* ready 534 arranged 992 *adv.* firmly 1103 [ON būinn]

bounden *pp.* bound, fastened 198, 1103 [OE bindan]

bourne. *See* **burne**

bow, bowed. *See* **bo3e**

boye3 *n. plur.* "boys," churls 806 [OF (em)boié]

brade. *See* **brode**

brathe *n.* violence 1170★ **braþe3** *plur.* violent emotions, agonies 346 [ON brāðr]

braundyſch *pres. 2 sing. subj.* "brandish," toss about 346 [OF brandir]

bray *pres. 2 sing. subj.* "bray," bellow, cry out 346 [OF braire]

brayde *pret. 3 plur.* brought 712 *pret. 3 sing.* aroused 1170 [OE bregdan]

brayne3 *n. plur.* brains 126 [OE bræg(e)n]

bred *n.* bread 1209 [OE brēad]

brede *v.* grow 415 stretch out 814 [OE bræden]

brede *n.* breadth 1031 [OE brǣdu]

bredful *adj.* brimful 126 [ON ★bredd-; cf. Norw. bredfuld]

bref *adj.* brief, fleeting 268 [OF bref]

breme *adj.* fierce 346 noble, glorious 863 [OE brēme]

brende *adj.* burned, refined 989

[ON brenna]

brent *pret. 3 plur.* "burned," shone 106 [ON brenna]

breſte *n.* breast 18, 222, 740, 1103, 1139 **bereſte** 854 [OE brēost]

breue *imp. sing.* "brief," tell 755 [ON brēfa, L breviāre]

brode *adj.* broad, wide 650, 1022, 1024 **brade** 138 [OE brād]

broʒ, broʒte. *See* **bryng**

brok *n.* brook 981 **broke** 141, 146 **brokeʒ** *gen. sing.* brook's 1074 [OE brōc]

broun *adj.* "brown," dark 537 shining 990 [OE brūn]

brunt *n.* blow 174 [? Cf. ON bruna]

bryd *n.* bride 769 [OE brȳd]

bryddeʒ *n. plur.* birds 93 [OE brid]

bryʒt *adj.* bright 75, 110, 989 *subst.* bright one 755 *adv.* brightly 769, 1048 **bryʒter** *comp.* brighter 1056 [OE beorht]

brym *n.* brim, brink 1074 **brymme** 232 [Cf. ON barmr, MHG brem]

bryng *v.* 853 *imper. sing.* 963 **boroʒt** *pp.* brought 628 **broʒ** 286 **broʒte** *pret. 3 sing.* brought 527 [OE bringan]

bur *n.* blow 1158 **burre** 176 [ON byrr]

burde *pret. 3 sing. impers.* "it befits" 316 [OE (ge)byrian]

burghe. *See* **borʒ**

burne *n.* man 1090 *voc.* "Sir" 397 **burneʒ** *plur.* people 712 **bourne** man 617 [OE beorn]

burniſt. *See* **bornyſt**

burre. *See* **bur**

buſtwys. *See* **boſtwys**

buſyeʒ *pres. 2 sing. refl.* "busy," occupy (yourself) 268 [OE bysgian]

by *prep.* by 107, 141, 152, etc. **be** 523 [OE bī, bi, be]

bycalle *pres. 1 sing.* call upon 913 **bycalt** *pp.* recalled, called back 1163 [OE be- + ON kalla; cf. OE ceallian]

bycawſe *conj.* because 296 [OE bī- + OF cause]

bycom *pret. 3 sing.* became 537 [OE becuman]

byde *v.* stay, abide, remain 399, 977 abide, endure 664 **bydeʒ** *pres. 3 plur.* lie, are situated 75 *pres. 2 sing.* abide 907 **bod** *pret. 3 sing.* remained 62 [OE bīdan]

byddeʒ *pres. perf. 3 sing.* has bidden 520 [OE biddan]

bydene *adv.* immediately 196 [?]

bye *v.* buy 732 **byye** 478 **boʒt** *pret. 3 sing.* bought 651 *pp.* 733, 893 [OE bycg(e)an]

byfalle *v.* befall 186 [OE bef(e)allan]

byfore *prep.* in front of 294, 598, 885 *conj.* before, earlier than 530 *adv.* previously 172 in advance 1110 **bifore** *prep.* in front of 49 [OE beforan]

byg *adj.* big 102 **bygger** *comp.* bigger 374 [? Cf. Norw. bugge]

bygly *adj.* habitable 963 [Cf. OI byggiligr]

bygynne *v.* 581 begin **bygyn** *imp. sing.* 547 **bygynneʒ** *pres. 2 sing.* do (you) begin 561 **bygonne** *pp.* begun 33 *pret. 3 plur.* began 549 [OE biginnan]

bygyng *n.* building 932 [Cf. ON bygging]

byʒe *n.* ring 466 [OE bēag, bēah]

byʒonde *prep.* beyond 141, 146, 158, etc. [OE begeondan] byhod. *See* bo3

byholde *v.* behold 810 [OE bihaldan]

bylde *n.* building 727, 963 [OE gebyld, bold]

bylde *pret. 3 plur.* built, aroused 123 [OE byldan]

byngyner *n.* (scribal error for bygyner) beginner 436★ [OE biginnan]

byrþ *n.* birth 1041 [Cf. OE ge)byrd, OI byrð] (*see* whate3)

byfech *v.* beseech 390 [OE besēcan]

byfeme *v.* "beseem," befit 310 [OE be- + ON sœma]

byfwyke3 *pres. 1 sing.* deceive, cheat 568 [OE beswīcan]

byta3te *pret. 1 sing.* committed, entrusted 1207 [OE betǣcan]

byte *v.* incite, arouse 355 bite 640 [OE bītan]

bytwene *adv.* in between 44 *prep.* between 140, 658 [OE betwēon(um)]

bytwyfte *prep.* "betwixt," between 464 [OE betweox]

bytyde *v.* "betide," befall 397 [OE be- + tīdan]

byye. *See* bye

C

caggen *pres. 3 plur.* bind 512 [? Cf. ON kögurr]

ca3t *pret. 3 sing.* caught, seized on (with to) 50 ca3te took 237 [AF cach(i)er]

calder. *See* colde

calle *v.* call 173, 182, 721 *pres. 1 plur.* call 430 *pp.* called 572 **called** *pp.* called 273 *pret. 3 sing.* called 542 **calde** *pret. 3 sing.* called 762 [OE ceallian, ON kalla]

calfydoyne *n.* chalcedony 1003 [OF calcidoine]

cambe *n.* comb 775 [OE camb]

can. *See* con

care *n.* care 50, 371, 861 **care3** *plur.* cares 808 [OE caru]

carp *v.* speak 381 **carpe** 949 *pret. 3 sing.* spoke 752 [ON karpa]

carpe *n.* discourse 883 [ON karpa]

cas *n.* case 673 [OF cas]

cafte *n.* intention 1163 [Cf. OI kast]

caftel *adj.* castle 917 [OE castel]

caufe3 *n. plur.* causes, cases 702 [OF cause]

cayre *v.* extend 1031 [ON keyra]

cete. *See* cyte

ceuer *v.* attain 319 [OE ācofrian, OF covrer]

chace *v.* chase 443 [OF chacier]

chambre *n.* chamber 904 [OF chambre]

chapel *n.* chapel 1062 [OF chapele]

charde *pret. 3 plur.* changed, turned back 608 [OE cierran]

charyte *n.* charity 470 [OF charité]

chayere *n.* chair, throne 885 [OF chaëre]

chere *n.* cheer, state of mind 407 facial expression 887, 1109 [OF chiere]

ches *pret. 3 sing.* chose 759 **chefe** 954 **chos** *pret. 1 sing.* found 187 **ichofe** *pp.* chosen 904 [OE cēosan]

cheuentayn *n.* chieftain 605 [OF chevetaine]

chyche *n.* niggard, cheapskate 605 [OF chiche]

chyde *v.* chide 403 [OE cīdan]

chylde *n.* child 723 **chylder** *plur.* children 714, 718 [OE cild]

cite. *See* cyte

clad *adj.* clad, clothed 22 [OE
  clāðod]
clambe. *See* **clym**
clanly *adv.* cleanly, expertly 2 [OE
  clǣnlīc]
clem *v.* claim 826 [OF clamer]
clene *adj.* clean, clear, pure 227, 289,
  682, etc. *adv.* clearly, fully 754,
  949 [OE clǣne]
clente *pp.* clenched, held fast 259
  [OE clenc(e)an]
cler *adj.* clear 74, 207, 227, 1011
  pure 1111 *adv.* free of charge 274
  clearly 882, 913 *n.* clearness 1050
  clere *adj.* pure 2* clear 620, 735,
  737 [OF cler]
clerke3 *n. plur.* clerks, clerics 1091
  [OE clerc]
cleuen *pres. 3 plur.* cleave, split apart
  66 [OE clēofan]
clos *v.* enclose, set 2 **clofe** enclose
  271 **clofed** *pret. 3 sing.* closed
  803 [OF clore]
clos *adj.* closed 183 secure 512 [OF
  clore]
clot *n.* clods, earth 22, 320 ground
  789 **clotte3** *plur.* clods 857 [OE
  clot]
cloyftor *n.* cloister 969 [OF cloistre]
clyffe *n.* cliff 159 **klyfe3** *plur.* cliffs
  66 **klyffe3** 74 [OE clif]
clym *v.* climb 1072 **klymbe** 678
  clambe *pret. 2 sing.* climbed 773
  [OE climban]
clynge *pres. 3 plur. subj.* wither, decay
  857 [OE clingan]
clypper *n.* shearer 802 [ON klippa]
clyuen *v.* "cleave," adhere to, belong
  to (with **vpon**) 1196 [OE clīfan,
  clifian]
cnawyng *n.* "knowing," knowledge,
  understanding 859 [OE

(ge)cnāwan]
cnoken *pres. 3 plur.* knock 727 [Late
  OE cnocian]
cofer *n.* coffer, treasure chest 259
  [OF cofre]
colde *adj.* cold 50, 808 **calder** *comp.*
  colder 320 [OE cald]
color *n.* color, complexion 22
  colour 215, 753 [OF color]
com *v.* come 676, 701 *pret. 3 sing.*
  came 155, 230, 574, 615, 645,
  749 *pres. 3 plur.* come 262 *pres. 2*
  sing. subj. come 598 *pres. 3 sing.*
  subj. come 723, 724, 749 **come**
  pret. 1 sing. came 582 **comme3**
  pres. 3 sing. comes 848 **cum** *imp.*
  sing. come 763 [OE cuman]
come *n.* coming 1117 [OE cyme]
comfort *n.* comfort 55 **comforte**
  357 **coumforde** *dat.* with
  comfort 369 [OF confort]
comly *adj.* comely, fair 259 **cumly**
  929 *subst. adj.* comely one, fair
  lady 775 [OE cȳmlīc]
comme3. *See* **com**
commune *adj.* common, belonging
  equally 739 [OF comun]
compas *n.* circuit, arc 1072 [OF
  compas]
companyny *n.* company 851 [OF
  compaignie]
con (1) *pres. 3 sing.* can, is able to
  665, 709, 729, 827, 921 *pres. 2*
  sing. can 381, 914 **conne** *pres. 2*
  plur. can 521 **couþe** *pret. 3 sing.*
  could 95 *pret. 3 plur.* 855 **cowþe**
  pret. 1 sing. subj. 134 **cowþe3**
  pret. 2 sing. 484 [OE cunnan]
con (2) (*verbal auxiliary*) *pres. 1 sing.*
  do 931 *pres. 3 sing.* does 495, 851,
  1093 *pres. 3 plur.* do 78, 1078
  pret. 1 sing. did 147, 149, 150, etc.

pret. 2 sing. 313, 437, 769, etc.
pret. 3 sing. 81, 88, 111, etc. *pret.
3 plur.* 103, 160, 509, etc. **can**
pret. 3 plur. did 499 **coneȝ** *pres.
2 sing.* do 482, 925 *pres. 3 sing.*
does 909 [OE onginnan]
conciens *n.* consciousness,
conviction 1089 [OF conscience]
contryſſyoun *n.* contrition 669 [OF
contriciun]
coppe *n.* top, summit 791 [OE cop]
corne *n.* grain 40 [OE corn]
coronde *pret. 3 sing.* crowned 767 *pp.*
1101 **corounde** *pret. 3 sing.* 415
pp. 480 [OF coroner]
coroun *n.* crown 237, 255 **coroune**
205 **croun** 1100 **croune** 427
corouneȝ *plur.* crowns 451 [AF
coroune]
corſe *n.* body, corpse 320 **corſes**
plur. corpses 857 [OF cors]
cortayſe *adj.* courteous 433 **corteȝ**
754 [OF corteis]
cortayſe *n.* courtesy 469, 480, 481
cortayſye 432, 444, 456, 468
courtayſye 457 [OF cortesie]
cortayſly *adv.* courteously 381 [OF
corteis]
corteȝ. *See* **cortayſe** *adj.*
corte. *See* **court.**
cortel *n.* kirtle, gown 203 [OE
cyrtel]
coruen *pp.* cut 40 **keruen** *pres. 3
plur.* 512 [OE ccorfan]
couenaunde *n.* agreement, covenant
563 **couenaunt** 562 [OF
covenant]
coumforde. *See* **comfort**
counſayl *n.* plan, course of action
319 [OF conseil]
counterfete *v.* resemble, counterfeit
556 [OF contrefet]

countes *n.* countess 489 [OF
contesse]
countre *n.* country 297 [OF
contrée]
court *n.* court 445 **corte** 701 [OF
cort]
courtayſye. *See* **cortayſe**
couþe, cowþe, cowþeȝ. *See* **con**
v. (1)
crafteȝ *n. plur.* powers, virtues 356
arts 890 [OE cræft]
craue *v.* crave 663 [OE crafian]
crede *n.* the Apostles' Creed 485
[OE crēda]
creſſe *n.* cress, trifle 343 [OE cresse]
creſte *n.* crest, crown 856 [OF
creste]
crokeȝ *n. plur.* sickles 40 [ON crōkr]
croun. *See* **coroun**
cryſolyt *n.* chrysolite 1009 [OF
crisolite]
cryſopaſe *n.* chrysoprase 1013 [OF
crisopace]
cryſtal *n.* crystal 74, 159 [OF cristal]
cryſtes. *See* **kryſt**
cum. *See* **com**
cumly. *See* **comly**
cure *n.* medical treatment, care 1091
[OF cure]
cyte *n.* city 792, 939, 1023 **cete** 927,
952 **cite** 1097 **cyty** 986 [OF
cité]

D

daleȝ *n. plur.* dales, valleys 121 [OE
dæl]
dam *n.* stream 324 [Cf. OI damm]
dampned *pp.* damned 641 [OF
dampner]
damyſel *n.* damsel 489 **damyſelle**
361 [OF dameisele]
dar *pres. 1 sing.* dare 1089 **dorſt** *pret.*

1 sing. "durst," dared 143 **dorſte** 182 [OE durran]

dare *v.* bow down, cower, abase oneself 839 **dard** *pret. 3 sing.* bowed down 609 [OE darian]

daſed *pp.* dazed 1085 [Cf. OI dasask]

date *n.* end, limit 493, 516, 528, 529, 540, 541 beginning 517 result 492 season 504, 505 **date3** *plur.* birth dates 1040 [OF date]

Dauid *n.* David 698 **dauid** 920

daunce *pres. 2 sing. subj.* may dance 345 [OF dancer]

daunger *n.* distress, frustration, lovesickness 250 **daungere** 11 [OF dangier]

day *n.* day 486, 510, 516, etc. **daye** 517, 541, 1210 **daye3** *plur.* 416, 554 *gen. sing.* of day 533 **dawe3** *plur.* days 283 [OE dæg]

day-glem *n.* "day-gleam," sun 1094 [OE dæg + glæm]

dayly *v.* dally (?); contend, dispute (?); speak courteously (?) 313*

debate *n.* debate 390 [OF debat]

debonere *adj.* debonair, courteous 162 [OF debonaire]

debonerte *n.* meekness, gentleness 798 [OF debonaireté]

declyne *v.* decline, become weaker 333 enter into (an agreement) 509 [OF decliner]

dede *adj.* dead 31 [OE dēad]

dede *n.* action 481 deed 524 [OE dæd]

degres *n. plur.* steps 1022 [OF degre]

del, dele *n.* See **doel**

dele *pres. 3 sing. subj.* dispenses, metes out 606 [OE dælan]

delfully *adv.* dolefully, grievously 706 [OF deol] Cf. **dol**

delit *n.* delight 1129 **delyt** 643,

1104,* 1105, 1116, etc. [OF delit]

delyuered *pret. 1 sing.* delivered, saved 653 [OF delivrer]

dem *v.* deem, judge 312 **deme** 336, 348, 360, 1183 *imper. sing.* judge 313, 349 *pres. 3 sing. subj.* may deem 324 **deme3** *pres. 2 sing.* deem, judge 325, 337 **demed** *pret. 1 sing.* spoke, said 361 [OE dēman]

demme *v.* be dammed, be blocked 223 [Cf. OE fordemman]

dene *n.* valley 295 [OE denu, dænu]

denned *pret. 3 sing.* made its den, dwelt 51 [OE denn]

dep *adv.* deeply 406 **depe** *adj.* deep 143 intense 215 *subst. plur.* deeps, depths 109 [OE dēop]

departed *pret. 1 plur.* separated, were parted 378 [OF departir]

depaynt *pp.* adorned 1102 [OF depeint]

depres *v.* vanquish, drive away 778 [OF depresser]

depryue *v.* deprive 449 [OF depriver]

dere *adj.* dear, precious, pleasing, excellent, noble 72, 85, 97, etc. *subst. plur.* dear ones 777; *adv.* for a high price 733 [OE dēore]

dere *v.* harm, thwart 1157 [OE derian]

dere3 *n. plur.* hindrances, obstacles 102 [OE derian; cf. OE daru]

derely *adv.* richly, splendidly 995 [OE dēorlīce]

derk *n.* darkness 629 [OE deorc]

derþe *n.* splendor, glory 99 [Cf. ON dȳrð]

derworth *adj.* precious 109 [OE dēorwurþe]

defe *n.* dais, raised platform 766 [OF deis]

defferte *n.* merit, just deserts 595 [OF desserte]

deffypele3 *n. plur.* disciples 715 [OE discipul]

deftyne *n.* destiny 758 [OF destinée]

determynable *adj.* definite, determined 594 [OF determinable]

deth *n.* death 323, 630, 653, 656 dethe 860 [OE dēaþ]

deuely *adj.* dismal, desolating 51★ [OE dēaf; cf. OI daufligr]

deuife *v.* observe 1129 deuyfe describe 99 deuyfe3 *pres. 3 sing.* describes 984, 995 deuyfed *pret. 3 sing.* described 1021 [OF deviser]

deuote *adj.* devout 406 [OF devot]

deuoyde *v.* do away with, get rid of 15 [OF devoyder]

deuyfe *n.* device 139 at my deuyfe in my opinion 199 [OF devis]

deuyfe (*v.*), deuyfe3, deuyfed. *See* deuife

deuyfement *n.* description 1019 [OF devisement]

dewyne *pres. 1 sing.* languish, pine 11 dowyne 326 [OE dwīnan]

do *n.* doe 345 [OE dā]

do *v.* do 424, 496, 520, 566 *pres. 1 sing.* place, put 366 did *pret. 1 sing.* did 102 *pret. 3 sing.* 1138 dyd caused 306 dyt did 681 dyden *pret. 3 plur.* did 633 dot3 *pres. 3 sing.* causes 330 takes 823 *pres. 2 sing.* do 338 make 556 *emphatic auxiliary* does 17, 293, 630 *imper. plur.* 521, 536 don *pp.* placed, put 250, 283 done 930 *pres. 3 plur.* do 511 done *pp.* put,

placed 1042 do way *imper. plur.* stop, cease 718 don to slake *pp.* brought to an end 942 to done to be done, possible 914 [OE dōn]

doc *n.* duke 211 [OF duc]

doel *n.* grief, sorrow 336, 339, 642 dol 326 del 250 dele 51 [OF doel]

doel-doungoun *n.* doleful dungeon 1187 [OF doel + donjon]

doel-dyftreffe *n.* tribulation 337 [OF doel + destrece]

dole *n.* part 136 [OE dāl]

dom *n.* understanding, judgment 157, 223 judicial decision, judgment 667 dome 580, 699 [OE dōm]

don, done. *See* do

dorft, dorfte. *See* dar

dot3. *See* do

double *adj.* double 202 [OF duble]

doun *adv.* down 30, 41, 125, 530, 538, 1094 *prep.* down 196, 230 [Late OE dūne]

doun *n.* "down," hilly upland 121 downe3 *plur.* 73, 85 [OE dūn]

doufour *n.* sweetness, good nature 429 [OF dousor]

doute *n.* doubt 928 [OF doute]

douth *n.* troop, company 839 [OE duguþ]

downe3. *See* doun, *n.*

dowyne. *See* dewyne

dra3 *imper. sing.* draw 699 drawen *pp.* drawn 1193 dro3 *pret. 3 plur.* went 1116 [OE dragan]

dred *pret. 1 sing.* feared 186 [OE andrǣdan]

drede *n.* dread 181 doubt 1047 [OE andrǣdan]

drem *n.* dream, vision 790, 1170

[OE drēam, ON draumr; cf. OS
drōm]

dreſſe *v.* ordain 495 **dreſt** *pp.*
erected, constructed 860 [OF
dresser]

dreue drive, pass 323 **dreued** *pret. 1
sing.* went 980 [OE drǣfan]

drof. *See* **dryf**

droʒ. *See* **draʒ**

drounde *pret. 3 sing.* drowned 656 [?
ON *drugna; cf. OI drukna]

drwry *adj.* cruel 323 [OE drēorig]

dryf *vt.* drive 777 **drof** *pret. 3 sing.*
drove 1153 *vi.* **dryue** *pres. 3 sing.*
sink 1094 **drof** *pret. 3 sing.* sank
30 **dryuen** *pp.* driven, brought
1194 [OE drīfan]

dryʒe *adj.* continual, incessant 823
[Cf. OI drjūgr, OE drēogan]

dryʒly *adv.* continually, incessantly
125, 223 [Cf. OI drjūgr, OE
drēogan]

dryʒtyn *n.* the Lord 324, 349 [OE
dryhten]

dryue, dryuen. *See* **dryf**

dubbed *pp.* adorned, arrayed 73, 202
dubbet 98 [OE dubbian, OF
adober]

dubbement *n. coll.* adornment,
splendor 121 **dubbemente**
109 [OF adubbement] Cf.
adubbement

due *adj.* due 894 [OF deü]

dunne *adj.* dark-colored 30 [OE
dun(n)]

durande *adj.* enduring 336 [OF
durer]

dyche *n.* ditch 607 [OE dīc]

dyd, dyden. *See* **do**

dyʒe *v.* die 306, 643 **dyed** *pret. 3
sing.* died 705 **dyʒed** 828 [ON
deyja]

dyʒt *v.* dispose, determine 360 *pp.*
established 920 adorned 987
dyʒte 202 [OE dihtan]

dylle *adj.* dull, slow 680 [OE *dyl;
cf. OE dol]

dym *adj.* dim 1076 [OE dim(m)]

dyne *n.* din, loud continued noise
339 [OE dyne]

dyſcreuen *v.* be seen 68 [OF
descrivre]

dyſpleſeʒ *imper. sing. pass.* be
displeased 422 *pres. 3 sing.*
displeases 455 [OF desplaisir]

dyſſente *pres. 3 plur.* descend 627
[OF descendre]

dyſſtreſſe *n.* distress 898 **dyſtreſſe**
280 [OF destresse]

dyſtryed *pret. 3 plur.* destroyed 124
[OF destruire]

dyt. *See* **do**

E

efte *adv.* again 328 afterwards 332
[OE eft]

elleʒ *adv.* else, otherwise 32, 130,
491, 567, 724 [OE elles]

emerad *n.* emerald 118 **emerade**
1005 [OF emeraude]

emperiſe *n.* empress 441 [OF
emperesse]

empyre *n.* empire 454 [OF empire]

enchace *v.* impel, urge 173 [OF
enchacier]

encloſe *v.* enclose, contain 909 [OF
enclos]

enclyin *adj.* lying prostrate 1206★
[OF enclin]

enclyne *v.* sink down 630
enclynande *pres. p.* bowing 236
[OF encliner]

encreſ *v.* increase 959 [OF encres-]

encroched *pret. 3 sing.* brought,

aroused 1117 [OF encrochier]

endele3 *adv.* endlessly, without end 738 [OE endelēas]

endent *pp.* inlaid 1012 **endente** 629 [OF endenter]

endorde *pp. as subst.* adored one 368 [OF adorer]

endure *v.* suffice 225 **endeure** endure 1082 **endured** *pp.* endured 476 [OF endurer]

endyte *pres. 3 plur.* proclaim, utter 1126 [OF enditer]

ene *adv.* once, one time 291, 953 [OE ǣne]

enle *adj.* single 849 [OE ānlīc]

enleuenþe *adj.* eleventh 1014 [OE endlyfta]

enpreſſe *n.* renown, glory 1097 [OF emprise]

enſens *n.* incense 1122 [OF encens]

entent *n.* intent, purpose 1191 [OF entente]

enter *v.* enter 966 **entred** *pret. 1 sing.* entered 38 **entre3** *pres. 3 sing.* enters 1067 [OF entrer]

enurned *pp.* adorned, decorated 1027 [OF aörner]

er *adv.* before 319, 372 **ere** 164 **er** *prep.* before 517 *conj.* before 188, 224, 324, 328, 372, 1030, 1140 **er þenne** before 631, 1094 [OE ǣr]

erber *n.* herb garden 38, 1171 **erbere** 9 [OF (h)erbier]

erde *n.* land, country 248 [OE eard]

ere *adv. See* **er**

ere *n.* ear 1153 [OE ēare]

erle *n.* earl 211 [OE eorl]

erly *adv.* early 392, 506 [OE ārlīce]

errour *n.* error, falsehood 422 [OF error]

erþe *n.* earth 840 **vrþe** 442, 893,

1125 [OE eorþe]

erytage. *See* **herytage**

eſchaped *pret. 3 sing. subj.* should escape 187 [OF eschaper]

eþe *adj.* easy 1202 [OE ēaþe]

euel *adv.* ill 310, 930 [OE yfele]

euen *adv.* exactly 740 [OE efen]

euen *v.* compete 1073 [OE efnan]

euenſonge *n.* evensong, vespers 529 [OE ǣfen-sang]

euentyde *n.* evening 582 [OE ǣfen-tīd]

euer *adv.* always, continually 144, 153, 180, 349, etc. ever, at any time 200, 239, 328, 609, etc. [OE ǣfre]

euermore *adv.* always, forever 591, 666, 1066 [OE ǣfre mā]

excuſed *pp.* excused 281 [OF excuser]

expoun *pres. 3 sing.* describe 37 [OF espondre]

expreſſe *adv.* expressly, explicitly 910 [OF expresse]

F

fable *n.* fable 592 [OF fable]

face *n.* face 67, 169, 434, 675,★ 809 [OF face]

fader *n.* father 639, 736 **fadere3** *gen. sing.* father's 872 [OE fæder]

fa3t *pret. 3 plur.* fought 54 [OE feohtan]

fande. *See* **fynde**

farande *adj.* suitable, fitting, seemly 865★ [OE faran]

fare *v.* fare, go 147 *pres. 1 plur.* get along, get on 467 **fares** *pres. 3 sing.* goes 129 [OE faran]

fare *n.* conduct 832 [OE fær; faru]

faſor *n.* maker 431 [OF faiseor]

faſoun *n.* fashion, form 983, 1101

[OF façon, fazon]

faſte *adv.* tenaciously 54, 150 [OE fæste]

faſure *n.* fashion, form 1084* [OF feisure]

fate3 *pres. 3 sing.* fades 1038 [OF fader]

faunt *n.* infant, child 161 [OF enfaunt]

fauor *n.* favor 968 **fauour** grace 428 [OF favor]

fax *n.* hair 213 [OF feax]

fay *n.* faith *in* **par ma fay** by my faith 489 **in faye** in truth 263 [OF fei]

fayle *v.* fail 317 **fayly** 34 **fayled** *pret. 3 sing.* failed, faded 270 [OF faillir]

fayn *adj.* happy, pleased 393, 450 [OE fægen]

fayr *adj.* fair, pleasing, comely 46, 147, 490, 810 **fayre** 169, 177, 747, 946, 1024, 1178 **feier** *comp.* fairer 103 [OE fæger]

fayr *adv.* courteously 714 **fayre** pleasingly 88, 884 [OE fægre]

fech *v.* fetch, deal (a blow) 1158 **feche** *pres. 3 sing. subj.* fetch, bring in 847 [OE fecc(e)an]

fede *adj.* withered, faded (?); wasted (?) 29* [OE ____]

feier. *See* **fayr**

fel *pret. 1 sing.* fell 1174 **felle** 57 *pret. 3 plur.* 1120 [OE feallan]

felde *pret. 1 sing.* felt 1087 [OE fēlan]

fele *pron.* many 21, 439, 716 *adj.* 874, 927, 1114 [OE fela]

felle *adj.* fell, cruel, deadly 367, 655 [OF fel]

felonye *n.* felony 800 [OF felonie]

fenyx *n.* phoenix 430 [OE and OF fenix]

fer *adv.* far 334, 1076 **fyrre** *comp.* further 103, 127, 152, 347, 544, 563 [OE feor(r)]

fere *n.* company *in* **in fere** together 89, 884, 1105 [OE gefēr]

fere3 *pres. 3 sing.* brings, leads 98 **feryed** *pp.* led, brought 946 [OE ferian]

fere3 *n. plur.* companions 1150 [OE gefēra]

ferly *adj.* amazing, marvelous 1084 *subst.* amazement 1086 [OE fǣrlic]

feryed. *See* **fere3** *v.*

feſte *n.* feast, rejoicing *in* **ma feſte** rejoice, make merry 283 [OF feste]

fete. *See* **fote**

fewe *adj.* few 572 [OE fēawe]

fla3t *n.* sod, turf 57 [OE *flæht, *fleaht]

flake *n.* spot, blemish 947 [Cf. Du vlak]

flambe *v.* flame, shine 769 **flaumbande** *pres. p.* flaming, shining 90 [OF flamber]

flauore3 *n. plur.* odors, scents 87 [OF flaur]

flayn. *See* **fly3e**

fle *v.* flee 294 [OE flēon]

fle3e *pret. 3 sing.* flew 431 **flowen** *pret. 3 plur.* 89* [OE flēogan]

fleme *v.* drive 1177 *pres. 3 sing. subj.* may banish 334 [OE flīeman]

fleſch *n.* flesh 306 [OE flǣsc]

fleſchly *adj.* fleshly, bodily 1082 [OE flǣsclic]

flet *n.* floor 1058 [OE flet(t)]

fleten *pret. 3 plur.* flowed, were wafted 21 **flot** *pret. 3 sing.* floated 46 [OE flotian, flēotan]

flode *n.* flood, water, river 736, 1058

flode₃ *gen. plur.* of waters 874
[OE flōd]

flok *n.* flock 947 [OE flocc]

flonc *pret. 1 sing.* rushed, flung 1165
[Cf. OI flengja]

flor *n.* flower 29, 962 **flour** 426
flowre₃ *plur.* flowers 208 [OF
flour, flur, flor]

flor-de-lys *n.* fleur-de-lys, iris 195
flour-de-lys 753 [OF flour de
lis]

flot. *v. See* fleten

flot *n. dat.* in company 786 **flote** *n.*
company 946 [OF flote]

floty *adj.* watery 127 [OE flotian +
-ig]

flour. *See* flor

flour-de-lys. *See* flor-de-lys

floury *adj.* flowery 57 [OF flour, flur,
flor + -ig]

flowen. *See* fle₃e

flowred *pret. 3 sing.* flowered 270
[Cf. OF florir]

flowre₃. *See* flor

flurted *adj.* figured 208 [OF fleureté]

fly₃e *v.* flay, scourge 813 **flayn** *pp.*
flayed, lashed 809 [OE flēan]

flyte *v.* dispute 353 [OE flītan]

fode *n.* food 88 [OE fōda]

folde *n.* land 334, 736 [OE folde]

folde *vt.* bend, bow down 813 *pp.*
having covered 434 [OE fealdan]

fol₃ed *pret. 1 sing.* followed 127 *pret.*
3 sing. 654 **folewande** *pres. p.*
following 1040 [OE folgian]

fon. *See* fyne *v.*

fonde *v.* attempt 150 seek out, visit
939 [OE fandian]

fonde 283. *See* fynde

fonge *v.* receive 479 *pret. 3 plur.*
took up 884 **fonge₃** *pret. 3 plur.*
obtain, win 439 [OE fōn]

fonte. *See* fynde

for *prep.* for, because of, on behalf of
50, 154, 244, 263, etc. as 211 in
spite of 890 **fore** in exchange for
734 **for to** *prep.* to, in order to
99, 333, 403, 613, etc. [OE for]

for *conj.* for, because 31, 71, 93, 117,
etc. [OE for]

forbede *pres. 3 sing. subj.* forbid 379
[OE forbēodan]

forbrent *pp.* burned up 1139 [OE
forbeornan]

fordidden *pret. 3 plur.* did for,
destroyed 124 [OE fordōn]

fordolked *pp.* severely wounded 11
[Cf. Late OE dolg]

fore. *See* for

foreſte *n.* forest 67 [OF forest]

foreuer *adv.* forever 261 [OE for +
ǣfre]

forfete *v.* forfeit 639 **forfeted** *pret. 3*
sing. forfeited 619 [OF forfet]

forgarte *pp.* forfeited, condemned
321 [Cf. OI fyrirgöra]

forgo *v.* give up the enjoyment of, do
without 328 **forgos** *pres. 3 sing.*
passes over 340 [OE forgān]

for₃ete *v.* forget 86 [OE forgitan]

forhede₃ *n. plur.* foreheads 871 [OE
forhēafod]

forlete *pret. 1 sing.* relinquished, lost
327 [OE forlǣtan]

forlonge *n. gen. plur.* furlongs' 1030
[OE furlang]

forloyne *pres. 1 sing. subj.* go astray,
err 368 [OF forloignier]

forme *adj.* first 639 [OE forma]

forme *n.* form 1209 [OF fo(u)rme,
furme]

formed *pret. 3 sing.* formed 747 [OF
fourmer]

forpayned *pp.* severely afflicted 246

[OE for- + OF pener]

forſake *imp. sing.* forsake 743 [OE forsacan]

forſer *n.* treasure chest 263 [OF forcer]

forſoþe *adv.* forsooth, in truth 21, 292 [OE forsōð]

forth *adv.* forth 98, 101, 510, 980, 1116 [OE forð]

fortune *n.* fortune 129, 306 **fortwne** 98 [OF fortune]

forty *adj.* forty 786, 870 [OE fēowertig]

forþe *n.* ford 150 [OE ford]

forþy *adv.* therefore 137, 234, 701, 845 [OE forðī, forðȳ]

fote *n.* bottom, lowest part 161 foot (unit of measure) 350, 970 **fete** *n. plur.* feet 1120 [OE fōt]

founden. *See* **fynde**

founce *n.* bottom 113 [AF founz]

foundemente3. *See* **fundament**

fowle3 *n. plur.* birds 89 [OE fugel]

fowre *adj.* four 870, 886 [OE fēower]

foyſon *n.* abundance *used as adj.* copious 1058 [OF foison]

fraunchyſe *n.* franchise, immunity from punishment 609 [OF franchise]

frayne3 *pres. 3 sing.* asks, desires 129 [OE frignan]

frayſte *pret. 1 sing.* examined 169 [ON freista]

fre *adj.* free, liberal, lavish 481, 796 *adv.* freely 299 [OE frēo]

frech *adj.* fresh 87 *subst.* fresh one 195 **freſch** *subst. plur.* fresh bodies 958* **freuch** *adj.* fresh 1086* [OF fresche]

freles *adj.* faultless, perfect 431 [?ON frȳju-lauss (OED); OF fraile

(MED)]

frely *subst. adj.* noble one, fair one 1155 [OE frēolīc]

frende *n.* friend 558, 1204 [OE frēond]

freſch, freuch. *See* **frech**

fro *prep.* from 10, 13, 46, 61, etc. to 803 *adv.* fro 347 *conj.* since 251, 375 **fro þᵗ** since 958 **fro me warde** in front of me 981 [ON frā]

frount *n.* forehead, face 177 [OF front]

frym *adv.* abundantly 1079 [OE freme]

fryt *n.* fruit 894* **fryte** 29 **fryte3** *plur.* fruits 87, 1078 [OF fruit]

fryth *n.* forest 89, 98, 103 [OE (ge) fyrhðe; cf. OS frīd-hof]

ful *adj.* full 1098 [OE full]

ful *adv.* full, very, quite 28, 42, 50, 80, etc. fully 860 [OE full]

fundament *n.* foundation 1010 **foundemente3** *plur.* foundations 993 [OF fondement]

furþe *n.* fourth 1005 [OE fēorða]

fyf *n.* five 849 **fyue** 451 [OE fif]

fyfþe *adj.* fifth 1006 [OE fifta]

fygure *n.* form, figure 170, 747, 1086 [OF figure]

fyldor *n.* gold thread 106 [OF fil d'or]

fylþe *n.* filth 1060 [OE fȳlð]

fyn *adj.* fine, thin 106 fine, excellent 170 **fyin** 1204 [OF fin]

fynde *v.* find 150 **fynde3** *pres. 3 sing.* finds 508, 514 **fande** *pret. 1 sing.* found 871 **fonde** *pp.* found 283 **founden** 1203 **fonte** 170, 327 [OE findan]

fyne *pres. 1 sing.* die 328 *imp. sing.* cease 353* **fon** *pret. 3 sing.* ended

1030 [OF finer]

fyne *adv.* completely 635 [OF fin]

fynger *n.* finger 466 [OE finger]

fyrre *comp. adj.* farther, more distant 148 [OE firra]

fyrſt *adj.* first 486, 999 *adv.* 316, 583 **fyrſte** 638 *n.* 549, 570, 571, 635, 1042 **fyrſte** 548 [OE fyrst]

fyrte *adj.* fearful 54★ [OE ge)fǣren]

fyue. *See* **fyf**

G

galalye *n.* Galilee 817

galle (1) *n.* gall, envy, rancor 915 **gawle** 463 [OE gealla]

galle (2) *n.* blemish, spot 189 scum 1060 [OE gealla, galla]

gardyn *n.* garden 260 [ONF gardin]

gareʒ *pres. 3 sing.* causes 331 **gart** *pret. 3 sing.* caused 1151 **garten** *pret. 3 plur.* caused 86 [ON ger(v)a]

garlande *n.* garland 1186 [OF garlande]

gart, garten. *See* **gare**ʒ

gate *n.* way, street 395, 526, 619 **gate**ʒ *plur.* streets 1106 [ON gata]

gawle. *See* **galle** (1)

gay *adj.* gay, bright 1124, 1186 **gaye** 7, 260 **gay** *subst.* gay one 189 **gaye** 433 [OF gai]

gayn *prep.* beyond 138 [ON gegn]

gayneʒ *pres. 3 sing.* avails 343 [ON gegna]

gef. *See* **gyue**

gele *v.* linger, tarry 931 [OE gǣlan]

gemme *n.* gem 118, 219, 266, 289, 999, 1010 **gemme**ʒ *plur.* gems 7, 253, 991 [OE gim, OF gemme]

generacyoun *n.* generation 827 [L generationem]

gent *adj.* fair, gentle, noble 1014, 1134 **gente** 118, 253, 265 [OF gent]

gentyl *adj.* gentle, of noble birth, excellent 264, 278, 605, 883, 895, 991 *subst.* gentle one 602 **gentyle** *adj.* gentle 632 **gentyleſte** *superl.* most excellent 1014 [OF gentil]

geſſe *v.* form an opinion, judge 499 [Cf. MDu gissen, gessen]

geſte *n.* guest 277 [OE giest, gæst; ON gestr]

gete *v.* get, obtain 95 [ON geta]

geuen. *See* **gyue**

gilofre cloves 43 [OF gilofre]

glace *v.* glide 171 [OF glacer]

gladande. *See* **glade**ʒ

glade *adj.* glad 136, 1144 **gladder** *comp.* gladder 231 **gladdeſt** *superl.* gladdest 1109 [OE glæd]

gladeʒ *pres. 3 sing.* gladdens, makes glad 861 **gladande** *pres. p.* gladdening 171 [OE gladian]

gladneʒ *n. plur.* joys, delights 136 [OE glædnes]

glas *n.* glass 114, 990, 1018 **glaſſe** 1025, 1106 [OE glæs]

glauereʒ *pres. 3 sing.* deceives 688 [? Cf. Wel. glafru]

glayre *n.* glair, egg white used in illuminating manuscripts 1026 [OF glaire]

glayue *n.* glaive, spear 654 [OF glaive]

gle *n.* music 95 joy, glee 1123 [OE glēo]

glem *n.* gleam 79 [OE glǣm]

glemande *pres. p.* gleaming 70, 990 [OE glǣm]

glene *v.* glean, gather 955 [OF glener]

glent *pret. 3 sing.* glanced (off),
glinted 70, 1026 *pret. 3 plur.* 1106
glente *pret. 3 sing.* glinted 1001
turned aside 671 [Cf. Sw. (dial.)
glänta]

glente *n.* light, flashes of light 114
glente3 *plur.* glances 1144 [Cf.
Sw. (dial.) glänta]

glet *n.* mud, slime 1060 [OF glette]

glod. *See* **glyde3**

glode *n.* scribal error for **golde** gold
1111★

glode3 *n. plur.* glades (?), bright
patches of sky (?) 79★ [? OE
★glǽd]

glory *n.* glory 70, 171, 934, 959,
1123 [OF glorie]

gloryous *adj.* glorious 799, 915 *adv.*
gloriously 1144 [AF glorious]

glowed *pret. 3 plur.* glowed 114 [OE
glōwan]

glyde3 *pres. 3 sing.* glides 79 **glod**
pret. 3 plur. proceeded 1105 [OE
glīdan]

gly3t *pret. 3 plur.* glinted, shone 114
[? Cf. OI gljā]

glymme *n.* radiance, brightness
1088 [? OE glǽm]

glyſnande *pres. p.* glistening, shining
165, 1018 [OE glisnian]

go. *See* **gon**

god *n.* (1) God 314, 342, 379, 445,
etc. **godde3** *gen. sing.* God's 591,
1193 **gode3** 63, 601, 822, 885,
943, 1054 [OE god]

god *n.* (2) goods 734 **goud** goodness
33 goods 731 **goude** good thing
33 [OE gōd]

god *adj.* good 310, 1202 **goude** 568,
818 [OE gōd]

godhede *n.* godhead, divine nature
413 [OE god; cf. OE godhād]

godneſſe *n.* goodness 493 [OE
gōdnes]

golde *n.* gold 2, 165, 213, 989, 1025
[OE gold]

golden *adj.* golden 1106 [OE gold]

golf *n.* gulf, abyss 608 [OF gouffre]

gome *n.* man 231, 697 [OE guma]

gon *v.* go 63 *pp.* gone 376, 820 **go**
pres. 3 sing. subj. would go 530
imp. sing. go 559 **got3** *pres. 3
sing.* goes 365 *pres. 3 plur.* go 510
imp. plur. go 535 **gos** 521 [OE
gān]

goſpel *n.* gospel 498 [OE godspel]

goſte *n.* soul, spirit 63, 86 [OE gāst]

goſtly *adj.* spiritual 185, 790 [OE
gāstlic]

gote *n.* stream 934 **gote3** *plur.*
streams 608 [OE gēotan]

got3. *See* **gon**

goud, goude. *See* **god** n. (2), **god**
adj.

grace *n.* 63, 194, 425, 436, etc. [OF
grâce]

gracios *adj.* gracious 189 *adv.*
graciously 260 **gracos** *adj.*
gracious 95 **gracous** 934 [OF
gracious]

grauayl *n.* gravel 81 [OF gravele]

graunt *n.* grant, permission 317 [AF
graunter]

graye *adj.* gray 254 [OE grǽg]

grayne3 *n. plur.* grain 31 [OF grain]

grayþely *adv.* aptly, fittingly 499
[ON greiðliga]

grece *n.* Greece 231

greffe *n.* grief 86 [OF grief]

greme *n.* anger, wrath 465 [ON
gremi]

grene *adj.* green 38, 1001, 1005 [OE
grēne]

greſſe *n.* grass 10, 245 blade of grass

31 [OE græs]

gret *adj.* great 250, 330, 511, 578, etc. **grete** 90, 237, 280, 470, 637 [OE grēat]

grete *v.* weep 331 [OE grētan, OE grēotan]

greue *n.* grove 321 [OE græfa]

greve *pres. 3 sing. subj.* might grieve 471 [OF grever]

grewe. *See* **grow**

gromylyoun *n.* gromwell 43 [OF gromil]

grouelyng *pres. p.* groveling, lying prostrate 1120 [ON grūfa + OE –ling]

grounde *n.* ground 10, 81, 434, 1173 basis, foundation 372, 384, 396, 408, 420 [OE grund]

grounde *pp.* *See* **grynde**

grym *adj.* grim 1070 [OE grim(m)]

grymly *adv.* grimly 654 [OE grimlīce]

grynde *v.* grind 81 **grounde** *pp.* ground, sharpened 654 [OE grindan]

grow *v.* grow 31 **grewe** *pret. 3 sing.* grew 425 [OE grōwan]

gryſte *n.* anger 465 [OE grist-, gyrst]

gulte *n.* guilt 942 **gylteȝ** *plur.* guilts 655 [OE gylt]

gyf. *See* **gyue**

gyfte *n.* gift 565 **gyfteȝ** *plur.* gifts 607 [OE gift]

gyle *n.* guile 671, 688 [OF guile]

gylteȝ. *See* **gulte**

gylteȝ *adj. subst.* guiltless one(s) 668, 799★ [Late OE gyltlēas]

gyltyf *adj. subst.* guilty one(s) 669 [OE gyltig]

gyng *n.* gang, company 455 [OE genge]

gyngure *n.* ginger 43 [OE gingiber,

OF gingimbre]

gyrle *n.* girl 205 [? OE *gyrela]

gyſe *n.* guise, style of dress 1099 [OF guise]

gyternere *n.* guitar player 91 [OF guiterne]

gyue *pres. 1 sing. subj.* give 707 **gef** *pret. 1 sing.* gave 174, 270, 734, 765, 1211 **geuen** *pp.* given 1190 **gyf** *imp. sing.* give 543, 546 [OE giefan]

3

3are *adv.* well, clearly 834 [OE gearwe]

3ate *n.* gate 728, 1037 **3ateȝ** *plur.* gates 1034, 1065 [OE geat, gæt]

3e *pers. pron. 2 plur.* 290, 515, 516, 521, etc. *pron. 2 sing. formal* you, thou 257, 307, 308, 371, etc. [OE ge] Cf. **yow, þou**

3ede (past tense of **go**) *pret. 3 sing.* went 526, 1049 *pret. 3 plur.* went 713 **yot** *pret. 3 sing.* went 10 [OE ēode]

3emen *n. plur.* yeomen, hired laborers 535 [OE geongman]

3er *n.* year 483 *as plur.* years 1079 **3ere** year 503, 505 *as plur.* years 588 [OE gēar, gēr]

3erned *pp.* yearned for, desired 1190 [OE geornan]

3et *adv.* yet, 19, 46, 145, 200, etc. **3ete** 1061 [OE gēt, gēta]

3ete *v.* grant (?); do (?) 558★

3if. *See* **if**

3on *adj.* yon, yonder 693 [OE geon]

3ong *adj.* young 412 **3onge** 474, 535 [OE geong]

3ore *adv.* formerly, in the past 586 [OE geāra]

3orefader *n.* forefather (Adam) 322

[OE geāra + fæder]

3ys *adv.* yes 635 [OE gēse]

H

had, hade, haf. *See* **haue**

hafyng *ger.* having, possession 450
   [OE habban]

halde *v.* hold, have 490 *pres. 1 sing.*
   consider 301 **halde3** *pres. 3 sing.*
   holds 454 **halden** *pp.* held 1191
   helde *pret. 3 sing.* held, occupied
   1002, 1029 [OE haldan]

hale3 *pres. 3 sing.* flows 125 [OF
   haler]

half *adv.* half 72 [OE healf]

half *n.* side 230 [OE healf]

halle *n.* hall 184 [OE heall]

halte *v.* waver, falter (?); *adj.* lame,
   halt (?) 1158*

han. *See* **haue**

happe *n.* fortune, good luck,
   happiness 16, 713, 1195 [ON
   happ]

harde *adj.* hard 606 [OE hearde]

hardyly *adv.* boldly, fearlessly 3, 695
   [OF hardi + OE līce]

harme *n.* harm 681 **harme3** *plur.*
   harms 388 [OE hearm]

harmle3 *adj.* harmless 676, 725 [OE
   hearm + lēas]

harpe *n.* harp 881 [OE hearpe]

harpen *pres. 3 plur.* harp, play the
   harp 881 [OE hearpian]

harpore3 *n. plur.* harpers, harp-
   players 881 [OE hearpere]

hate *adj.* hot, fierce 388 [OE hāt]

hate *n.* hate, hatred 463 [OE hete]

hated *pp.* hated 402 [OE hatian]

hat3. *See* **haue**

haþel *n.* man, person 676 [OE hæleþ
   + æðel]

haue *v.* have, possess 132, 661, 928

verbal auxiliary w/pp. have 704,
   967 **haf** 14, 194, 242, 244, etc.
   pres. 1 sing. have, possess 577
   pres. 3 plur. have, possess 917
hauen *pres. 1 plur.* have, possess
   859 **hat3** *verbal auxiliary w/pp.*
   has 249, 273, 274, 286, etc.
   pres. 3 sing. has, possesses 441,
   446, 465, 625, 770 *pres. 2 sing.*
   have, possess 935, 971 **han** *verbal
   auxiliary w/pp.* have 373, 554,
   776 **had** *verbal auxiliary w/pp.*
   had 170, 1140, 1148 *pret. 3 sing.*
   had, possessed 1034 *pret. 3 plur.*
   had, possessed 1045 *pp.* had 1140
   hade *pret. 1 sing.* had, possessed
   134, *verbal auxiliary w/pp.* had
   164, 476, 550, 1090, etc. *pret.
   3 sing.* had, possessed 209, 502,
   812, 841, etc. **hade ben** *verbal
   auxiliary w/pp.* would have been
   1194 [OE habban]

hawk *n.* hawk 184 [OE heafoc]

haylſed *pret. 3 sing.* hailed, greeted
   238 [ON heilsa]

he *pers. pron. nom. 3 sing. masc.* he
   302, 332, 348, 350, etc.; used as
   neut. it 1001, 1140 [OE he, hē]

hed *n.* head 209 **hede** 1172 **heued**
   459, 465, 974 [OE hēafod]

he3t *n.* height 1031 [OE hīehþo]

helde *v. See* **halde**

helde *adv.* likely, probably 1193 [Cf.
   OI heldr]

hele *n.* health, happiness 16, 713
   [OE hǽlu]

helle *n.* hell 442, 651, 840, 1125 *gen.
   sing.* hell's 643 [OE hel(l]

hem *pers. pron. dat., acc. 3 plur.* them
   69, 70, 75, 79, etc. **hen** 532
   reflexive themselves 551 *dat.* to
   them 717 for them 728 *as nom.*

they 1044 [OE him, hiom, heom]

hemme *n.* hem 217 edge, border 1001 [OE hem(m)]

hen. *See* **hem**

hende *adj.* gentle 184 **hynde** *subst.* gracious one 909 [OE gehende]

hente *v.* obtain 669 take, seize 1195 *pres. 1 sing.* receive 388 [OE hentan]

her (1) *poss. pron. fem. 3 sing.* her 4, 6, 131, 170, etc. *masc.* his 687, 688 **hir** *fem. poss.* her 22, 191, 197, 428 *pers. pron. fem. 3 sing. acc.* her 188 **hyr** *fem. poss.* her 163, 169, 178, 220, etc. *pers. pron. fem. 3 sing. acc.* 8, 9, 164, 167, etc. [OE hire]

her (2) *poss. pron. 3 plur.* their 92, 93, 96, 106, etc. [OE hiera]

her (3) *adv.* here 263, 519 **here** 262, 298, 389, 399, etc. [OE hēr]

here *v.* hear 96 **herde** *pret. 1 sing.* heard 873, 879, 1132 [OE hīeran]

hereinne *adv.* herein, in this place 261, 577 [OE hēr inne]

herneȝ *n. plur.* brains 58 [Late OE hærnes; cf. ON hjarni]

hert *n.* heart 17, 51, 174, 179, 682, 1082, 1136 **herte** 128, 135, 176, 364 [OE heorte]

herytage *n.* heritage 417 **erytage** 443 [OF heritage, eritage]

hefte *n.* behest, commandment 633 [OE hǣs]

hete *pres. 1 sing.* promise, assure 402 **hyȝt** *pp.* "hight," were called 950 *pret. 3 sing.* "hight," was called 999 **hyȝte** *pret. 3 sing.* promised 305 [OE hātan]

hete *n.* heat 554, 643 [OE hǣtu]

heterly *adv.* bitterly 402 [OE hetelice; ON hatr-liga]

heþen *adv.* hence, from here 231 [ON heðan]

heue *v.* lift up 314, 473 [OE hebban]

heued. *See* **hed**

heuen *v.* lift up, exalt 16 [OE hafenian]

heuen *n.* heaven 473, 490, 500, 873, 1126 *w/ definite article* the heavens 988 **heueneȝ** *plur.* the heavens 423, 620 **heuenȝ** 441 **heueneffe** 735 [OE heofon]

heuenryche *n.* the kingdom of heaven 719 [OE heofonrīce]

heuy *adj.* heavy, profound 1180 [OE hefig]

hider *adv.* hither, to this place 517 **hyder** 249, 763 [OE hider]

hiȝe. *See* **hyȝ**

hil *n.* hill 976 **hyl** 789, 979 **huyle** 41 **hyul** 1205 **hylleȝ** *plur.* hills 678★ [OE hyll]

hir. *See* **her** (1)

his *poss. pron. 3 sing. masc.* his 285, 526, 715, 819, etc. **hys** 307, 312, 354, 355, etc. **hysfe** 418 [OE his]

hit *pers. pron. 3 sing. neut. nom., acc.* it 10, 13, 30, 41, etc. *3 plur.* they 88, 895, 1199 *poss. pron. 3 sing. neut.* its 108, 120, 224 **hyt** *pers. pron. 3 sing. neut. nom., acc.* it 270, 271, 283, 284, etc. [OE hit]

ho *pers. pron. 3 sing. fem. nom.* she 129, 130, 131, 177, etc. **fcho** 478 **ho** *masc.* (?) he 479 [OE hēo, hīo]

hol *adj.* whole, complete 406 [OE hāl]

holteȝ *n. plur.* woods 921 [OE holt]

holtewodeȝ *n. plur.* woods 75 [OE

holtwudu]

holy *adv.* wholly 418 [OE hāl]

holy *adj.* holy 592, 618, 679 [OE hālig]

homly *adj.* belonging to the household, familiar 1211 [OE hām + lic]

honde *n.* hand *in* **com on honde** came to hand, appeared 155 *coll.* hands 49, 218 **honde3** *plur.* hands 706 [OE hond]

hondelynge3 *adv.* with the hands 681 [OE handlinga]

hondred. *See* **hundreth**

hone *v.* remain, stay, be situated 921 [Cf. OIr ōn, ōin, h)ūan; MnScot hūne]

honour *n.* honor 424, 475, 852, 864 [OF h)onor]

hope *n.* hope 860 [Late OE hopa]

hope *pret. 1 sing.* supposed 142, 185, *pres. 1 sing.* believe 225 **hoped** *pret. 1 sing.* supposed 139 [OE hopian]

horne3 *n. plur.* horns 1111 [OE horn]

houre3. *See* **oure** *n.* (2)

how *adv.* how 334, 690, 711, 1146 [OE hū]

hue *n.* outcry, shout 873 [OF hu, hui, huy, heu]

huee *n.* hue, color 842 **hwe** appearance 896 **hwe3** *plur.* colors 90 [OE hīew, hīw]

hundreth *n.* hundreds 1107 **hundreþe** hundred 869 **hondred** 786 [OE hundred, ON hundrað]

hurt *pp.* hurt 1142 [OF hurter]

huyle. *See* **hil**

hwe3. *See* **huee**

hyde *n.* hide, skin 1136 [OE hӯd]

hyder. *See* **hider**

hy3 *adj.* high 39, 678 **hy3e** 395, 401, 596, 1024, 1051, 1054 *adv.* high **hy3** 473, 773 **hy3e** 454 **hi3e** 207 [OE hēah]

hy3t *n.* height *in* **on hy3t** on high 501 **he3t** height 1031 [OE hīehþo]

hy3t *v. See* **hete** *v.*

hyl, hylle3. *See* **hil**

hyl-coppe *n.* hilltop 791 [OE hyll + cop(p)]

hym *pers. pron. 3 sing. masc. dat., acc.* him 324, 349, 360, 404, etc. himself 478, 711 721, 732, etc. *as nom.* he 662 *plur.* them 635, 715 [OE him]

hymſelf *pron.* himself 680, 808, 811, 812, 826, 896, 1134 *as nom.* himself 825 [OE him + self]

hynde. *See* **hende**

hyne *n. plur.* agricultural laborers 505, 632 servants 1211 [OE hīne]

hyr. *See* **her** (1)

hyre *v.* hire 507 **hyred** *pret. 1 sing.* hired 560 [OE hӯrian]

hyre *n.* service 523 employment 534 wages 539, 583, 587 [OE hӯr]

hys, hysſe. *See* **his**

hyt. *See* **hit**

hytſelf *pron.* itself 446 [OE hit + self]

hytte3 *pres. 3 sing.* happens, chances 132 [Late OE hyttan]

hyul. *See* **hil**

I

I *pers. pron. 1 sing. nom.* I 3, 4, 7, 8, etc. [OE ic]

iacyngh *n.* jacinth 1014 [OF iacinte]

iaſper *n.* jasper 999, 1026 **iaſporye** 1018 [OF jaspre]

ichofe. *See* **ches**

Ierusalem *n.* Jerusalem 792, 793, 805, 816, etc. **Iherusalem** 804

Iefu *n.* Jesus 453, 711, 717, 721, 820 **iesu** 458

if *conj.* if 147, 264, 265, 313, etc. ʒif 45, 662 ʒyf 482 **inf** scribal error for **if** 1185★ [OE gif]

ilk *adj.* same, very 995 **ilke** 704 [OE ilca]

ille *adv.* wrongfully 681 ill, poorly 1177 [ON illr]

in *prep.* in, on, into 2, 5, 8, 9, etc. **inne** 656 [OE in]

inf. *See* **if**

inlyche *adv.* alike 546, 603 [OE iliche]

inne *adv.* in 940 [OE inne]

innocens *n.* innocence 708 [OF innocence]

innocent *n.* innocent 625, 720 **innofent** 684, 696 **innoffent** 666 **inofcente** 672 [OF innocent]

innogh *adv.* enough 660 *adj.* 661 **innoghe** *n.* 625, 649 *adv.* 636, 648 **innoʒe** 624 **inoghe** 612 **inoʒe** 637 [OE genōg]

innome *pp.* taken, trapped 703 [OE geniman]

ins. *See* **is**

into *prep.* into 245, 509, 525, 582, 628 [OE in-tō]

inwyth *adv.* within 970 [OE in(n + wið]

Iohan *n.* John 788, 836, 867, 985,★ etc. **Ion** 383, 818 **Ihoan** 984 **Ihan** 1020

ioly *adj.* bright, beautiful 929 **iolyf** 842 [OF jolif, joli]

ioparde *n.* risk, hazard 602 [OF iu parti]

Iordan *n.* Jordan 817

ioueler. *See* **iueler**

ioy *n.* joy 234, 266, 395, 796 **ioye** 128, 577, 1126, 1197 [OF joie]

ioyfol *adj.* joyful 288, 300 [OF joie + OE full]

ioyleʒ *adj.* joyless 252 [OF joie + OE –lēas]

ioyned *pret. 3 sing.* joined, added 1009 [OF joindre]

is *pres. 3 sing.* is 26, 33, 40, 63, etc. **ins** scribal error for **is** 309★ [OE is]

ifrael *n. gen.* Israel's 1040

Iudee *n.* Judea 922 **Iudy** *gen.* of Judea 937

iuel *n.* jewel 249, 253, 277 **iuele** 23★ *plur.* jewels 929 **iuelle** jewel 795, 1124 **iueleʒ** *plur.* jewels 278 [OF joel]

iueler *n.* jeweler 264, 265, 276, 289, etc. **iuelere** 252 **ioueler** 734★ [OF juelìer]

Iueʒ *n. plur.* Jews 804

iugged *pret. 1 sing.* judged 7 *pret. 3 plur.* 804 [OF jugier]

iuftyfyet *pp.* justified 700 [OF justifier]

iwyffe *adv.* indeed, certainly 151, 394, 1128 **iwyfe** 279 [OE gewis]

K

kafte *pp.* cast, cast out, cast off 1198 **keft** 861 **kefte** 66 **keften** *pret. 3 plur.* 1122 [ON kasta]

kene *adj.* keen, sharp 40 [OE cēne]

kenned *pret. 3 sing.* taught 55 [OE cennan]

keruen. *See* **coruen**

keft, kefte, keften. *See* **kafte**

keue *v.* sink 320 **keued** *pp.* having descended 981 [ON kefja]

klyfeʒ, klyffeʒ. *See* **clyffe**

klymbe. *See* **clym**

knaw *v.* know 410, 541, 794, 1109
    pres. 1 sing. 673 **knawe** *pres.*
    3 plur. 505 *pres. 2 plur.* 516
    knawen *pp.* known 637 **knew**
    pret. 1 sing. knew 66, 164, 168,
    998, 1019 **knewe** *pret. 3 plur.*
    890 [OE (ge)cnāwan]

knelande *pres. p.* kneeling 434 [OE
    cnēowlian]

knew, knewe. *See* **knaw**

knot *n.* group, throng 788 [OE
    cnotta]

kryſt *n.* Christ 55, 458, 776 **kryſte**
    569 **kryſteʒ** *gen.* Christ's 904,
    1208 **cryſtes** 383 [OE Crīst]

kryſten *adj.* Christian 461 **kryſtyin**
    n. 1202★ [OE Cristen]

kyn *n. gen.* of kind *in* **quat kyn** of
    what kind 755, 771, 794 **kynnes**
    gen. plur. of kinds *in* **alle kynnes**
    of all kinds 1028 [OE cynna]

kynde *n.* nature, character 55, 74,
    270, 271, 752 [OE gecynde]

kynde *adj.* natural-born, rightful;
    kind, genial 276 [OE gecynde]

kyndely *adv.* kindly 369 **kyntly** 690
    [OE gecyndelīce]

kyndom *n.* kingdom 445 [OE
    cynedōm]

kyng *n.* king 448, 468, 480, 596
    [OE cyning]

kynnes. *See* **kyn**

kyntly. *See* **kyndely**

kyrk *n.* church 1061 [Cf. OE circe,
    ON kirkja]

kyſte *n.* chest, coffer; coffin 271 [Cf.
    ON kista]

kytheʒ *n. plur.* regions 1198 [OE
    cӯðð]

kyþe *v.* show, reveal 356 [OE cӯðan]

L

labor *v.* spend labor upon, work on
    504 [OF laborer]

labour *n.* labor 634 [OF labor]

lad. *See* **lede** *v.*

lade *pp.* laden, loaded 1146 [OE
    hladan]

laden. *See* **ledden**

lady *n.* lady 453, 491 [OE hlǣfdige]

ladyly *adj.* ladylike 774 [OE
    hlǣfdige]

ladyſchyp *n.* ladyship, rank as a lady
    578 [OE hlǣfdige + -scipe]

laften *pret. 3 plur.* left 622 [OE lǣfan]

laʒt *pret. 1 sing.* took, seized 1128
    laʒte 1205 [OE lǣccan]

lamb *n.* lamb, Lamb (Christ) 407
    lambe 757, 771, 1046 **lombe**
    413, 741, 795, 802, etc. **lomp**
    815 **lompe** 945 **loumbe** 861,★
    867 **lambes** *gen. sing.* Lamb's
    785 **lombeʒ** 872 [OE lamb]

lande *n.* land, countryside 802★
    londe 148, 937 [OE land]

langour *n.* languor, sorrow 357 [OF
    langour]

lantyrne *n.* lantern 1047 [OF
    lanterne]

lappeʒ *n. plur.* hanging sleeves 201
    [OE læppa]

large *adj.* large 201, 609 [OF large]

laſſe *comp. adj.* less 491 *n.* 599, 600,
    601, 853 **les** *comp. adj.* 864, 876,
    888, 901 *comp. adv.* 865★ **leſſe**
    comp. adj. 339, 852 [OE lǣssa]

laſte *n.* last 547, 570, 571 [OE lætest]

laſte *v.* last 956 **laſteʒ** *pres. 3 plur.* last
    1198 [OE lǣstan]

laſte *pp.* loaded, filled 1146 [OE
    gehlæstan]

laſteʒ. *See* **laſte** *v.*

late *adv.* late 392, 574, 615 *adj.* late 538 [OE læt, late]

laueȝ *pres. 3 sing.* pours out 607 [OE lafian]

launceȝ *n. plur.* boughs, branches 978 [OF lance]

laweȝ *n. plur.* laws 285 [OE lagu]

layd *pp.* laid 958 **layde** 1172 [OE lecgan]

ledden *n.* voice, speech 878 **laden** 874 [OE læden]

lede *v.* lead 774 *pres. 1 sing.* 409 *pres. 2 plur.* 392 **lad** *pp.* led 801 [OE lædan]

lede *n. voc.* man 542 [OE leod]

lef *n.* leaves, foliage 77 **leueȝ** *n. plur.* leaves, pages 837 [OE lēaf]

lef *adj.* "lief," dear, beloved 266 *subst.* beloved one 418 [OE lēof]

legg *n.* leg 459 [ON leggr]

leghe. *See* **lyȝ**

legyonnes *n. plur.* legions 1120 [OF legion]

leke *n.* linen, wimple (?) 210★ [Du laken]

lelly *adv.* loyally, faithfully 305 [OF lēal + OE -lice]

leme *v.* drive (?) *in* **of leme** drive away, banish 358★ [OE flēman]

lemed *pret. 3 sing.* gleamed, shone 119, 1043 [OE leoma]

lemman *n.* beloved, loved one 763, 796, 805, 829 [OE leof + man]

lenge *v.* linger, stay 261 *pres. 2 sing.* 933 [OE lengan]

lenger. *See* **long**

lenghe *n.* length 416 **on lenghe** for a long time 167 [OE lengu]

lenþe *n.* length 1031 [OE lengþu]

lere *adj.* face★ 210 *n.* 398 [OE hlēor]

lere *n.* recompense (?) 616★

lefande *pres. p.* opening 837 [OE lēsan]

les, leffe. *See* **laffe**

left *conj.* lest 187, 865★ [OE þȳ læs þe]

lefte *pret. 1 sing.* lost 9 **lefteȝ** *pret. 2 sing.* 269 [OE –lēosan]

lefyng *n.* lying, falsehood 897 [OE lēasung]

let *pret. 3 plur.* let 715 *imp. sing.* 901, 912, 964 *imp. plur.* 718 *pret. 3 sing.* 20 **lette** 813 [OE lætan]

lette *pret. 3 sing.* hindered, obstructed 1050 [OE lettan]

lettrure *n.* learning, knowledge 751 [OF lettreure]

leþeȝ *pres. 3 sing.* abates, is assuaged 377 [OE liþian]

leue *n.* leave, permission 316 [OE lēaf]

leue *v.* believe 311 *pres. 1 sing.* 469, 876 *pres. 2 sing.* 865★ **leueȝ** *pres. 3 sing.* believes 304★ **leuen** *v.* believe 69 *pres. 2 plur.* 425 [OE gelēfan]

leued *pp.* "leaved," having leaves 978 [OE lēaf]

leueȝ. *See* **lef** *n.*

liureȝ *n. plur.* garments, clothing 1108★ [OF livree]

lo *interj.* lo, behold 693, 740, 822 [OE lā]

loȝe *n.* water, pool 119 [Wel llwch]

loke *v.* look 934 *imper. sing.* 463 *pres. 1 sing. subj.* may look 710 **loked** *pret. 1 sing.* looked 167, 1145 [OE lōcian]

lokeȝ *n. plur.* looks, appearance 1134 [OE lōcian]

lokyng *n.* looking, gaze 1049 [OE –lōcung]

lombe, lombeȝ, lomp, lompe, loumbe. *See* **lamb**

londe. *See* **lande**

lone *n.* lane, street 1066 [OE lone]

long *n.* a long time 586 [OE lang]

long *adj.* long (in time) 597 **longe** long (in distance) 1024 [OE lang]

longande *pres. p.* belonging 462 [OE gelang]

longe *adv.* long, throughout the length of the time specified (*w/ gen.*) 477, 533★ [OE lange]

lenger *comp. adv.* longer (in time) 168, 180, 600, 977 [OE lengra]

longed *pret. 3 sing. impersonal w/acc. of person* caused longing in *in* me **longed** [it] caused longing in me, I longed 144 [OE longian]

longeyng *n.* longing 244, 1180, 1152 [OE longung]

lorde *n.* lord; Lord (God) 285, 362, 403, 407, etc.; *voc.* 678, 699, 1199 [OE hlaford]

lorde *interj.* Lord! 108, 1149 [OE hlaford]

lore *n.* lore, knowledge, custom 236 [OE lār]

loſe *v.* lose 265 be lost, perish 908 **loſte** *pp.* lost 1092. [OE losian] Cf. **leste**

lote *n.* (1) word, speech 238, 896 noise 876 [ON lāt]

lote *n.* (2) lot, fortune 1205 [OE hlot]

loþe *n.* grief 377 [OE lāþ]

loude *adj.* loud 878 [OE hlūd]

loue *v.* (1) love 285★ (?), 342 (?), 1124 (?), 1127 (?) **loueʒ** *pres. 3 sing.* loves 302★ (?), 308 (?), 403, 407 [OE lufian]

loue *v.* (2) honor, praise 285★ (?), 342 (?), 1124 (?), 1127 (?) **loueʒ** *pres. 3 sing.* honors 302★ (?), 308

(?) [OE lofian]

louely, loueloker. *See* **lufly**

loute *pres. 2 sing.* lurk (?) 933★ [OE lutian]

louyly *adj.* lawful 565 [OE lagu + -lic]

lowe *adv.* low 236, 547 **loweſt** *superl. adj.* lowest 1001 [ON lāgr]

luf *n.* love 467, 851 *gen. sing.* of love 11, 1152 [OE lufu]

lufly *adj.* lovely 962 **louely** 693 **loueloker** *comp. adj.* lovelier 148 **lufly** *adv.* beautifully 880, 978 [OE luflic, luflīce]

lufſoum *adj. subst.* lovely one 398 [OE lufsum]

lureʒ *n. plur.* losses 339, 358 [OE lyre]

lurked *pret. 1 sing.* stole along, proceeded 978 [Cf. Norw. lurka]

lyf *n.* life 247, 305, 392, 409, etc. **lyueʒ** *gen.* of life 477, 578, 908 [OE līf]

lyfed *pret. 2 sing.* lived 483 **lyued** *pp.* lived 477, 776 **lyuyande** *pres. p.* living 700 [OE lifian]

lyfte *pp.* lifted, raised 567 [ON lyfta]

lygyngeʒ *n. plur.* lodgings 935★ [Cf. ON liggja]

lyʒ *v.* lie, sleep 930 **leghe** *pret. 3 sing.* lay 214 **lys** *pres. 3 sing.* lies 360 is, exists 602 [OE licgan]

lyʒe *n.* lie 304 [OE lyge]

lyʒt *n.* light 69, 119, 1043, 1046, 1050, 1073★ [OE leoht]

lyʒt *adj.* light (in weight) 682 **lyʒte** bright, cheerful 238, 500 [OE leoht]

lyʒte *adv.* lightly 214 [OE leohte]

lyʒt *pret. 3 sing.* alighted, descended 943 *pp.* 988 **lyʒte** *pret. 2 sing.* 247 [OE līhtan] ly3tly *adv.* lightly, easily 358 [OE lēohtlīce]

lyk *adj.* like, similar 432, 501, 896 [OE gelīc]

lyk *prep.* like 874 **lyke** 735 [OE gelīc; gelīce]

lyke3 *pres. 3 sing. impers.* pleases 566 [OE līcian]

lykne3 *pres. 3 sing.* likens, compares 500 [OE gelīc]

lykyng *n.* pleasure 247 [OE līcung]

lym n. limb, member 462 **lyme3** *plur.* limbs 464 [OE lim]

lyne *n.* line, lineal descent 626 [OE līne, OF ligne]

lynne *adj.* linen 731 [OE līnen]

lys. *See* ly3

lyſte *pret. 3 sing. impers.* "list," was pleasing to 146, 181, 1141 [OE lystan]

lyſte *n.* desire 173 joy, happiness 467, 908 [OE lystan]

lyſten *v.* listen to, hear 880 [OE hlystan]

lyth *n.* limb 398 [OE liþ]

lyttel *adv.* little 172, 301 *adj.* little 387, 574, 604, 1147 *n.* little 575 [OE lytel]

lyþe *v.* soften, soothe 357 **lyþe3** *imp. sing.* soothe 369 [OE liþian]

lyþer *n.* evil 567 [OE lyþer]

lyued, lyuyande. *See* **lyfed**

lyue3. *See* **lyf**

M

ma *poss. adj.* my *in* **par ma fay** by my faith 489 [OF par ma fei]

ma *v. See* **make** *v.*

ma *n. See* **man** *n.*

mad *adj.* mad 267, 1199 **madde** 290 **mad** *adv.* madly 1166 [OE gemǣdd]

madde *pres. 2 sing. subj.* act madly, rave 359 [OE gemǣdd]

maddyng *n.* madness 1154 [OE gemǣdd]

make *v.* make 176, 304, 474 *pres. 1 sing.* 281 **ma** *v.* make 283 **mad** *pp.* made 274, 486, 953 *pret. 3 sing.* 539 **made** *pp.* made 140 *pret. 2 sing.* 371 *pret. 3 sing.* 522, 1149 **man** *pres. 3 plur.* make 512 **mat3** *pres. 3 sing.* makes 610 [OE macian]

make *n.* mate 759 [OE gemaca]

makele3 *adj.* matchless, peerless 435, 757, 780, 784 **makelle3** 733 [OE gemaca + -lēas]

malte *v.* melt *in* **malte in** become absorbed in, comprehend 224 *pret. 3 sing.* melted *in* **malte to** melted into, was reduced to 1154 [OE meltan]

man *n.* man 69, 386, 675, 685, 1195 **ma** 323 **mon** 95, 310, 340, 520, 603, 661 **manne3** *gen. sing.* man's 223 **mane3** mankind's 940 man's 1154 **men** *plur.* men 290, 331, 336, 802,★ etc. [OE man(n), mon(n)]

man *indef. pron.* one, a man, a person 165, 314, 334 **mon** 194, 799 [OE man, mon]

man *v. See* **make** *v.*

manayre *n.* manor, mansion, abode 1029 **maner** 918 [OF manoir]

mankyn *n.* mankind 637 [OE man(n)cyn(n)]

mare. *See* **more**

marere3 *n.* (spiritual) vitality (?) [Vantuono]; scribal error for **manere3** manners (?) 382★

margarys *n. plur.* pearls 199 **mariorys** 206 **margyrye** *sing.*

pearl 1037 [OF margerie]

marked *n.* market 513 [OE market]

marre *pres. 2 sing. subj.* lament 359 [OF marrir]

marreȝ *pres. 2 sing.* mar 23 [OE mirran]

mary *n.* Mary 383 **marye** 425

maryag *n.* marriage 778 **maryage** 414 [OF mariage]

mas *n.* mass 1115 **meſſe** 497 [OE mæsse, messe]

maſcelleȝ *adj.* spotless 732 **maſkelles** 744, 781 **maſkelleȝ** 756, 768, 769, 780 **maſkeleȝ** 745, 900, 923 [L macula + OE -lēas]

maſcle *n.* spot 726 **maſklle** 843 [L macula]

mate *adj.* dejected, discouraged 386 [OF mat]

mate *v.* discourage, subdue 613 [OF mater]

matȝ. *See* **make**

mathew *n.* Matthew 497

may *pres. 1 sing.* may, can 487, 783 *pres. 2 sing.* 296, 347, 694, 703, etc. *pres. 3 sing.* 300, 310, 312, 355, etc. *pres. 2 plur.* 918 *pres. 3 plur.* 29, 336, 447, 669, etc. **moun** *pres. 2 plur.* 536 [OE magan]

may *n.* maiden 435, 780, 961 [OE mæg]

mayden *n.* maiden 162 **maydenneȝ** *plur.* virgins 869 **maydeneȝ** maidens 1115 [OE mægden]

maynful *adj.* mighty, powerful 1093 [OE mægen + ful]

mayſter *n.* master 462, 900 [OF maistre]

mayſterful *adj.* masterful, overbearing 401 [OF maistre + -ful]

me *pers. pron. 1 sing. acc.* me 10, 13, 20, 21, etc. *dat.* to me 19, 155, 233, 235, etc. for me 239, 565, 1187 *refl.* myself 66, 366, 1191 [OE mē]

mede *n.* meed, reward 620 [OE mēd]

meke *adj.* meek 404, 815, 832, 961 [ON mjúkr]

mekeneſſe *n.* meekness 406 [ON mjúkr + OE -nes]

mele *v.* speak 925 **meled** *pret. 1 sing.* spoke 589 **meleȝ** *pres. 3 sing.* says, tells 497 [OE mǣlan]

melle *v.* tell 797, 1118 [OE meþlan]

melle *n.* middle *in* **in melle** *prep.* amid, among 1127 [ON ī milli, ī millum]

membreȝ *n. plur.* members, limbs 458 [OF membre]

men. *See* **man** *n.*

mendeȝ *n. plur.* (construed as *sing.*) amends, recompense 351 [OF amendes]

mendyng *n.* amending, improvement 452 [OF amendes]

mene *v.* mean 293, 951 **meneȝ** *pres. 2 sing.* 937 [OE mǣnan]

menſk *n.* honor 783 **menſke** graciousness, courtesy 162 [ON mennska]

menteene *v.* maintain 783 [OF maintenir]

merci *n.* mercy 576 **mercy** 356, 623, 670 **merſy** 383 [OF merci]

mere *n.* stream, body of water 158 **mereȝ** *plur.* streams 140, 1166 [OE mere]

merked *pp.* situated 142 [OE mearcian]

merſy. *See* **merci**

meruayle *n.* wonder, amazement
157, 1130 **merwayle** miracle
1081 **meruayle3** *plur.* marvels
64 [OF merveille]

meruelous *adj.* marvelous 1166 [OF
merveillos]

mes *n.* meal, feast 862 [OF mes]

meſchef *n.* misfortune 275 [OF
meschief]

meſſe. *See* **mas**

meſure *n.* measure, worth, value
224 [OF mesure]

mete *v.* meet 329, 918 **meten** *pres. 1
plur.* 380 [OE mētan]

mete *n.* food 641 [OE mete]

mete *adj.* fitting, suitable, proper
833, 1063 [OE gemǣte]

meten *pp.* measured 1032 [OE
metan]

meued *pret. 3 sing.* moved 156
meuen *pres. 3 plur.* exist 64 [OF
mouvoir]

meyny *n.* company, retinue 542,
892, 899, 925, etc. [OF meyné]

mirþe *n.* mirth 1149 **myrþe** melody
92 **myrþe3** *plur.* delights 140
[OE myrgþ]

myrþe3 *pres. 3 sing.* gladdens,
delights 862 [OE myrgþ]

mo *n.* more, greater part 340 more,
a greater number 850, 1194 *adj.*
more 151, 870 [OE mā]

mod *n.* mood, state of mind 401
mode 738, 832 [OE mōd]

mode3 *n. plur.* modulations, melody
884 [L modus]

moder *n.* mother 435 [OE mōder]

mo3t, mo3te, mo3ten. *See* **my3t** *v.*

mokke *n.* muck, filth 905 [OE –
moc; cf. ON myki]

mol. *See* **mul**

molde3 *n. plur.* clods of earth 30

[OE molde]

mon *n.* (1), *indef. pron. See* **man**

mon *n.* (2) complaint, lamentation
374 [OE *mān]

mone *n.* moon 923, 1044, 1045,
1056, etc. [OE mōna]

mony *adj.* many 160, 340, 775 *n.*
many 572 [OE manig]

moote. *See* **mot**

more *comp. adj.* more 128, 157, 212,
234, etc. *n.* 132, 133, 552, 577,
etc. *adv.* 144, 145, 156, 168, etc.
moreover 565 **mare** *adv.* more
145 [OE māra]

morne *pres. 2 sing. subj.* mourn 359
[OE murnan]

mornyf *adj.* mournful 386 [OE
murnan]

mornyng *n.* mourning 262 [OE
murnung]

moſte *v. See* **mot** *v.*

moſte *adj. superl.* most 1131 [OE
mǣst]

mot *pres. 3 sing.* must 31, 320, 663
pret. 3 sing. subj. may 397 **moſte**
pres. 2 sing. must 319, 348 *pres. 3
plur.* 623 [OE mōt, mōste]

mot *n.* mote, spot, blemish 843
mote 726, 764, 924, 960, 972
moote 948 [OE mot]

mote *n.* (1) castle, fortress 142 city
936, 937, 948, 973 **mote3** *plur.*
cities 949 [OF mote]

mote *n.* (2) disputation 855 [OE
gemōt]

mote3 *pres. 2 sing.* argue 613 [OE
mōtian]

motele3 *adj.* spotless 925, 961*
moteles 899 [OE mot + -lēas]

moul. *See* **mul**

moun. *See* **may** *v.*

mount *n.* mount, hill 868 [OE

munt]

mounteȝ *pres. 3 sing.* increases 351
[OF munter]

mouth *n.* mouth 183, 803 [OE
mūþ]

much *adj.* 244, 604, 776, 1118, 1130
adv. 234, 303, 374, 576 *n.* 1149
[OE micel]

mul *n.* mold, earth 905 **mol** 382
moul 23 [OE molde]

munt *n.* purpose, intention 1161
[OE myntan]

my *poss. pron.* my 15, 16, 17, 18,
372,*etc. **myn** (before h or
vowel) my, mine 128, 174, 176,
179, *etc. reflex.* myself 243 *subst.*
mine, my own property 566
myne my 335 [OE mīn]

myddeȝ *n.* middle, midst *in* **in
myddeȝ** *prep.* amidst, in the
middle of 222, 740 **in mydeȝ**
835 [OE on middan]

myȝt (*pret. of* **may**) *pret. 3 sing.*
might, could 69, 135, 176, 722,
etc. pret. 3 plur. 579 **myȝteȝ** *pret.
2 sing.* 317 **moȝt** *pret. 3 sing.* 34,
194, 223, 224, *etc. pret. 3 plur.*
92, 1028 *pret. 1 sing.* 188 *pret. 2
sing.* 1051 **moȝte** *pret. 3 sing.* 475
moȝten 1196 [OE mihte]

myȝt *n.* might, strength 765 **myȝte**
1069 [OE miht]

mykeȝ *n. plur.* friends, chosen ones
572 [L amicus]

mylde *adj.* mild 961, 1115 *subst.* mild
ones 721 [OE milde]

myn. *See* **my**

mynde *n.* mind 156, 224, 1130,
1154 [OE gemynd]

mynge *v.* have in mind, think 855
[OE mynegian]

mynne *v.* call to mind, remember

583 [ON minna]

mynyſter *n.* minster, cathedral 1063
[OE mynster]

myrþe, myrþeȝ. *See* **mirþe**

myry *adj.* bright, pleasant, delightful
23, 158, 781, 936 **myryer** *comp.*
merrier 850 **myryeſte** *superl.*
fairest, brightest 199 **myryeſt**
435 [OE myr(i)ge]

mys *n.* (1) cloak, robe 197* [OF
amit, amist]

mys *n.* (2) loss, sorrow 262 **myſſe**
364 [OE missan]

myſelf *pron.* me 414 myself 1175
myseluen 52 [OE mē + self]

myſerecorde *n.* mercy 366 [OF
misericorde]

myſetente *pp.* not given proper
attention, misstated 257 [OE
mis- + OF tendre]

myſſe *v.* lack, feel the want of 329
pres. 1 sing. 382 [OE missan]

myſſeȝeme *v.* fail to take care of 322
[OE misgīman]

myſte *n.* mystical things, spiritual
mysteries 462 [OE mist, OF
mystique]

myſterys *n. plur.* mysteries, truths
known only by divine revelation
1194 [OF mistere]

myte *n.* mite, small amount 351 [OF
mite, MDu mîte]

myþe *pres. 2 sing. subj.* conceal (one's
feelings) (?); mutter (?) 359*

N

naȝt, naȝte. *See* **nyȝt**

name *n.* name 998, 1039 **nome** 872
[OE nama]

nature *n.* nature 749 [OF nature]

naule *n.* navel 459 [OE nafela]

nauþeles *adv.* nevertheless 877

nowþeleſe 889 nawþeles 950
[OE nāwiht, nōwiht + þy + læs]

nauþer *conj.* neither 465, 484, 485
    nawþer 1044, 1087 **noþer** 848*
    adv. either 751 [OE nawþer]

nawhere *adv.* nowhere 534, 932 [OE
    nāhwǣr]

nawþer. *See* nauþer

ne *adv.* not 35, 65, 293, 350, etc.
    emphatic, with one or more additional
    negatives 4, 362, 403, 898, etc.
    conj. nor 262*, 334, 347, 465,
    etc. [OE ne, ni]

nece *n.* niece 233 [OF nièce]

nedde *pret. 3 sing. impers. (with*
    dat.) was necessary 1044 [OE
    nēodian]

nede *n.* need 1045 [OE nīd]

nede3 *adv.* necessarily, of necessity
    25, 344 [OE nēdes]

nemme *v.* mention, name 997* [OE
    nemnan]

nente *adj.* ninth 1012 [OE nigoþa]

ner *prep.* near 286 **nere** 404 **nerre**
    comp. adj. nearer 233 [OE nēar]

neſch *adj. subst.* mild or gentle
    treatment 606 [OE hnesce]

neuer *adv.* never 4, 19, 71, 262, etc.
    in no way, not at all 333, 376,
    841, 852, etc. *w/ subj.* ever 571
    [OE nǣfre]

neuermore *adv.* nevermore, at no
    future time 724 [OE nǣfre +
    māra]

neuerþeles *adv.* nevertheless,
    notwithstanding 900
    neuerþeleſe 912, 913 [OE
    nǣfre + þy + læs]

new *adv.* anew 662 **nwe** 1080, 1123
    newe *adj.* new 894 **nw** 527 **nwe**
    155, 792, 879, 882, etc. *subst.*
    new one 943 [OE nīwe]

nie3bor *n.* neighbor 688 [OE
    nēahgebūr]

nis *pres. 3 sing.* is not 100 **nys** 951
    [OE nis]

niy3t. *See* ny3t

no *adj.* no 32, 69, 95, 100, 848,* etc.
    adv. no 347, 951, 977, 1190 [OE
    nān, nōn]

noble *adj.* noble 922, 1097 [OF
    noble]

no3t *n.* nothing 274, 337, 520, 657,
    955, *adv.* not 563, 588 [OE
    nōwiht]

nom *pret. 3 plur.* received 587 [OE
    niman]

nome. *See* name

non *pron.* not any, no one 215, 443,
    455, 544, etc. *adj.* no 206, 209,
    219 **none** 440 [OE nān]

not *adv.* not 29, 34, 92, 135, etc.
    [OE nōwiht]

note *n.* (1) matter, circumstance 155,
    922 [OE notu]

note *n.* (2) note, song 879 **note3**
    plur. notes 883 [OF note]

noþer. *See* nauþer

noþyng *n.* 1157 nothing **noþynk**
    496, 587 [OE nā-þing]

now *adv.* now 271, 287, 313, 333,
    etc. *conj.* now that, since 283,
    327, 377, 389, etc. [OE nū]

nowþeleſe. *See* nauþeles

nw, nwe. *See* new

ny3t *n.* night 116, 1071 **ny3te** 243
    na3t 523 **na3te** 1203 **niy3t** 630*
    [OE niht]

nys. *See* nis

O

o *prep. See* of *prep.*

O *interj.* O 23, 241, 745, 1182 [L O]

obes *pres. 3 plur.* obey, do obeisance

to 886 [OF obēir]

odour *n.* odor, fragrance 58 [OF odor, odur]

of *prep.* of 3, 55, 69, 72, 1018,★ etc. by 11, 248 for 12, 1126 from 31, 33, 36, 70, etc. with 25, 119, 207, 216, etc. in, on 74, 426, 481, 860, etc. to 84 about 226, 583, 689, 797, etc. between 371 due to 457 **o** of 309, 429, 792 [OE of]

of *adv.* off 237, 358 about 925, 1118 [OE of]

offys *n.* office, position 755 [OF office]

ofte *adv.* often 14, 340, 388 **ofter** *comp.* more often 621 [OE oft]

oȝe *pres. 3 sing. impers.* [it] befits, is due (to) 552 **owe** *pres. 1 sing.* owe 543 **oȝte** *pres. 3 sing. impers.* [it] befits, [it] behoves 341 **aȝt** *pret. 3 sing.* ought (to) 1139 [OE āhte]

oȝt *n.* something, anything 274, 1200 [OE ō(wi)ht]

oȝte. *See* **oȝe**

olde *adj.* old 941, 942 **alder** *comp.* older 621 **aldest** *superl. subst.* eldest 1042 [OE ald]

on *prep.* on, upon 41, 60, 62, 78, etc. in 97, 425, 874, 1079, 1095 to 155 at 167, 243 for 510 *adv.* upon 45 on 255 [OE an, on]

on *indef. art.* 9, 1079. *See* **a** (1)

on *n.* one 293, 378, 557,★ 953 **oneȝ** *gen. sing.* one's 864 **on** *adj.* one 530, 551, 860★ [OE ān]

one *adj.* alone 243 own 312 [OE ān]

onende. *See* **anende**

onflydeȝ *pres. 3 sing.* unfold, open (?); sway (?); hang (?) 77★

onfware *v.* answer 680 [OE ondswarian]

open *adj.* open 183 **vpen** 1066 **vpon** 198 [OE open]

or *conj.* or 233 [OE oþer]

orient *adj.* oriental 255 **oryent** *n.* orient 3 **oryente** 82 [OF orient]

oþer *conj.* or 130, 138, 141, 211, etc. [OE oþer]

oþer *adj.* other 118, 206, 209, 219, etc. *pron.* other 955 *plur.* others 449, 585, 773, 778 *gen. plur.* others' 450 [OE ōþer]

ouer *prep.* over 318, 324, 454, 773, 1166 upon 1205 *adv.* overly 473 [OE ofer]

ouerte *adj.* unconcealed, evident 593 [OF overt]

ouerture *n.* opening, aperture 218 [OF overture]

our *poss. pron. 1 plur.* our 851 **oure** 304, 322, 455, 483, etc. [OE ūre]

oure *n.* (1) mercy (?) 690★ [OE ār]

oure *n.* (2) hour 530, 551 **houreȝ** *plur.* hours 555 [AF houre]

out *adv.* out 282, 642, 777, 1137, 1177 **oute** 3 **out of** *prep.* out of, from 365, 649,★ 1058, 1163, 1170 [OE ūt, of]

outryȝte *adv.* straight out 1055 [OE ūt + rihte]

owe. *See* **oȝe**

owne *adj.* own 559 [OE āgen]

P

pace *n.* passage 677 [OF pas]

pakke *n.* group, company 929 [MLG pak]

pale *v.* pale, grow dim 1004 [OF palir]

pane *n.* side 1034 [OF pan]

par *prep.* by *in* **par ma fey** by my

faith 489 [OF par ma fei]

paradys *n.* paradise 248, 321
paradyſe 137 [OF paradis]

parage *n.* noble lineage 419 [OF
parage]

paraunter *adv.* perchance, perhaps
588 [OF par aventure]

parfyt *adj.* perfect 638, 1038 **perfet**
208 [OF parfit]

part *n.* part, share 573 [OF part]

partleȝ *adj.* having no part (of) 335
[OF part + OE lēas]

paſſe *v.* pass 299, 707, 1110 **paſſed**
pret. 3 sing. subj. surpassed 428
pp. past 528 **paſſeȝ** *pres. 3 sing.*
surpasses 753 [OF passer]

pater *n.* Pater Noster, the Lord's
prayer 485 [L pater]

pay *v.* pay 635 *imper. sing.* 542 **paye**
v. please 1201 **payed** *pp.* paid
584, 603, *pret. 3 sing.* pleased
1165 *pret. 3 sing. impers.* [it] was
pleasing (to) 1177 **payeȝ** *pres. 3
sing.* pays 632 [OF payer]

paye *n.* satisfaction, pleasure, liking
1, 1164, 1176, 1188, 1189, 1200
[OF paie]

payment *n.* payment 598 [OF
paiement]

payne *n.* pain 664, 954 **payneȝ** *plur.*
pains 124 [OF peine]

paynted *pret. 3 sing.* painted 750 [OF
peindre]

payred *pp.* impaired, weakened 246
[OF empeirer]

pechche *n.* patch 841 [ME pacche]

penaunce *n.* penance 477 [OF
peneance]

pene. *See* **peny**

penſyf *adj.* pensive 246 [OF pensif]

peny *n.* penny 546, 560, 614 **pene**
510, 562 [OE pening]

pere *n.* peer, equal 4 [OF per]

pereȝ *n. plur.* pear trees 104 [OE
pere]

perfet. *See* **parfyt**

perle *n.* pearl 1, 12, 24, 36, etc.
perleȝ *plur.* pearls 82, 192, 193,
204, etc. [OF perle]

perre *n.* gems, jewelry 730, 1028
[OF pierrie]

pertermynable *adj.* able to
determine thoroughly, judging
perfectly 596 [L per + OF
termine + able]

peryle *n.* peril 695 [OF peril]

pes *n.* peace 742, 952, 953, 955 [OF
pais]

pitouſly *adv.* piteously, with pity 798
pytoſly 370 [OF pitos, piteus]

place *n.* place 175, 405, 440, 679,
1034 [OF place]

planeteȝ *n. plur.* planets 1075 [OF
planete]

plateȝ *n. plur.* plates, flat sheets of
metal 1036 [OF plate]

play *v.* play 261 [OE plegan]

playn *adj.* smooth, polished 178
playn *adv.* plainly, clearly 689
[OF plain]

playn *n.* plain 104 **playneȝ** *plur.*
plains 122 [OF plain]

playned. *See* **pleny**

playnt *n.* plaint, expression of sorrow
815 [OF plaint]

pleny *v.* complain 549 **playned** *pret.
1 sing.* mourned 53 *pp.* lamented
242 [OF plaindre]

pleſaunt *adj.* pleasant 1 [OF plaisant]

pleſe *v.* please 484 [OF plaisir]

plete *v.* plead, contend 563 [OF
plaitier]

plye *v.* express, signify 1039 [OF
emplier]

ply3t *n.* state, condition 1075 **plyt**
1114, 1015 plight, precarious
situation 647 [OE pliht, OF
ploit]

plontte3 *n. plur.* shrubs, saplings 104
[OE plante]

pobbel *n.* pebble 117 [OE papel-
stān]

pole *n.* pool 117 [OE pōl]

porchace *imper. sing.* purchase 744
porchaſe3 *pres. 3 plur.* strive for
439 [OF porchasser]

pore *adj.* poor 573 **pouer** 1075 [OF
povre]

porfyl *n.* embroidered border 218
[OF porfil]

porpos *n.* purpose 508 **porpoſe**
intended result 185 intention
267 [OF porpos]

portale3 *n. plur.* portals, gates 1036
[OF portal]

poſſyble *adj.* possible 452 [OF
possible]

pouer. *See* pore

poule *n.* Paul 457

pourſent *n.* precinct, space
immediately surrounding a
building 1035 [OF porceinte]

powdered *pp.* sprinkled, scattered
44 [OF poudrer]

poyned *n.* wristband 217 [OF
poignet]

poynt *n.* instance 309 point 594 note
891 [OF point]

pray *n.* prize 439 [OF preie]

pray *v.* pray 484 ask 524★ **prayed**
pret 3 plur. asked, beseeched 714
pret. 3 sing. 1192 [OF preier]

prayer *n.* prayer 355 **prayere** 618
[OF preiere]

prayſe *v. in* to prayſe to be praised,
deserving praise 301 **prayſed** *pp.*

prized 1112 [OF preisier]

precios *adj.* precious 4, 36, 204,
216, etc. **precious** 48, 82, 1212
precos 60, 192 [OF precios]

pref *n.* proof *in* put in pref to
proven to be 272 [OF prueve]

pres *n.* press, crowding 1114 [OF
presse]

pres *pret. 1 plur.* advance, hasten
forward, press on 957 [OF
presser]

pres *adj.* precious, "of great price"
730 [OF pris]

preſe *n.* praise (?); worth, value (?)
419★

preſent *n.* presence 1193 **preſente**
389 [OF present]

preſte *n.* priest 1210 [OE prēost]

preued. *See* proued

prince *n.* prince 1201★ **prynce3** *gen.*
sing. prince's 1164, 1176, 1189
prynces 1 **prynſe3** 1188 [OF
prince]

priuy *adj.* personal, intimate, dear 24
pryuy 12 [OF privé]

profered *pret. 3 sing.* proffered 235
proferen *pres. 3 plur.* proffer
1200 [OF purofrir]

profeſſye *n.* prophecy 821 [OF
profecie]

profete *n.* prophet 797 **prophete**
831 [OF prophete]

proper *adj.* well-made, excellent 686
[OF propre]

property *n.* property, essential
quality 446 **properte3** *plur.*
properties 752 [OF proprieté]

prophete. *See* profete

profeſſyoun *n.* procession 1096 [OF
procession]

proudly *adv.* proudly 1110 [OE
prūtlīce]

proued *pret. 1 sing.* proved, established as genuine 4 **preued** *pp.* 983 [OF prover]

pryde *n.* pride 401 [Late OE prȳde]

prynce3, prynces, prynſe3. *See* **prince**

prys *n.* value, worth 193, 272, 419, 746 [OF pris]

pryſe *v.* prize, esteem highly 1131 [OF prisier]

pryuy. *See* **priuy**

pure *adj.* pure, without blemish 227, 745, 1088 [OF pur]

purly *adv.* clearly, purely 1004 [OF pur + OE līce]

purpre *adj.* purple 1016 [OE purpure]

put *pp.* put, placed 267, 272 [Late OE putian]

pyece *n.* woman 192★ **pyſe** 229 [OF pece]

py3t *pp.* placed, set 117, 193, 216, 228 *pret. 3 sing.* 742, 768 adorned, set (with gems) 192, 205, 217, 229, 241, 991 **py3te** *pp.* adorned 218, 240 [OE ★piccan]

pykes *pres. 3 plur.* pick up, obtain 573 **pyked** *pp. in* **pyked of** set with 1036 [Cf. OE pīcung]

pyle *n.* castle, stronghold 686 [?]

pymalyon *n.* Pygmalion 750

pynakled *pp.* having pinnacles or turrets 207 [OF pinacle]

pyne *n.* pain, anguish 330 pains, toil, effort 511 [Early ME pīne]

pyonys *n. plur.* peonies 44 [OE peonie]

pytoſly. *See* **pitouſly**

pyſe. *See* **pyece**

pyte *n.* pity 355 **pyty** 1206 [OF pité]

Q

quat. *See* **what**

quatſo *pron.* whatever 566 [OE swā hwæt swā]

quayle *n.* quail 1085 [OF quaille]

quelle *v.* kill 799 [OE qwellan]

queme *adj.* pleasant 1179 [OE cwēme]

quen *conj. See* **when**

quen *n.* queen 432, 433, 444, 448, etc. **quene** 415, 423, 456, 468, etc. [OE cwēn]

quere. *See* **where**

quereſoeuer *conj.* wherever 7 [OE swā hwær swā + ǣfre]

query *n.* query, inquiry 803 [L quærere]

queþerſoeuer *conj.* whether 606 [OE hwæþer + swā + ǣfre]

quo, quom. *See* **who**

quod *pret. 1 sing.* said 241, 279, 325, 421, etc. *pret. 3 sing.* 569, 758, 781 [OE cweþan]

quoynt *adj.* skilled 889 [OF cointe]

quy. *See* **why**

quyke3 *adj.* lifelike 1179 [OE cwicu]

quyt, quyte. *See* **whyt**

quyte3 *pres. 2 sing.* requite, reward 595 [OF quiter]

qwyte. *See* **whyt**

R

raas *n.* haste 1167 [ON rās]

ran *pret. 3 sing.* ran 646, 1055 **runne** *pp.* accumulated 523 **runnen** fallen, deteriorated 26 *pres. p.* running 874 [OE rinnan, ON rinna]

rande3 *n. plur.* borders, banks 105 [OE rand]

rapely *adv.* quickly, hastily 363, 1168

[ON hrapaliga]

rafch *adj.* hasty, rash 1167 [Cf. MDu rasch]

raue (1) *pres. 1 sing.* rave 363 [OF raver]

raue (2) *v.* go astray, err 665 [Cf. OI rāfa]

rauþe *n.* ruth, sorrow, pity 858 [OE hreow, ON hryggð]

rauyfte *pp.* ravished, enraptured 1088 [OF ravir]

rawe *n.* row 545 **rawe3** *plur.* hedgerows 105 [OE rāw]

raxled *pret. 1 sing.* stretched (after waking) 1174★ [OE raxan]

ray *n.* ray, beam of light 160 [OF rai]

raykande *pres. p.* running, flowing 112 [ON reika]

rayfe *v.* raise, restore to life 305 [ON reisa]

rayfon. *See* **refoun**

rebuke *imper. sing.* rebuke 367 [OF rebuch(i)er]

recen *v.* count; recount, relate 827 [OE (ge)recenian]

rech *pres. 1 sing.* care, feel concern 333 [OE reccan]

recorde *n.* record, account 831 [OF record]

red *adj.* red 1111 **rede** 27 [OE rēad]

rede *v.* read 709 *pres. 1 sing.* advise 743 [OE rǣdan]

refete *v.* refect, refresh with food 88 [OF refet]

reflayr *n.* odor, fragrance 46 [OF flair]

reget *v.* get back, redeem 1064 [L re- + ON geta]

regioun *n.* region 1178 [AF regiun]

regne *n.* kingdom 501 **rengne** 692 [OF regne]

regretted *pp.* regretted, lamented

243 [OF regretter]

reiate3 *n. plur.* royal dignities 770 [OF reauté]

reken *adj.* elegant, beautiful 5, 92, 906 [OE recen]

reles *n.* remission *in* **w'outen reles** without cessation, continually 956 [OF reles]

relufaunt *adj.* gleaming, resplendant 159 [L relūcentem]

reme *n.* realm 448, 735 [OF reaume]

reme *v.* cry out, lament 1181 **remen** *pres. 2 plur.* 858 [OE hrēman]

remnaunt *n.* remnant, remaining part 1160 [OF remenant]

remorde *pp.* afflicted with remorse 364 [OF remordre]

remwe *v.* remove, take away 427, 899 [OF remuer]

rengne. *See* **regne**

renoun *n.* renown 986, 1182 [OF renon]

renowle3 *pres. 3 plur.* renew 1080 [OF renoveler]

rent *pp.* rent, torn 806 [OE rendan]

reparde *pp.* kept back, withheld 611 [ME parran]

repayre *v.* be present 1028 [OF repairer]

repente *pres. 3 sing. impers. subj.* [it] causes to feel regret 662 [OF repentir]

reprene *v.* reprehend, find fault with 544★ [OF repreigne]

requefte *n.* request *in* **make requefte** ask, beg 281 [OF requeste]

rere *v.* rise 160 **rert** *pp.* exalted 591 [OE rǣran]

refcoghe *n.* rescue, deliverance 610 [OF rescoure]

reſet *n.* refuge, shelter 1067 [OF recet]

reſonabele *adj.* reasonable 523 [OF reson(n)able]

reſoun *n.* reason 52, 665 **rayſon** cause 268 **reſouneʒ** *plur.* statements, arguments 716 [OF reson]

reſpecte *n.* respect *in* **in reſpecte of** in comparison with 84 [L respectus]

reſpyt *n.* respite, cessation of suffering 644 [OF respit]

reſſe *n.* race, rush of water 874 [ON rās, OE ræs]

reſt *v.* rest 679 [OE restan]

restay *vi.* stop, stay **reſtayed** *pret. 3 plur. trans.* held back, restrained 716 *pp.* 1168 [OF resteir]

reſte *n.* rest 858, 1087 [OE rest]

reſtored *pp.* restored 659 [OF restorer]

retrete *v.* reproduce 92 [OF retrait(i)er]

reue *n.* reeve, overseer 542 [OE gerēfa]

reuer *n.* river 1055 **reuereʒ** *plur.* rivers 105 [OF rivere]

rewarde *n.* reward 604 [ONF reward]

rewfully *adv.* ruefully, regretfully 1181 [OE hrēow]

riche *adj.* rich 993 **rych** 68, 105, 1036, 1182 **ryche** 646, 770, 906, 1097 [OE rīce]

rode *n.* rood, cross 646, 705, 806 [OE rōd]

roghe *adj.* rough 646 [OE rūh]

rokkeʒ *n. plur.* rocks 68 [OF roke]

ronk *adj.* luxuriant 844 impetuous 1167 [OE ranc]

ros. *See* **rys**

roſe *n.* rose 269, 906 [OE rose]

rot *n.* rot, decay 26 [OE rotian]

rote *n.* root 420 [Late OE rōt]

rote *v.* rot, decay 958 [OE rotian]

rounde *adj.* round 5, 657, 738 [OF ronde]

rourde *n.* noise, sound 112 [OE reord]

route *n.* company, crowd 926 [AF rute]

rownande *pres. p.* whispering, murmuring 112 [OE rūnian]

ruful *adj.* rueful, sorrowful 916 [OE hreow]

runne, runnen. *See* **ran**

ryal *adj.* royal 160, 193 **ryalle** 191, 919 [OF roial]

ryally *adv.* royally 987 [OF roial]

rybe *n.* ruby 1007 [OF rubi]

rych, ryche *adj. See* **riche**

ryche *n.* kingdom, realm 601, 722, 919 [OE rīce]

rycheʒ *n.* richness, wealth 26 [OF richeise]

ryf *adj.* abundant 770, 844 [Late OE rȳfe]

ryʒt *adv.* just, precisely 298, 461, 520, 673, 723, etc. **ryʒte** 672 [OE rihte]

ryʒt *n.* right 496, 580, 622, 665, etc. **ryʒte** 696, 708 [OE riht]

ryʒte *adj.* right 672, 703 [OE riht]

ryʒtwys *adj.* righteous 675, 685, 697 *subst.* righteous one 689 **ryʒtywys** 739★ [OE rihtwīs]

ryʒtwyſly *adv.* righteously 709 [OE rihtwīslīce]

rys *v.* rise 1093 **ryſe** 103 **ryſeʒ** *pres. 3 sing.* arises 191 **ros** *pret. 3 sing.* rose 437, 506, 519 [OE rīsan]

S

ſadde *adj.* serious, dignified 887 **ſade**

211 [OE sæd]

fade *v. See* **fay**

faf *adj.* safe 672, 684, 720 **faue** 696 [OF sauf]

faffer *n.* sapphire 118, 1002 [OF safir]

faghe *n.* saw, saying 226 **fawe3** *plur.* speeches 278 [OE sagu]

fa3 689. *See* **say**

fa3 1021, 1147. *See* **se**

fa3t *adj.* at peace, reconciled, free from strife 52 **fa3te** 1201 [Late OE seht, sæht]

fake *n.* charge, accusation 800 sake, good, advantage 940 [OE sacu]

fakerfyfe *n.* sacrifice 1064★ [OF sacrifice]

falamon *n.* Solomon 689

fame *adj.* same 1099, 1101 [ON same]

famen *adv.* together 518 [OE samen]

fample *n.* example, parable 499 [OF example]

fange. *See* **fonge** *n.*

fant. *See* **faynt**

fardonyfe *n.* sardonyx 1006 [L sardonyx]

faue *v.* save 674 **faue3** *pres. 3 sing.* saves 666 [OF salver]

faue *adj. See* **faf**

fauerly *adj.* acceptable, satisfactory 226 [OF savouré]

faule *n.* soul 845 **fawhe** (scribal error for **sawle**) 461★ [OE sāwol]

fauter *n.* Psalter 593, 677, 698 [OE (p)saltere]

fawe3. *See* **faghe**

fawhe. *See* **faule**

fay *v.* say 226, 256, 258, 391, 1041 **faye** 482 *pres. 1 sing. 3* **fays** *pres. 2 sing.* 295, 297, 409, 694 *pres. 3 sing.* says 867 **fayt3** *pres. 2 sing.*

say 315 *pres. 3 sing.* says 457, 501, 697, 836 **fay3** *pres. 2 sing.* say 615 **fat3** *pres. 3 sing.* says **fa3** 689 **fayde** *pret. 3 sing.* said 289, 338, 398, 494, etc. *pret. 1 sing.* 589, 962 677 **fayd** *pret. 3 sing.* 593 *pret. 1 sing.* 1175 **fyde** *pret. 3 sing.* 433 **fade** 532★ **fayden** *pret. 3 plur.* 534, 550 **fade** *pret. 1 sing.* 784 [OE secgan]

faynt *n.* saint 457, 818 **fant** 788 **faynte3** *plur.* saints 835 [OF saint]

fcale *n.* surface, outside 1005 [OF escale]

fchadowed *pret. 3 plur.* shadowed, shaded 42 [OE sceadwian]

fchafte3 *n. plur.* shafts, beams of light 982 [OE sceaft]

fchal *pres. 1 sing.* must 328, 329 *pres. 3 sing.* 332, 344 *verbal auxiliary forming future tense* shall, will *pres. 1 sing.* 283, 569 *pres. 2 sing.* 265, 298, 315 *pres. 3 sing.* 348, 356, 405, 416, etc. **fchalte** *pres. 2 sing.* 564 [OE sceal]

fcharpe *adv.* sharply 877 [OE scearpe]

fchede *v.* depart 411 *pret. 3 sing.* shed 741 [OE sc(e)ādan]

fchene *adj.* beautiful, shining 42, 80, 203, 1145 *subst.* fair one, shining one 166, 965 [OE scīene]

fchente *pp.* punished 668 [OE scendan]

fchep *n.* sheep 801 [OE scēap]

fchere *v.* cut, shear 165 **fchere3** *pres. 3 sing.* cuts, cleaves 107 **fchorne** *pp.* having been cut or sheared 213 [OE sceran]

fcheued *pret. 3 sing.* showed 692 **fchewe3** *pres. 3 sing.* shows 1210

[OE scēawian]

ſcho. *See* ho

ſchon. *See* ſchyneȝ

ſchore *n.* shore 107, 166, 230 [OE scora]

ſchorne. *See* ſchere

ſchot *pret. 3 sing.* shot 58 [OE scēotan]

ſchowted *pret. 3 sing.* made a loud noise 877 [? ON skūta]

ſchrylle *adv.* clearly, brightly 80 [ME shrille; Cf. LG schrell]

ſchulde (*past tense of* ſchal) *pret. 1 sing.* ought (to) 153, 903 *pret. 3 sing.* was about to 186 ought to 314, 634, 668, 924 *pret. 3 sing. subj.* would 186, 1072, 1162 could 1159 *pret. 3 plur. subj.* should 930 [OE sc(e)olde]

ſchylde *v.* prevent, forbid 965 [OE scildan]

ſchyldereȝ *n. plur.* shoulders 214 [OE sculdor]

ſchym *adj.* bright 1077 [OE scima]

ſchymeryng *n.* shimmering 80 [Late OE scymrian]

ſchyneȝ *pres. 3 sing.* shines 28, 1074 ſchynde *pret. 3 plur.* shined 80 ſchon *pret. 3 sing.* shone 166, 213, 982, 1018 *pret. 3 plur.* 1057 [OE scīnan]

ſchyr *adj.* bright, shining 213, 284 ſchyre 42 ſchyr *adv.* brightly 28 ſchyrrer *comp. adj.* brighter 982 [OE scīr]

ſclade. *See* ſlade

ſcrypture *n.* engraved characters 1039 [L scriptura]

ſe *v.* see 96, 146, 296, 914, 675, 964, 969 ſene 45 ſe *pres. 1 sing.* see 377, 385, 932 ſeȝ *pres. 3 sing.* sees 302 *pret. 1 sing.* saw 158,

175, 200, 1155 *pret. 3 sing.* saw 531 *pret. 3 sing. subj.* saw 698 ſen *pp.* seen 164 ſene 194, 787, 1143 ſyȝ *pret. 3 sing.* saw 788, 985, 1032 ſyȝe *pres. 2 sing. subj.* see 308 *pres. 1 sing.* saw 986, 1033 ſegh *pret 3 sing.* saw 790 ſeghe *pret. 1 sing.* saw 867 ſaȝ 1021, 1147 [OE sēon]

ſech *imper. sing.* seek 354 ſoȝt *pp.* having been asked for 518 ſoȝte *pret. 3 sing.* sought 730 [OE sēcan]

ſecounde *adj.* second 652, 1002 [OF second]

ſede *n.* seed 34 [OE sǣd]

ſegh, ſeghe, ſeȝ. *See* ſe

ſelden *adv.* seldom 380 [OE seldan]

ſelf *adj.* the same 203 þe ſelf god God himself 1046 þe ſelf sunne the sun itself 1076 þe hyȝe godeȝ ſelf the high God himself 1054 [OE self]

ſely *adj.* fortunate, blessed 659 [OE gesǣlig]

ſembelaunt *n.* face, expression 1143 ſemblaunt demeanor 211 [OF semblant]

ſeme *adv.* fittingly, becomingly 190 *adj.* decorous, well-behaved 1115 [ON sēm-r]

ſeme *n.* seam 838 [OE sēam]

ſemed *pret. 3 sing. subj.* may have seemed 760 [ON søma]

ſemly *adj.* fair, seemly 34, 45, 789 [ON sømilig-r]

ſende *pres. 3 sing. subj.* send 130 [OE sendan]

ſen, ſene. *See* ſe

ſengeley *adv.* apart from others, by itself 8 [OF sengle]

ſerlypeȝ *adj.* separate, distinct 994

[ON sēr + OE –lēpes]

fermoun *n.* discourse, account 1185 [OF sermon]

fertayn *adv.* certainly, assuredly 685 [OF certain]

feruaunt *n.* servant 699 [OF servant]

ferued *pp.* deserved 553 [OF deservir]

ferueȝ *pres. 3 sing.* avails, profits 331 [OF servir]

fefed *pp.* seised, put in possession of *in* **fefed in** having been put in possession of, being the legal possessor of 417 [OF seisir]

fet (1) *pret. 3 sing.* sat 1054 **fete** 161 *pret. 3 plur.* 835 [OE sittan]

fet (2) *pret. 3 sing.* put 255 caused to become (*see* **vayn**) 811 *imper. sing.* put, place 545 *pp.* built, erected 1062 **sete** *v.* cause to be 1201 **fette** *pret. 1 sing.* set 8 *pret. 3 sing. subj.* should have caused to be 52 *pp.* set 222, 838 **fetten** *pres. 2 plur.* cause to become 307 [OE settan]

feuen *adj.* seven 838, 1111 [OE seofon]

feuenþe *adj.* seventh 1010 [OE seofoþa]

fexte *adj.* sixth 1007 [OE sexta]

feyfoun *n.* season 39 [OF seson]

fir *n.* sir 257, 439 [OF sire]

fkyfte *v.* arrange, change 569 [OE sciftan]

fkyl *n.* reason 312 **fkylle** arrangement, ordinance 674 **fkylleȝ** *plur.* arguments 54 [ON skil]

flade *n.* valley 141 **fclade** 1148 [OE slæd]

flaȝt *n.* slaughter 801 [OE slæht]

flake *v.* abate, cease *in* **don to flake** brought to an end 942 [OE slacian]

flayn *pp.* slain 805 [OE slēan]

flente slope, hillside 141 [ON *slent]

flepe *pres. 3 plur.* sleep 115 [OE slēpan]

flepyng-flaȝte fit of sleep, trance 59 [OE slēpan + slæht]

flode *pret. 1 sing.* slid, slipped 59 [OE slīdan]

flyȝt *adj.* slight, slim 190 [ON slēttr]

fmal *adj.* small, slender 6, 190 **fmale** 90 [OE smæl]

fmoþe *adj.* smooth 6, 190 [OE smoð]

fo *adv.* so 2, 5, 6, 19, etc. such, such a 95, 616, 774 thus 22, 97, 338, 461, etc. then 1187 *with subj. expressing wish* may 487, 850 *correl. adv.* **so . . . a** as . . . as 1057 [OE swa]

foberly *adv.* soberly 256 [OF sobre]

fobre *adj.* sober, solemn 391, 532 [OF sobre]

fodanly *adv.* suddenly 1095, 1098, 1178 [OF soudain]

foffer. *See* **fuffer**

foȝt, foȝte. *See* **fech**

folace *n.* solace 130 [OF solas]

folde *pret. 3 sing.* sold 731 [OE sellan]

fommoun. *See* **fumoun**

fonde *n.* sending, dispensation 943 [OE sond]

fone *adv.* soon, quickly 537, 626, 1078, 1197 [OE sōna]

fonge *n.* song 882, 888, 891 **fange** 19 [OE sang]

fonge *pret. 3 plur.* sang 1124 **fongen** 94, 882, 888 [OE singan]

fonne. *See* **funne**

for *n.* pain, suffering, bodily injury 940 scribal error for **for** 700★

ſore 130 [OE sār]

ſore *adv.* sorely, laboriously 550 [OE sāre]

ſorʒ *n.* sorrow 663 ſorʒe 352 [OE sorh]

ſorquydryʒe *n.* arrogance, presumption 309 [OF s(o)urcuiderie]

ſoth *adj.* true 482, 1185 ſoþe *n.* truth 653 for ſoþe in truth, indeed 21, 292 [OE sōþ]

ſothfol *adj.* truthful 498 [OE sōþ]

ſotyle *adj.* tenuous, transparent 1050 [OF soutil]

ſoþe. *See* ſoth

ſoun *n.* voice 532 [AF soun, OF son]

ſounande *adj.* resounding, sonorous 883 [OF soner]

ſpace *n.* space 61, 1030 space of time 438 [OF espace]

ſpakk. *See* ſpeke

ſparred *pret. 1 sing.* darted, sprang 1169 [?]

ſpech *n.* text 704 ſpeche speech 37, 235, 400, 471, 793, 1132 [OE spræc]

ſpecial *adj.* special 235 ſpecyal 938 [OF especial]

ſpede *pres. 3 sing. subj.* cause to prosper 487 [OE spēdan]

ſpeke *pres. 1 sing.* speak 422 *pret. 3 sing.* spoke 438 ſpakk 938 ſpekeʒ *pres. 3 sing.* speaks to, makes 594 ſpoken *pp.* spoken 291 [OE sprecan]

ſpelle *n.* speech, discourse 363 [OE spell]

ſpelle *pres. 1 sing.* speak, tell 793 [OE spellian]

ſpennd *pret. 1 sing.* clasped 49 ſpenned *pp.* captured, imprisoned 53 [ON spenna]

ſpent *pp.* employed, uttered 1132 [OE spendan]

ſpoken. *See* ſpeke

ſponne *pret. 3 sing. subj.* would shoot, would spring 35 [OE spinnan]

ſpornande *pres. p.* stumbling 363 [OE spornan]

ſpot *n.* spot, blemish 12, 36, 48, 60, 764, 1068 spot, place 25, 49, 61 ſpote 13 ſpotte blemish 24, 36 ſpotteʒ *plur.* spots, blemishes 945 [ME spot; Cf. MDu spotte]

ſpoteʒ *adj.* spotless 856 [ME spot; Cf. WFlem. spotteloos]

ſpotty *adj.* spotty 1070 [ME spot]

ſprang. *See* ſpryng

ſprede *v.* be spread 25 [OE sprǣdan]

ſprent *pret. 3 sing.* spurted 1137 [OE gesprintan]

ſpryng *v.* spring 453 ſprang *pret. 3 plur.* sprang 61 ſprange 13 [OE springan]

ſprygande *adj.* scribal error for ſpryngande springing, sprouting (?) 35★ [OE springan]

ſpyce *n.* spice (endearment for pearl-maiden) 235, 938 ſpyſe spice-bearing plants 104 ſpyceʒ *plur.* spice-bearing plants 35 ſpyſeʒ 25 [OF espice]

ſpyryt *n.* spirit 61 [OF esperit]

ſpyt *n.* spite, malacious act 1138 [OF despit]

ſtable *adj.* stable 597 [OF stable]

ſtable *v.* stand firm, be stable 683 [OF esstablir]

ſtage *n.* station, rank 410 [OF estage]

ſtale *n.* position 1002 [OE stalu or steall, or OF estal]

ſtalked *pret. 1 sing.* walked cautiously 152 [OE bestealcian]

ſtalle v. stall, bring to a stand 188
     [OF estaller; OE forþteallian]
ſtande v. (prog.) standing 514 pres.
     2 plur. stand 515 ſtonde 533
     ſtandeȝ pres. 3 sing. stands 547
     ſtonden pret. 3 plur. stood 113
     ſtanden pp. stood, been standing
     519, 1148 ſtod pret. 1 sing. stood
     182, 184, 1085 pret. 3 sing. stood
     597, 1023 ſtande vt. (reflexive)
     stand, cause to stand 867 ſtode
     pret. 3 sing. stood, caused to stand
     740 [OE standan]
ſtare v. stare 149 ſtaren pres. 3 plur.
     shine 116 [OE starian]
ſtart v. jump, leap 1159, 1162 [OE
     styrtan]
ſtayre adj. steep 1022 [OE *stæger]
ſtele v. steal, come quietly 20 [OE
     stelan; cf. OE stalian]
ſtep n. footsteps 683 [OE stepe]
ſtepe adj. brilliant 113 [OE stēap]
ſtere v. govern 623 restrain 1159
     [OE stīeran]
ſterneȝ n. plur. stars 115 [ON
     stjarna]
ſteuen n. speech 188 noise 1125 [OE
     stefn fem.]
ſtod, ſtode. See ſtande
ſtok n. stump, post 380 by ſtok
     oþer ſton by (sign)post or (mile)
     stone, i.e. along the way [OE
     stoc(c)]
ſtoken pp. shut, closed 1065 [OE
     *stecan]
ſton n. stone 380, 822, precious
     stone 206, 994, 1006 ſtoneȝ
     plur. precious stones 113, 997
     [OE stān]
ſtonde, ſtonden. See ſtande
ſtonge pret. 3 sing. stung 179 [OE
     stingan]

ſtore n. large group 847 [OF estor]
ſtote v. stop, stand still 149 [MDu,
     MLG stōten (?)]
ſtounde n. time, moment 20, 659
     [OE stund]
ſtout adj. proud 779 ſtoute stately
     935 [OF estout]
ſtrange adj. strange 175 [OF
     estrange]
ſtrateȝ. See ſtrete
ſtray adv. astray, out of the right way
     179 [OF estraié]
ſtrayd pret. 3 sing. strayed 1173 [OF
     estraier]
ſtrayn v. lead, compel to go 691
     ſtreny strain, exert 551 ſtrayneȝ
     pres. 3 sing. strains, constrains
     128 [OF estreindre]
ſtrech v. walk, proceed 971 ſtreche
     spread 843 [OE streccan]
ſtreȝt adj. straight 691 [OE strehte,
     pp. of streccan]
ſtrem n. stream 125, 1159, 1162 [OE
     strēam]
ſtremande adj. streaming, emitting a
     stream of light 115 [OE strēam]
ſtrenghþe n. strength, intensity 128
     [OE strengðu]
ſtreny. See ſtrayn
ſtreſſe n. distress 124 [OF destresse]
ſtrete n. street 971, 1059 ſtreteȝ plur.
     streets 1025 ſtrateȝ 1043 [OE
     strǣt]
ſtrok. See ſtryke
ſtronde n. strand, shore 152 [OE
     strand]
ſtronge adj. strong 531 adv. strongly
     476 [OE strong, stronge]
ſtrot n. strife, contention 353, 848
     [OE strūtian]
ſtroþe-men n. plur. woodsmen 115
     [OE strōd + men]

ſtryf *n.* strife 248, 776, 848 [OF estrif]

ſtryke *vi.* strike, pass 1125 **ſtryke3** *pres. 3 sing.* comes 570 **ſtrok** *pret. 3 sing. trans.* struck 1180 [OE strīcan]

ſtrynge *n.* string 91 [OE streng]

ſtryuen *pres. 3 plur.* strive 1199 [OF estriver]

ſtyf *adj.* unyielding 779 [OE stīf]

ſtyke3 *pres. 2 sing.* remain fixed, stay 1186 [OE stician]

ſtylle *adj.* still, silent 20 *adv.* still, motionless 182, 1085 forever 683 [OE stille]

ſtynſt *imper. sing.* cease, desist 353 [OE styntan]

ſuch *adj.* such 26, 407, 1043, 1099 *pron.* such 727 **ſuche** *adj.* 58, 171 *pron.* 719 [OE swylc]

ſuffer *v.* suffer 954 **ſoffer** 940 **ſuffred** *pp.* suffered, endured 554 [OF sof(f)rir]

ſuffyſe *v.* suffice 135 [OF suffire]

ſulpande *adj.* defiling 726 [?]

ſum *adj.* some 428 *pron.* some *in of al & ſum* in full, for everything 584 **ſumme** *pron.* some 508 [OE sum]

ſumkyn *adj.* some kind of 619 [OE sum + cynn]

ſumme. *See* ſum

ſommoun *n.* summons 1098 **ſumoun** 539 [OF somondre]

ſumtyme *adv.* at some time 620 at one time 760 [OE sum + tīma]

ſunne *n.* sun 28, 519, 538, 982, etc. **ſonne** 530 [OE sunne]

ſunnebeme3 *n. plur.* sunbeams 83 [OE sun(n)bēam]

ſupplantore3 *n. plur.* supplanters 440 [OF supplanteor]

ſure *adj.* sure 1089 *adv.* securely 222 [OF sur]

ſute *n.* suit, pattern of clothing 203 **in ſute** of the same pattern 1108 [AF sute]

ſve *v.* proceed 976 **ſwe** *pres. 3 plur.* follow 892 [OF sivre]

ſwalt *pret. 3 sing.* died 816 **ſwalte** *pret. 1 sing. subj.* died 1160 [OE sweltan]

ſwange (1) *pret. 3 plur.* labored, toiled 586 [OE swincan]

ſwange (2) *pret. 3 sing.* rushed 1059 **swangeande** *pres. p.* swirling, rushing 111 [OE swingan]

ſware *v.* answer 240 [ON svara]

ſware *adj.* square 837, 1023 [OF esquarré]

ſware *n.* square, side 1029 [OF esquire]

ſwat *pret. 3 plur.* sweated 586 **ſwatte** suffered, sweat (blood) 829 [OE swætan]

ſwe. *See* ſve

ſweng *n.* toil, labor 575 [OE sweng]

ſwepe *v.* sweep, move swiftly along 111 [OE swēop; cf. ON svipa]

ſwefte. *See* ſwyſt

ſwete *adj.* sweet 19, 94, 763, 1122 *subst.* sweet one 240, 325 *adv.* sweetly 111, 1057 [OE swēte]

ſwetely *adv.* sweetly 717 [OE swētelīce]

ſweuen *n.* sleep, dream 62 [OE swef(e)n]

ſwone *n.* swoon 1180 [OE geswōgen]

ſwyſt *adj.* swift 571 **ſwefte** *adv.* swiftly 354* [OE swift]

ſwymme *v.* swim 1160 [OE swimman]

ſwyþe *adv.* swiftly, without delay

354, 1059 [OE swīðe]

ſyde *v. See* **ſay**

ſyde *n.* side 975, 1137 **ſydeȝ** *plur.* sides 6, 73, 198, 218 [OE sīde]

ſyȝ, ſyȝe. *See* **ſe**

ſyȝt *n.* sight, spectacle 226, 839, 952, 968, 1151 sight, faculty of vision 985 **ſyȝteȝ** *plur.* sights 1179 [OE sihð]

ſyluer *n.* silver 77 [OE siolfor]

ſympelneſſe *n.* simpleness, simplicity 909 [OF simple]

ſymple *adj.* simple, unpretentious 1134 [OF simple]

ſyn. *See* **ſyþen**

ſynge *v.* sing 891 [OE singan]

ſynglerty *n.* singularity, uniqueness 429 [OF senglerté]

ſynglure *n.* singleness, uniqueness 8 [OF single]

ſyngnetteȝ *n. plur.* signets, seals 838 [OF signet]

ſynne *n.* sin 610, 726, 811 **ſynneȝ** *plur.* sins 823 [OE syn(n)]

ſynneȝ *pres. 3 sing.* sins 662 [OE syngian]

ſyon *n.* Sion, Zion 789, 868 [eccl. L Siōn]

ſyt *n.* sorrow, grief, trouble 663 [ON *syt]

ſytole *adj.* of the citole (medieval stringed instrument) 91 [OF citole]

ſyþen *conj.* since 245 *adv.* afterwards 643, 1207 **ſyþen** *conj.* since 13 **ſyn** 519 [OE siþþan]

ſyþeȝ *n. plur.* times 1079 [OE siþ]

T

tabelment *n.* tier, course of masonry 994 [AF tablement]

table *n.* tier 1004 [OF table]

tached *pp.* attached, inherent 464 [OF atachier]

take *v.* take 539, 552, 599, 944, 1067, 1158 *pres. 2 sing.* 387 *imper. sing.* 559 **takeȝ** *pres. 3 sing.* takes 687 **taken** *pp.* taken 830 **tan** 614 **toke** *pret. 3 sing.* took 414, 808 *pret. 3 plur.* 585 **totȝ** goes, proceeds 513 [Late OE tacan]

tale *n.* tale, account 257, 311, 590, 897, 998 **talle** 865* [OE talu]

tan. *See* **take**

tech *imper. sing.* guide, direct 936 [OE tǣcan]

teche *n.* blemish 845 [OF teche]

telle *v.* tell 134, 653 **telleȝ** *pres. 2 sing.* tell 919 **tolde** *pret. 3 sing.* uttered 815 [OE tellan]

temen *pres. 3 plur.* attach themselves, belong 460 [OE tīman]

temple *n.* temple 1062 [OE templ]

tempte *v.* test, try 903 [OF tempter]

tender *adj.* tender 412 [OF tendre]

teneȝ *n. plur.* afflictions, suffering 332 [OE tēona]

tenoun *n.* construction, joinery 993 [OF tenon]

tente *n.* attention, heed 387 [OF atente]

tenþe *adj.* tenth 136, 1013 [Early ME tenþe]

terme *n.* term, appointed time 503 **termeȝ** *plur.* terms, words of precise meaning 1053 [OF terme]

that. *See* **þat** *adj.*

the. *See* **þe**

theme *n.* theme, topic 944 [OF tesme, L thema]

then, thenne. *See* **þen** *adv.*

this. *See* **þis**

thow. *See* **þou**

throne *n.* throne 1113 **trone** 835, 920, 1051, 1055 [OF trone]

thys. *See* **þis**

to *prep.* to 10, 20, 21, 22, etc. for 1, 136, 508, 588, etc. upon, on 167, 209 as 468 before 700 at 1120 *pleonastic* 1073 **for to** to 99, 333, 403, 613, 1118, 1129 **lyk to** like 432, 896 **to hym warde** toward him 820 [OE tō]

to *adv.* too 481, 492, 615, 1070, 1075, 1076, 1118 forth (indication of direction) in **to ne fro** to (n)or fro, back and forth 347 [OE tō]

todrawe3 *pres. 2 sing.* dispel 280 [OE tō + dragan]

togeder *adv.* together 1121 [OE tōgædere]

to3t *adj.* settled, binding 522 [OE tēon (?)]

toke. *See* **take**

token *n.* token *in* **in token of** as a sign of 742 [OE tācan]

tolde. *See* **telle**

tom *n.* leisure 134 time 585 [ON tōm]

tong *n.* tongue 225 **tonge** 100, 898 [OE tunge]

topaſye *n.* topaz 1012 [OF topaze]

tor *n.* tower (= heaven) 966 [OE torr]

tor *adj.* hard, difficult 1109 [OE tor-]

torente *pp.* rent through 1136 [OE torendan]

toriuen *pp.* split asunder, shattered 1197 [OE to- + ON rīfa]

torre3 *n. plur.* hills 875 [OE torr]

tot3. *See* **take**

touch *v.* touch 714 **towched** *pret. 3 sing.* touched 898 [OF tochier]

toun *n.* town 995 [OE tūn]

towarde *prep.* to, toward 67, 438, 974, 1113 [OE tōweard]

towched. *See* **touch**

towen *pp.* pulled, drawn *in* **in twynne towen** separated 251 [OE tēon]

trauayle *n.* toil, travail 1087 [OF travail]

trauayled *pret. 3 plur.* labored, toiled 550 [OF travaillier]

tras *n.* course, way *in* **trone a tras** made their way, took their course 1113 [OF trace]

traw *v.* believe 487 **trawed** *pret. 1 sing.* believed 282 **trawe3** *pres. 2 sing.* believe 295 **trowe** *pres. 1 sing.* believe 933 [OE trēowian, trūwian]

trawþe *n.* truth 495 [OE trēowþ]

trendeled *pret. 3 sing.* rolled 41 [OE trendel]

tres *n. plur.* trees 1077 [OE trēow]

treſor *n.* treasure 331 **treſore** 237 [OF tresor]

trone *n. See* **throne**

trone *pret. 3 plur.* went, marched (*see* **tras**) 1113 [Cf. OSwed trina]

trowe. *See* **traw**

true *adj.* true 311 **trw** 831 **trwe** 421, 725, 822, 1191 *adv.* truly, faithfully 460 [OE trēowe]

try3e *v.* try, put to the test 311 **tryed** *pp.* tried, brought to trial 702, 707 [OF trier]

trylle *v.* quiver, shake (?); trail, hang down (?) 78★ [Cf. MDu trillen; Cf. Sw. and Norw. trilla]

twayned *pp.* divided in two, parted 251 [OE twēgen]

twelfþe *adj.* twelfth 1015 [OE twelfta]

twelue *adj.* twelve 992, 993, 1022,

1030, 1035, 1078, 1079 [OE twelf]

two *adj.* two 483, 555, 674, 949 [OE twā]

twye3 *adv.* twice 830 [Late OE twiges]

twynne *n.* twain *in* **in twynne** in two parts, asunder 251 [OE twinn]

twynne-how *adj.* twin-hued, bi-colored 1012 [OE twinn + hīew]

ty3ed *pp.* tied 464 [OE tīgan]

ty3t *v.* (1) betake themselves, come 718 *pp.* appointed 503 [OE tyhtan]

ty3t *v.* (2) *pp.* set firmly, fixed 1013 **ty3te** *pret. 3 sing.* set down in writing 1053 [?]

tyl *conj.* until 976 **tyl . . . þat** until 548, 979 **tylle** *prep.* to 676 [ONorthumb. til]

tyme *n.* time 503, 833 [OE tīma]

tynde *n.* twig, branch 78 [OE tind]

tyne *v.* lose, cease to enjoy 332 [ON tȳna]

tyste *adv.* scribal error for **tryste** (?) steadfastly 460★ [Cf. OI traustr]

tyt *adv.* quickly 728 **as tyt** at once 645 [Cf. ON tītt]

þ

þa. *See* **þat** *rel. pron.*

þa3 *conj.* though 52, 55, 134, 306, etc. **þo3** 345 [OE ðēah, þēah, þēh; ON *þōh]

þare. *See* **þer**

þat *rel. or demonst. pron.* that, who(m), which, that which 15, 37, 50, 54, etc. **þᵗ** 17, 53, 271, 302, etc. **þa** *plur.* that, who 856 [OE þæt]

þat *conj.* that, so that, that which 119, 185, 269, 312, etc. **þᵗ** 35, 102,

137, 185, etc. *pleonastic* **þat** 334, 548, 979 **þᵗ** 65 [OE þæt]

þat *adj.* that 12, 13, 14, 25, etc. **that** 253, 481, 937 **þᵗ** 142, 226, 235, 760, etc. [OE þæt]

þay *pers. pron. 3 plur. nom.* they 80, 94, 509, 510, etc. [ON þeir]

þe *def. art.* the 28, 67, 69, 70, etc. **the** 109, 121, 445, 541, etc. [Late OE þe]

þe *adv.* the (with *comp. adj.*) 152, 168 by that 234, 576, 852, 864, 876, 888, 901 **the** 169 *correl. adv.* the . . . the, by how much . . . by so much 103, 127-8, 180, 600, 621, 850 [OE þē, þȳ]

þe *pers. pron. 2 sing acc., dat.* you (thee), to you, for you 244, 263, 266, 274, etc. used as *nom.* you (thou) 267, 316, 341, *reflex.* yourself (thyself) 268, 474, 703 [OE þē]

þede *n.* land, country 483 [OE þēod]

þef *n.* thief 273 [OE þēof]

þen *adv.* then 277, 398, 494, 623, etc. **then** 589 **thenne** 361 **þenne** 155, 177, 213, 253, etc. **after þenne** afterwards 256 **er þenne** before 1094 [OE þenne]

þen *conj.* than 134, 181, 212, 232, etc. **þenn** 555 [OE þenne, þanne]

þenk *v.* consider, intend 1151 **þenke** think of 22 **þenkande** *pres. p.* thinking 370 **þo3t** *pret. 1 sing.* thought 137, 1138, 1157 [OE þenc(e)an]

þenn. *See* **þen** *conj.*

þenne *adv.* (1). *See* **þen** *adv.*

þenne *adv.* (2) thence 631 [OE þanone]

þer *adv.* there (indefinite subject, or

as placeholder for subject where subject follows verb) 21, 113, 151, 161, etc. there, in that place 28, 53, 61, 62, etc. **þere** 167, 194, 742, 942, 1155 **þare** 830,* 1021 **þore** 562 **þer** *conj.* (or *rel. adv.*) where 26, 30, 41, 47, etc. **þere** 835, 838 [OE þǣr]

þeras *conj.* wherever 129 where 818, 1173 [OE þǣr + all-swā]

þerate *adv.* there, in that place 514 [OE þǣr æt]

þere-ine *adv.* therein, in that place 633 **þerinne** 447, 644, 724, 1061 in that matter 1168 [OE þǣrin]

þerfor *adv.* therefore 1197* [OE þǣr + fore]

þerof *adv.* of it, of that 99, 161, 410, 968, 1069, 1084 [OE þǣr of]

þeron *adv.* of that 387, after that 645 on that 1042 [OE þǣron]

þeroute *adv.* outdoors 930 [OE þǣrūt]

þerto *adv.* to that place 172, to that 664, 833 in that 1140 [OE þǣrtō]

þeſe. *See* **þis**

þike *adv.* thickly 78 [OE þicce]

þis *adj. sing.* this 65, 260, 295, 315, etc. **þys** 250, 277, 286, 297, etc. **this** 733 **thys** 841 **þis** *plur.* these 42 **þiſe** 287, 997, 1022, 1119 **þyſe** 931 **þiſe** *sing.* this 533 **þeſe** *plur.* these 752 **þys** *pron. sing.* this 421 **þyſſe** 370 *plur.* these 505 **þiſe** 384 **þeſe** 551 **þyſe** 555 [OE þis, ðæs]

þo *adj.* those 73, 85, 109, 138, 777, 1179 that 136 *pron.* those ones 557 [OE þā]

þo *adv.* then 451 **þoo** 873 [OE þā]

þo3. *See* **þa3**

þo3t. *See* **þenk, þynk**

þo3te *n.* thought 524 [OE þoht]

þole *v.* suffer 344 [OE þolian]

þonc *n.* thanks, gratitude [OE þonc]

þoo. *See* **þo**

þore. *See* **þer**

þos *pron. plur.* those ones 515 **þoſe** *adj.* those 93, 127 [OE þās]

þou *pers. pron.* 2 *sing. nom.* thou, you (*sing.*) 247, 264, 265, 269, etc. **þow** 411 **thow** 337 [OE þū]

þouſande3 *n. plur.* thousands 926 **þowſande3** *gen. plur.* of thousands 1107 **þowſande** *sing.* thousand 786, 869, 870 [OE þūsend]

þrange *adv.* grievously, painfully 17 [OE geþrang; Cf. ON þröngr]

þre *adj.* three 291, 292, 1034 [OE þrī]

þrete *v.* complain 561 [OE þrēatian]

þro *adj.* angry, violent 344 excellent, bold 868 [ON þrār]

þrowe3 *pres. 3 sing.* peals 875 [OE þrāwan]

þrych *v.* oppress 17 **þry3t** *pp.* brought, thrust 670 thrust, stabbed 706 thrust together, crowded 926 [OE þrycc(e)an]

þryd *adj.* third 1004 **þrydde** 299 **þryde** 833 [OE þridda]

þryf *v.* thrive **þryuen** *pp.* noble, excellent 868 successful, prosperous 1192 [ON þrífask]

þry3t. *See* **þrych**

þryuen. *See* **þryf**

þᵗ. *See* **þat**

þunder *n.* thunder 875 [OE þunor]

þur3 *prep.* through 10, 114, 271, 323, etc. [OE þurh]

þur3outly *adv.* thoroughly,

completely 859 [OE þurh-ūt + līce]

þus *adv.* thus 526, 569, 573, 673,★ 829 therefore 673★ (second occurrence) [OE þus]

þy *poss. adj. 2 sing.* thy, your (*sing.*) 266, 273, 275, 294, etc. **þyn** (before a vowel) thine, your 559, 567, 754 [OE þīn]

þyder *adv.* thither, to that place 723, 946 [OE þider]

þyn. *See* þy

þynk *pres. 3 sing. impers.* [it] seems (with *dat.*) 552, 553, 590 **þoȝt** *pret. 3 sing.* appeared, seemed 19, 153 [OE þync(e)an]

þys, þyſe. *See* þis

þyſelf *pron. 2 sing. nom. emphatic* you (*sing.*), you yourself 298, 313 *dat. emphatic* by yourself 779; *reflex.* yourself 473 **þyſeluen** *acc. reflex.* yourself 341

þyſſe. *See* þis

U

ueray. *See* veray

ueſture *n.* vesture, raiment 220 [OF vesture]

uoched *pp.* called, summoned 1121 [OF voch(i)er]

uyne. *See* vyne

V

valeȝ *n. plur.* vales, valleys 127 [OF val]

vayl *v.* avail, prevail 912 [OF vail]

vayn *n.* vanity, emptiness *in* **in vayn** of no worth 811 **in vayne** to no purpose, as worthless 687 [OF vain, L *in vanum*]

vayned. *See* wayneȝ

vch *adj.* each 31, 323, 603, 803, etc.

vche 5, 33, 310, 839, 845 **vch a** every 78, 375, 436, 461 **vche a** 117, 217, 1066, 1080 [OE ylc]

vchon *pron.* each one 450, 546, 595 **vchoneȝ** *gen.* each one's 863, 1103 [OE ylc + ān]

veray *adj.* true 1184 **ueray** 1185 [AF veray]

verce *n.* verse 593 [OE fers; Cf. OF vers]

vered *pret. 3 sing.* raised up, uplifted 254 **vereȝ** *pres. 3 sing.* raises up, uplifts 177 [?]

vergyneȝ. *See* vyrgyn

vergynte *n.* virginity 767 [AF virginite]

vertues *n. plur.* virtues (an order of angels, traditionally the fifth in the celestial hierarchy) 1126 [AF vertu]

veued. *See* weue

vmbegon *pp.* having gone around, surrounding, encompassing 210 [OE ymb-gān]

vmbepyȝte *pp.* set round, adorned 204, 1052 [OE ymbe + ME piche(n) Cf. pyȝt]

vnavyſed *adj.* unadvised, rash 292 [OE un- + OF avisé; cf. MDu ongeavijst]

vnblemyſt *adj.* unblemished 782 [OE un- + OF belmir]

vncortoyſe *adj.* uncourteous, uncourtly 303 [OE un- + OF corteis]

vndefylde *adj.* undefiled 725 [OE un- + OE fýlan, OF defouler]

vnder *n.* undern, the third hour (about 9 a.m.) 513 [OE undern]

vnder *prep.* under 923 [OE under]

vnderſtonde *v.* understand *in* **to vnderſtonde** to be understood,

to wit, namely 941 [OE
understondan]

vnhyde *v.* reveal 973 [OE un- +
hȳdan]

vnlapped *adj.* uncovered, loose,
unbound 214 [OE un- + læppa]

vnmete *adj.* improper, unfitting 759
[OE unmǣte]

vnpynne *v.* open, unbolt 728 [OE
un- + pinn]

vnreſounable *adj.* unreasonable 590
[OE un- + OF reson(n)able]

vnſtrayned *adj.* unconstrained,
untroubled 248 [OE un- + OF
estrei(g)n]

vnto *prep.* unto 362, 712, 718, 772,
1169, 1212 [Cf. OS untō]

vntrwe *adj.* untrue, false 897 [OE
untrēowe]

vp *adv.* up 35, 177, 191, 254, etc.
[OE up]

vpen. *See* open

vpon *adj. See* open

vpon *prep.* upon 57, 370, 814, 824,
etc. into 59 in 545 to 1196
vpone upon 1054 *adv.* on it 208
upon 640 [OE up + on]

vrþe. *See* erþe

vrþely *adj.* earthly 135 [OE eorþ-līc]

vtwyth *adv.* outwardly, from
without 969 [OE ūt + wiþ]

vus *pers. pron. 1 plur. acc. and dat.* us,
to us 454, 520, 553, 556, etc.
used as subject 552 we (second
occurrence) [OE ūs]

vyf. *See* wyf

vygour *n.* strength, vigor 971 [AF
vigour]

vyne *n.* vineyard 504, 507, 521, 525,
etc. uyne 502 [OF vine]

vyrgyn *adj.* virgin 426 vergyneȝ *n.
plur.* virgins 1099 [AF virgine]

vys *n.* face, visage 750 vyſe 254 [OF
vis]

vyſayge *n.* face, visage 178 [OF
visage]

vyueȝ. *See* wyf

W

wace. *See* watȝ

wade *v.* wade 143, 1151 [OE wadan]

wage *v.* offer security or certainty (?)
(MED); bring reward (?) (OED)
416★ [ONF wagier]

wakned *pret. 1 sing.* awoke 1171 [OE
wæcnan]

wal *n.* wall 1017, 1026 walle *coll.*
walls 917 [OE wall]

wale *v.* perceive, distinguish 1000,
1007 [Cf. OI val]

walk *v.* walk 399 welke *pret. 1 sing.*
walked 101 *pret. 3 sing.* 711 [OE
wealcan]

wallande *pres. p.* welling, flowing
forth 365 [OE weallan]

walle. *See* wal

walte *pp.* removed 1156 [OE
wæltan]

wan. *See* wynne *v.*

wanig *Scribal error for* wrang wrong
Morris (?); *scribal error for* waning
diminution (Gollanz), harm
(Vantuono) (?) 558★

war *adj.* aware 1096 [OE wær]

warde *adv. expressing direction of
movement or relative position* (w/
pers. pron. and prep.) *in* to hym
warde toward him 820 fro me
warde across from me 981 [OE
weard]

ware. *See* were

warpe *v.* utter, sing 879 [OE
weorpan]

waſcheȝ *pres. 3 sing.* washes 655

wefch *pret. 3 sing.* washed 766
[OE wæscan]

waffe. *See* **wat3**

wate. *See* **wot**

water *n.* body of water 107, 299,
318, 1077, etc. water 111, 122,
139, 143, etc. *gen sing.* of the
water 230 [OE wæter]

wat3 *pret. 1 sing.* was 412, 584, 1088,
1096, etc. *pret. 2 sing.* were 372,
375, 474 *pret. 3 sing.* was 15, 45,
53, 97, etc. *pret. 3 plur* were 1065,
1123 **wace** *pret. 3 sing.* was 65
waffe *pret. 3 plur.* were 1108,
1112 [OE wæs]

wawe3 *n. plur.* waves 287 [OE
wagian]

wax *pret. 3 sing.* flowed 649 **wex**
grew 538, 648 [OE weaxan]

way *n.* way 350, 580 **waye3** *plur.*
ways 691 [OE weg]

way *adv.* away 718 [OE a-weg]

wayne3 *pres. 3 sing.* brings 131
vayned *pp.* brought, carried 249
[OE wægen, bewægnan]

wayted *pret. 1 sing.* waited, watched
14 [OF waitier]

we *pers. pron. 1 plur. nom.* we 251,
378, 379, 380, etc. [OE wē]

webbe3 *n. plur.* fabrics 71 [OE
web(b)]

wedde *v.* wed 772 [OE weddian]

weddyng *n.* wedding 791 [OE
weddung]

wede *n.* garment, clothing 748, 766
wede3 *plur.* clothing 1102, 1112,
1133 [OE wæd, wæde]

weete. *See* **wete**

wel *adv.* well 164, 302, 411, 505, 673
much 145, 148 very 528, 537 *adj.*
fortunate 239, 1187 [OE wel]

welcum *interj.* welcome 399 [OE
wilcuma]

wele *n.* wealth 14 weal, well-being
133, 342, 394 **wele3** *plur.* joys
154 [OE wela]

welke. *See* **walk**

welkyn *n.* sky, the heavens 116 [OE
wolcen]

welle *n.* well 365, 649 [OE wielle]

welne3 *adv.* nearly, almost 528
welnygh just 581 [OE welnēah]

wely *adj.* happy, blissful 101 [OE
welig]

wemle3 *adj.* without spot or blemish
737 [OE wam(m + lēas]

wemme *n.* blemish, flaw 221, 1003
[OE wam(m]

wende *v.* go away, depart 643 **went**
pret. 3 sing. went, passed through
1130 **wente** *pret. 3 plur.* went
525 departed 631 *pret. 1 sing.* 761
[OE wendan]

wene *pres. 1 sing.* ween, suppose,
believe 47, 201 *v.* doubt 1141
wende *pret. 1 sing.* supposed,
believed 1148 [OE wēnan]

wer (1) *pret. 3 sing.* wore 205 [OE
werian]

wer (2). *See* **were**

were *pret. 3 plur.* were 6, 87, 621,
739, etc. *pret. 3 sing. subj.* were,
would be 32, 263, 452, 849, etc.
was 139, 1142, 1156 *pret. 2 sing.*
subj. were 264 *pret. 1 sing subj.*
were 287, 1167 would be 288
wer *pret. 3 plur.* were 68, 641
pret. 3 sing. subj. were, would be
490, 930, 1092 *pret. 2 sing. subj.*
were 972 **ware** *pret. 3 plur.* were
151, 1027 **wern** *pret. 3 plur.* were
71, 73, 82, 110, etc. *pret. 2 plur.*
were 251, 378 **werne** *pret. 3 plur.*
were 585 **wore** *pret. 3 sing. subj.*

might be 142, *pret. 3 plur.* were 154, 574 *pret. 3 sing.* was 232 [OE wǣron, wǣre, wǣren]

werke *n.* work 599 [OE weorc]

werkmen *n. plur.* workmen 507 [OE weorcmann]

werle *n.* covering, attire; circlet (?) 209* [?]

wern, werne. *See* were

weſch. *See* waſcheʒ

weſternays *adj.* askew, awry 307* (?MED) *adv.* wrongfully, perversely (?OED)[OE western(e, westreis; OF bestorneis]

wete *adj.* wet 761 **weete** 1135 [OE wǣt]

weþer. *See* wheþer

weue *v.* go 318 **veued** *pp.* brought, conveyed 976 [Cf. ON viefa]

weuen *pres. 3 plur.* weave 71 [OE wefan]

wex. *See* wax

whalleʒ *n. gen. sing.* whale's 212 [OE hwæl]

wham. *See* who

what *interrog. adj.* what 249, 392, 475, 479, etc. *interrog. pron.* what 331, 336 *rel. adj.* what 463, 794 *indef. adj.* whatever 523 *adv.* why 1072 **quat** *rel. pron.* what 186, 293, *interrog. adj.* 755, 771 [OE hwæt]

whateʒ *n. plur.* fortunes *in* byrþ whateʒ birth order, fortunes of birth 1041 [OE hwatu]

when *conj.* when 332, 335, 347, 405, etc. **quen** 40, 79, 93, 115, etc. [OE hwanne]

where *conj.* where 68, 617 **quere** 376 **quere þ**ᵗ where 65 [OE hwǣr]

whete *n.* wheat 32 [OE hwǣte]

wheþer *adv.* and yet, however 581, 826 [OE hwæþ(e)re]

wheþer *conj.* whether 130, 604 **weþer** 565 [OE hwæþer]

who *pron.* who 1138 you who 344 **quo** who 427, 678, 709, 747, 827 one who 693 **quom** *dat.* whom 453 **wham** 131 [OE hwā]

why *adv.* why 329, 338, 515, 634 **quy** 561 **wy** 290, 533, 564 **why** *interj.* why 769 [OE hwī]

whyle *adv.* formerly 15 [OE hwīle]

whyt *adj.* white 163, 178, 197, 1133 **whyte** 219 **quyt** 207, 842, 1011, 1150 **quyte** 220, 844, 1137 **qwyte** 1102 [OE hwīt]

with. *See* wyth

wlonc *adj.* excellent 903 **wlonk** lush, lovely 122, 1171 [OE wlonc]

wo *n.* woe 56, 154 **woe** *dat.* in woe 342 [OE wā]

wod *n.* wood 122 [OE wudu]

wode *adj.* mad, insane 743 [OE wōd]

wod-ſchaweʒ *n. plur.* thickets, groves 284 [OE wudu + sc(e)aga]

woʒe *n.* wall 1049 [OE wāg]

woghe *n.* evil, wrong 622 [OE wōh]

wolde (1) (*pret. of* **wyl**) *pret. 3 sing.* would 304, 488, 772, 1195 would wish 451 *pret. 1 sing.* would 390, 910, 977, 1155 *pret. 2 sing* 391 *pret. 1 plur.* would wish 849 **woldeʒ** *pret. 2 sing.* would 410 [OE wolde]

wolde (2) *v.* be the cause of, be responsible for 812 [OE wealdan, waldan]

woldeʒ. *See* wolde (1)

wolen *adj.* woolen 731 [Late OE wullen]

wolle *n.* wool 844 [OE wull]

wommon *n. gen.* woman's, womanly 236 [OE wīfman]

won *v.* dwell 298, 315, 644, 918 **wony** 284 **wone3** *pres. 3 plur.* dwell 404 **wonys** *pres. 3 sing.* dwells 47 [OE wunian]

won *n.* dwelling place, palace 1049 **wone3** *plur.* barns 32 dwelling places 917, 924, 1027 [ON vān]

wonde *v.* hesitate, flinch 153 [OE wandian]

wonder *adj.* wondrous 221, 1095 [OE wundor-]

wone3. *See* **won** *v.* and *n.*

wonne. *See* **wynne** *v.*

wont *pp. adj.* accustomed 15 customary **wonte** 172 [OE gewunod]

wonted *pret. 3 sing.* wanted, lacked 215 [ON vanta]

wony, wonys. *See* **won** *v.*

worchen *v.* work 511 **wyrke3** *imp. plur.* work 536 **wro3t** *pret. 3 plur.* worked 555 did 631 *pp.* created 638 *pret. 3 sing.* made 748 committed 825 *pp.* committed 824 **wro3te** *pret. 3 plur.* worked 525 **wro3ten** committed 622 [OE wyrcan]

worde *n. coll.* words, speech 294 **worde3** *plur.* statements 291 words 307, 314, 367, 819 [OE word]

wore. *See* **were**

worlde *n.* world 65, 293, 424, 476, etc. [OE weorold]

worſchyp *n.* worship, honor 394, 479 [OE weorðscipe]

worte3 *n. plur.* plants, herbs 42 [OE wyrt]

worþe *adj.* (1) worthy 100 **worþy** 494, 616 [OE weorþ + y]

worþe *adj.* (2) worth 451 [OE weorþ]

worþe *pres. 3 sing. subj.* let there be 362* **worþen** *pp.* changed, converted 394 [OE weorðan]

worþy. *See* **worþe** *adj.* (1)

worþyly *adj. subst.* worthy one 47 **worthyly** *adj.* worthy 846 **worþly** 1073 *adv.* worthily, becomingly 1133 [OE weorðlic]

wot *pres. 1 sing.* know 47, 201, 1107 **wate** 502 **woſt** *pres. 2 sing.* know 411 **woſte** 293 **wyſte** *pret. 1 sing.* knew 65, 376 **wyſte3** *pret. 2 sing.* knew 617 [OE witan]

woþe *n.* danger 375 **woþe3** perils 151 [ON vāðe]

wounde *n.* wound 650, 1135, 1142 [OE wund]

wra3te *pret. 3 sing.* suffered anguish, was wracked 56 [OE wærcan]

wrang *adv.* wrongly 614 *n.* wrong 631 **wrange** *n.* wrong 15 *adv.* wrongly 488 [Late OE wrang]

wrathþe *n.* wrath 362 [OE wrǣððu]

wreched *adj.* wretched 56 [OE wrecca]

writ *n.* scripture 997 **wryt** 592 [OE writ]

wro *n.* nook or corner; passage 866 [ON rā]

wro3t, wro3te, wro3ten. *See* **worchen**

wroken *pp.* rescued, delivered 375 [OE wrecan]

wroþe *adj.* angry, indignant 379 [OE wraþ]

wryt. *See* **writ**

wryte3 *pres. 3 sing.* writes 1033 **wryten** *pp.* written 834, 866, 871 [OE wrītan]

wryþe *v.* turn aside 350, 488

wryþen twist oneself about, strain 411 [OE wriðan]

wᵗ. *See* **wyth**

wᵗdroȝ *pret. 3 sing.* withdrew, removed 658 [OE wið + dragan]

wᵗinne *prep.* within 440, 679, 966 *adv.* within, on the inside 1027 [Late OE wiþinnan]

wᵗnay *imper. sing.* deny, refuse 916 [OE wiþ- + OF neier]

wᵗoute, wᵗouten. *See* **wythouten**

wy. *See* **why**

wyde *adj.* wide 1135 [OE wīd]

wyf *n.* wife 846 **vyf** 772 **vyueȝ** *plur.* wives 785 [OE wīf]

wyȝ *n.* man, person 100, 131, 722 **wyȝeȝ** *plur.* men, people 71, 579 [OE wiga]

wyȝt *n.* person 338 **wyȝte** 494 [OE wiht]

wyȝte *adj.* strong, courageous 694 [ON vīgt]

wyl *aux. v. forming fut. 3 sing.* will 350, 443, 965 *pres. 1 sing.* will, intend 558 *pres. 2 sing. subj.* wish to, would 794 [OE willan]

wyl *conj.* until 528 [OE þā hwīle þe]

wylle *n.* will 56, 131 [OE willa]

wylneȝ *pres. 2 sing.* wish 318 [OE wilnian]

wyn *n.* wine 1209 [OE wīn]

wyngeȝ *n. plur.* wings 93 [ON vængir]

wynne *v.* win, attain 579, 694, 722 **wan** *pret. 1 sing.* came 107 **wonne** *pp.* won 32 arrived 517 [OE winnan]

wynne *adj.* pleasant, delightful, winsome 154, 647 [OE wyn(n)]

wynter *n.* as *adj.* winter 116 [OE winter]

wyrd *n.* fate, destiny 249 **wyrde** 273

[OE wyrd]

wyrkeȝ. *See* **worchen**

wys *adj.* wise 748 [OE wīs]

wyſchande *pres. p.* wishing for, desiring 14 [OE wȳscan]

wyſe *n.* way, manner, fashion 101, 1095 guise, state of things 133 [OE wīse]

wyſe *v.* show, appear 1135 [OE wīsian]

wyſte, wyſteȝ. *See* **wot**

wyt *n.* wit, intellect 903 **wytte** 294 [OE wit]

wyth *prep.* with 40, 54, 80, 94, etc. **wᵗ** 74, 204, 254, 296, etc. **with** 200, 202, 837 [OE wið]

wythouten *prep.* without 36, 48, 390, 782, etc. **wᵗoute** 644, 695 **wᵗouten** 12, 24, 60, 189, etc. beyond 1104★ [Late OE wiþūtan]

wytte. *See* **wyt**

wyþer *adj.* opposite 230 [OE wiþer]

Y

ydel *adj.* idle 514, 515, 531, 533 [OE īdel]

yȝe *n.* eye 302, 567, 1153 **yȝen** *plur.* eyes 183, 200, 254, 296 [OE ēage]

yle *n.* isle 693 [OF ile]

ynde *n.* indigo 76, 1016 [AF ynde]

yor. *See* **your**

yot. *See* **ȝede**

your *poss. pron.* your 257, 258, 305, 306, etc. **yor** 761 [Late OE ēower]

yow *pers. pron. 2 plur.* you 470, 524, 928 *sing.* you 287, 471, 913, 951 [OE ēow]

yſaye *n.* Isaiah 797, 819

yuore *n.* ivory 178 [OF yviore]

Abbreviations

adj.	adjective	LG	Low German
acc.	accusative	*masc.*	masculine
adv.	adverb	MDu	Middle Dutch
AF	Anglo-French	ME	Middle English
art.	article	MED	Middle English Dictionary
aux.	auxiliary	MHG	Middle High German
Cf.	*confer* (compare)	MLG	Middle Low German
CF	Central French	MnScot	Modern Scottish
coll.	collective	*n.*	noun
comp.	comparative	*neut.*	neuter
conj.	conjunction	*nom.*	nominative
correl.	correlative	Norw.	Norwegian
dat.	dative	OE	Old English
def.	definite	OED	Oxford English Dictionary
demonst.	demonstrative	OF	Old French
dial.	dialect	OI	Old Icelandic
Du.	Dutch	OIr	Old Irish
eccl.	Ecclesiastical	ON	Old Norse
etc.	*et cetera* (and others)	ONF	Old North French
F	French	OS	Old Saxon
fem.	feminine	OSwed	Old Swedish
fut.	future	*p.*	participle
gen.	genitive	*pass.*	passive
ger.	gerund	*perf.*	perfect
imp.	imperative	*pers.*	personal
impers.	impersonal	*plur.*	plural
indef.	indefinite	*poss.*	possessive
inf.	infinitive	*pp.*	past participle
interj.	interjection	*prep.*	preposition
interrog.	interrogative	*pres.*	present
L	Latin	*pret.*	preterite

prog.	progressive
pron.	pronoun
refl.	reflexive
rel.	relative
sing.	singular
subj.	subjunctive
subst.	substantive
superl.	superlative
Sw.	Swedish
trans.	transitive
v.	verb
vi.	intransitive verb
voc.	vocative
vt.	transitive verb
w/	with
Wel.	Welsh
WFlem	West Flemish

How to Read the
Manuscript Hand

The *Pearl* manuscript is written throughout in a minuscule alphabet, with capital letters, for the most part, only used decoratively. With the exception of the capital "I," which is regularly used for the first person pronoun, majuscules appear, with a few exceptions, only at the beginning of stanzas; decorated capitals, in blue ink, with flourishes in red, are used at the beginnings of stanza groups. The minuscule alphabet consists of 27 characters, as shown below; most of these will be easily recognizable to the modern reader, but there are several notable differences in the characters and the way they are used from the alphabet in use today. A very detailed description of the miniscule alphabet with graphic depictions from the Pearl manuscript can be found at the Cotton Nero A.x. Project website, under "Transcription/The Alphabet."

Minuscule Alphabet

In the *Pearl* manuscript, the letter "i" is used for what appears as two separate letters in the modern English alphabet, the vowel "i" and the consonant "j." It is also the only letter in the alphabet where a majuscule is regularly used in the poem. A "long i" is invariably used for the first person pronoun, and sometimes to begin words, where it usually stands for the consonant "j," but sometimes for the vowel "i." (When a capital "I" is called for at the beginning of a stanza, where decorative capitals normally appear, a more elaborate form of the letter, with a crossbar at the top, appears; as shown in the examples of majuscules on page 277.)

The letter "s" has two forms in the manuscript, a "long s" which is used everywhere except at the ends of words, and which looks something like an "f" without the crossbar, and a shorter "s" which more nearly resembles a modern printed "s" in form. The "long s" is represented in the transcription of the manuscript by the character "ſ" (which appears in italics as "*ſ*"). As there is no phonemic or phonetic difference between the long and short "s," most editions of *Pearl* do not distinguish between them, but I have preserved the distinction between the two in the manuscript transcription, as it is intended to serve in part as a key to reading the manuscript hand, in this appendix, and in the glossary.

The letters "u" and "v" are both used to stand for what appears as both the vowel "u" and the consonant "v" in the modern English alphabet. The letter "v" is used word-initially for both the vowel and the consonant, and the letter "u" is used for both the vowel and the consonant within words. In addition, "w" is sometimes used where we find a "u" in modern English, as in the spellings *fortwne* ("fortune"), *blwe* ("blue"), *trwe* ("true"), and also where we find a "v" or "u" in modern English, as in *wawes* ("waves") and *bycawse* ("because"). The letter "v" is sometimes used where a "w" is found in modern English, as in *vyf* 772 ("wife") and *vyueȝ* 785 ("wives").

There are two letters in the alphabet used in *Pearl*, thorn (þ) and yogh (ȝ), which no longer form part of the English alphabet. The thorn invariably stands for "th," although the letters "th" are also used at times, especially in initial position when the first letter of the word is capitalized. The character yogh is used for what is really two different letters: word-finally, it usually stands for the letter "z," which is normally used to form the plurals of nouns, and the present first person singular endings of verbs, for example, where an "s" would be used in modern English (although the short "s" is also occasionally used for this purpose in the manuscript). Although phonemically this is really a different letter than the yogh used elsewhere than at the ends of words, it is not possible to distinguish the form of the character in the manuscript from the character employed in the other uses of the yogh outlined below, so no distinction has been made between the two letters in the transcription. It should also be noted that there are a few words in which yogh is used word-finally where it does not stand for "z," for example *þurȝ* ("through"), *þaȝ* ("though"), and *borȝ* ("burg"), where "gh" is found in modern English, and *faȝ* ("saw"), *boȝ* ("bow") and *forȝ* ("sorrow"), where "w" is found in modern English; these uses, however, are relatively rare.

In word-initial position yogh is used where a "y" is found in modern English, as in *ȝet* ("yet"), *ȝe* ("ye"), *ȝore* ("yore"), *ȝonge* ("young'), *ȝere* ("year"); in *byȝonde* ("beyond"), this usage is found in the initial letter of the second element of a compound word. Very rarely, yogh is used in word-initial position where we find a "g" in modern English, e.g. *ȝates* ("gates"). Within words, yogh has several values. Rarely, and only after "a," "o," "l," or "r," it is used where we use "w" in modern English, as in *folȝed* ("followed"), *sorȝe* ("sorrow") and *boȝe* ("bow"). Most often, it is used where we find "gh" in modern English, especially before "t," as in *nyȝt* ("night"), *soȝte* ("sought"), *myȝt* ("might"), *noȝt* ("nought"), *lyȝt* ("light"), but also before other letters, as in *hiȝe* ("high") and *nieȝbor* ("neighbor"). In word-final position, "gh" is usually substituted for yogh in this usage—sometimes with a comma-shaped abbreviation above the "h" to indicate a final "e," as in *lenghe* ("length"), *nygh* ("nigh"), and *innoghe* ("enough").

The vowels "i" and "y" are used interchangably where "i" is used in modern English, with "y" more commonly used than "i"; "y" is also generally used rather than "i" at the ends of words, as in modern English.

The letter "q" is sometimes found where we use "w" in modern English, as in *quere* 7 ("where"), *quen* 40 ("when"), *quat* 186 ("what"), *quyt* 207 ("white"), *quo* 427 ("who"), *quy* 561 ("why"), *queþer* 606 ("whether"); however, forms of these words with "w" are also found: *where* 68, *when* 332, *what* 248, *whyt* 163 ("white"), *who* 344, *why* 329, and *wheþer* 130 ("whether").

The letters "i," "m," "n," and "u" are sometimes difficult to distinguish in the manuscript as all of them are composed of "minims," a stroke of the pen identical with the letter "i." The letters "n" and "u" are both composed of two minims, for example, and so cannot be distinguished from each other graphically; it is necessary to rely on the context to determine which letter is meant. When any combination of these four letters appears in the manuscript, the reading is ambiguous apart from context; for example, a series of three minims could be read as "m," "in," "iu," "ui," or "ni"; a series of four minims could be read as "mi," "un," "nu," "ini," etc. At times a "dotted i," with an oblique line above it, similar to an acute accent, is used to clarify the ambiguity, but in most cases the reader must decide from context which letters are meant.

As capital letters are seldom used in the manuscript, there is not a complete alphabet of majuscules; examples of those which are found are given below.

Examples of Majuscules

A very detailed description with graphic depictions from the *Pearl* manuscript of many of these capital letters can be found at the Cotton Nero A.x. Project website, under "Transcription/Capital Letters." For examples of illuminated capitals (reproduced in black and white), see the illustrations printed opposite the translation.

Another feature of the script that may cause difficulty in deciphering it is the use of combined letters, examples of which are given below. The principle behind the combining of letters is often the use of the final vertical stroke of the initial letter as the initial vertical stroke of the following letter, or as part of it. In combinations beginning with a long "s," such as "st" and "sc," the top stroke of the "s" is continued downward without a break to form the vertical stroke of the following letter. After "o" and sometimes "b," a form of "r" which resembles the Arabic numeral "2," or a capital "R" without the initial vertical stroke, is used. When the letter "b" is combined with a following vowel, it can easily be mistaken for the letter "l," except that the bottom of the vertical stroke curves to the right and connects with the following letter. Combinations with the letter "p" consist of the initial vertical stroke and a horizontal stroke, with the bow of the "p" replaced by the vertical stroke of the following letter. There are other forms of combined letters besides those shown below; letters combined in the poem include ba, be, bo, br, da, de, do, go, ha, he, ho, hr, or, pa, pe, po, pp, sc, sp, st, sv, and some three letter combinations: dor, por, hor, and ppe (the list is not exhaustive). A very detailed description with graphic depictions from the manuscript of many of these combined letters can be found at the Cotton Nero A.x. Project website, under "Transcription/Joined Letters."

Examples of Combined Letters

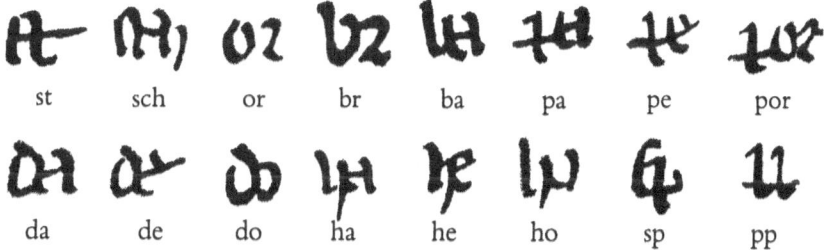

| st | sch | or | br | ba | pa | pe | por |

| da | de | do | ha | he | ho | sp | pp |

Another difficulty in reading the script is the frequent use of conventional abbreviations. Since Latin was the universal scholarly language of the Middle Ages, most of these abbreviations were derived from those commonly in use in Latin manuscripts; the standard reference work on these abbreviations is Adriano Capelli's *Lexicon Abbreviaturarum*; a translation of the introduction to this work into English, *The Elements of Abbreviation in Medieval Latin Paleography*, by David Heimann and Richard Kay, is also available for those who do not read Italian. However, there are a number of abbreviations used in *Pearl* which cannot be found in Cappelli. A very detailed description with graphic depictions from the manuscript of many of these abbreviations can be found at the Cotton Nero A.x. Project website, under "Transcription/Abbreviations."

Many of these conventional abbreviations consist of symbols above words, which stand for omitted letters. One of the most frequently used is a horizontal macron, the *linnea retta o leggermente curvata* or "straight or slightly curved line" of Cappelli (*Lexicon* xxiv; *Elements* 13–14), which when used over a vowel stands for an omitted "n" or "m"; see abbreviations for *in*, *hym*, and *innoghe* below (this symbol is also used as a general sign of abbreviation, as described below).

A symbol resembling a question mark written backwards, the *punto interrogativo rivolto* or "backward question mark" of Cappelli (*Lexicon* xxxiv; *Elements* 23) above a letter stands for the omitted letters "er" or "re" following that letter; see abbreviations for *neuer*, *oper*, *per*, and *precios* below.

A symbol resembling a question mark lying on its left side, a "modern tilde" (Cotton Nero A.x Project), or a flattened miniscule "u" above a letter stands for "ur" or "ru" following that letter; see abbreviations for *your*, *floury*, and *true* below.

A symbol resembling a comma or single quotation mark above an "h" at the end of a word stands for a final "e"; see abbreviation for *innoghe* below.

An abbreviation symbol which appears several times in *Pearl* above the cross stroke of letter "g" in the word "grace" and related words, and which takes various forms, but which is meant to represent a "superscript single lobed a" (Cotton Nero A.x Project) stands for the letters "ra"; see the abbreviation for *gracous* below.

Some abbreviations are additions to letters below the line rather than signs appearing above the line. A "p" with a horizontal stroke added to the bottom of the descender stands for "per"; a "p" with a loop joining the left end of the horizontal stroke representing the bottom of the bow with the descender stands for "pro" (see abbreviations for *pertermynable* and *profete* below).

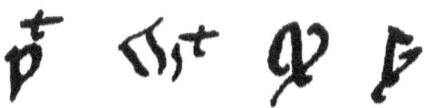

Other abbreviations appear on the same line as the other letters; in this manuscript, a symbol resembling a large numeral "9" with the top loop on the base line and with the vertical stroke descending below the line and leaning sharply to the right, the *grossa virgula* or "outsize comma" of Capelli (Capelli, *Lexicon* xxiv–xxvi; *Elements* 15) represents word-final "us" (see abbreviation for *gloryous* below).

The abbreviations discussed above are used to represent omissions within words; there are also a number of whole-word abbreviations used in the poem. The most common of these is the symbol which is used almost invariably for the word "and" in the manuscript. This abbreviation takes its form from a system of shorthand developed by Cicero's secretary Tiro, known as "Tironian" notation. In this manuscript the "Tironian *nota*" (Cotton Nero A.x Project) is invariably crossed with an oblique line.

A wavy line, usually with two peaks, or a "superscript miniscule u" (Cotton Nero A.x Project) stands for the omitted letters "ou"; in *Pearl*, this abbreviation is only used above the letter thorn, in abbreviation for the word *þou*.

A thorn with a superscript "t" stands for *that*; a "w" with a superscript "t" for *with*. A "q" with the upright stroke crossed below the bow at a forty-five degree angle by a hook-shaped stroke, hook upwards, with the hook sometimes making a loop with the top of the "q" (see illustration) is a common medieval abbreviation for the Latin word *quod*, and in this manuscript is used for Middle English *quod*, meaning "said." A long "s" with a similar obligue crossing stroke stands for the word *sir*.

Many whole-word abbreviations developed from Latin abbreviations for *nomina sacra*, or sacred names, which were abbreviated not simply for convenience, but also to express reverence for God, as the Hebrews used the tetragrammaton. The scribe uses two abbreviations for the name of Jesus in *Pearl*, for example: one consists of the letters "Ihu" with a macron above the last two letters, and the other of the letters "Ihc" with a macron above the the last two letters.

The "h" in these abbreviations does not stand for Christ's middle initial (though it has sometimes been taken for that) but was developed from the Greek capital *eta*, or long "e," which resembles a Roman capital "H"; the "c" originally stood for one form of the Greek capital *sigma*, or "s." Over time, the Greek abbreviation for the name of Jesus, consisting of the first three letters of his name in the Greek alphabet, with an abbreviation symbol indicating the suspension of the ending, was adopted by scribes who were ignorant of its origin, and who transcribed the *epsilon* as a lower-case Roman "h" and the *sigma* as a lower-case Roman "c" (Clemens and Graham 89). In this case the macron stands not for an omitted "m" or "n" as it does when it appears above a vowel in this manuscript, but as a general symbol of abbreviation indicating the suspension of the word ending or the omission of letters within the word.

The scribe also uses several forms of a conventional abbreviation for "Jerusalem." His regular abbreviation for this word is the letters "Ilrm" with a macron above the "m"; once he uses the letters "Ihrm," with a macron above the "m," and once he uses the letters "Irlm" with a macron above the "m." The macron in these abbreviations again is a general symbol of abbreviation, rather than a symbol representing specific missing letters.

In two other abbreviations, the scribe's abbreviation for "Israel," which consists of the letters "Isrl" with a macron above the "r," and the scribe's usual abbreviation for the name "John," which appears in various forms, but most commonly as the letters "Iohn" with a macron above the "n," the macron seems to stand for the letters "ae" and "a" respectively.

In order to learn to read the manuscript it is also necessary to learn how to pronounce Middle English, as most readers vocalize words in their heads even when reading silently; knowledge of the rules of pronunciation is also essential for classroom discussion of the poem. While a complete guide to the pronunciation of the poem, including dialectal variations in pronunciation, is beyond the scope of this work, knowledge of a few basic rules will enable the student of Middle English to at least approximate the proper pronunciation. Continued linguistic study and especially repeated practice in reading aloud, as well as listening to and imitating sound models, will be necessary for those who wish to master this skill (a CD of the entire poem recited in Middle English by Allen Gaylord is available from the Chaucer Studio). The rules of thumb given here are intended simply to give the beginner the essential information necessary to begin this process.

Most consonants are pronounced as in Modern English, the main difference being that consonants which are silent in Modern English, for example, "k" before "n" and "gh" before "t" as in "knight," "l" before "f" as in "half," "g" before "n" as in "gnaw," and "w" before "r" as in "write," were still pronounced in Middle English.

Word-finally, in the dialect of the Northwest Midlands in which *Pearl* was written, the letter "b" was evidently unvoiced and pronounced as "p," as can be seen in the variant spellings *lombe* ("lamb," line 846) and *lomp* ("lamb," line 815). This pronunciation allowed the poet to pun on "lamb" and "lamp" in *lambe ly3t* (line 1046), which can be read as both "lamp light" and "lamb light."

"C" was pronounced as a "hard c" or "k," as in Modern English "kill"; "ch" was pronounced like the "ch" in Modern English "church," and not like "sh" as in Modern English "chivalry."

"D" word-finally was evidently unvoiced and pronounced as "t," as can be seen from the spelling of past-tense weak verbs with "t" rather than "d," as in *justyfyet* ("justified," line 700), and by the spelling of words with etymological "t" with "d" instead, as in *marked* ("market," line 513).

"G" was usually pronounced as a "hard g," as in Modern English "gill," and not as a "soft g" like "j" as in "Jill"; however, when followed by "e" and either "m" or "n" it was sometimes pronounced like "j," for example in *gemme* ("gem"), *generacyoun* ("generation"), and *gentyl* ("gentle"). Medially, "gg" usually represents a "hard g," but in words which in Modern English have a "soft g" it may represent the "j" sound, as in *iugged* ("judged"). Word-finally, "g" was sometimes unvoiced and pronounced like "k," as can be seen from the rhyming of *among* with *wlonc* and *honc* in stanza XV, 6.

Yogh (3) was pronounced in several different ways, according to its position in the word. Initially, yogh was pronounced like "y," as in Modern English "yet." It had the same sound after the vowels "e," "i," or "y," for example in the Middle English words *y3e* ("eye") and *hi3e* ("high"), which unlike their Modern English counterparts were pronounced with two syllables. Within words or at the ends of words, yogh or "gh" sometimes represented the sound of "w," as in *fol3ed* ("followed"), or *inno3e* ("enough"), which we know from its use in rhyme was pronounced "enow" rather than with an "f" sound as in Modern

English "enough." Before "t" and after "e," "i," or "y," yogh or "gh" was pronounced like the "ch" in German *ich* (for example, in Middle English *ry3t*, "right"); before "t" and after "a" and "o" it was pronounced like the "ch" in Scottish *loch* or German *Bach* (for example, in Middle English *so3te*, "sought"). It had the same value word-finally in the word *þa3*, "though." However, at the ends of words it more often represented the unvoiced sound of "s" as in Modern English "sill"—though it may also at times have represented the voiced sound of "z" as in Modern English "zeal" (Vantuono 176).

"H" was silent in words derived from French such as *herytage* ("heritage"). This sometimes led to the loss of initial "h" as in *erytage* ("heritage") or *erbere* ("herb garden"). It was pronounced before the "w" in words beginning in Modern English with "wh," such as "where" and "whether."

Consonantal "i" was pronounced as "j," for example in *ieul* ("jewel") and *ioy* ("joy").

"K" was pronounced before "n," even where it is silent in Modern English, as in *knaw* ("know") and *knelande* ("kneeling").

"L" was pronounced before "f," even where it is silent in Modern English, as in *half* ("half").

"Q" was sometimes pronounced as in Modern English, as in *quen* ("queen") and *quelle* ("quell, kill"), and sometimes as "w," as in *quen* ("when") and *quat* ("what").

"S" word-finally usually represents the voiced sound in Modern English "sill," rather than the unvoiced "z" sound which it has in the same position in Modern English.

Thorn (þ) or "th" can represent either the sound of "th" in Modern English "the" or "clothe," or the unvoiced sound as in Modern English "thick" or "cloth."

Consonantal "v" usually represents the same sound as in Modern English, but sometimes represents "w," as in *veued* ("weaved") or *vyf* ("wife").

The greatest difference between the pronunciation of Middle English and Modern English is in the pronunciation of vowels and dipthongs. To accurately reproduce the pronunciation of the vowels in *Pearl*, including regional variations in pronunciation local to the northwest Midlands, would require a great deal of study, instruction, and practice; however, by following the guidelines given below, with a reasonable amount of practice and either self-correction or expert guidance, a rough approximation of the proper pronunciation can be achieved which will be sufficient for reading the poem aloud and for class discussion.

The English language beginning around the fifteenth century underwent a change in the pronunciation of long vowels known as the "Great Vowel Shift," in which the place of articulation of these vowels shifted upward, for no known reason. Short vowels were not affected by this phenomenon, so their pronunciation is approximately the same in Middle English as in Modern English, although there are a number of exceptions to this rule. As other European languages did not undergo the Great Vowel Shift, the easiest way to approximate the pronunciation of long vowels in Middle English is to pronounce them as they would be pronounced in a modern European language such as French or Italian.

Long "a" was pronounced like the vowels in French *madame,* or like the "a" in Modern English "father," for example in *name* ("name") and *cas* ("case").

Long "e" had two differing pronunciations, according to whether the vowel was "open" or "closed"; open vowels were pronounced with the jaw lowered, and closed vowels with the jaw raised. If open, long "e" was pronounced like the "ea" in Modern English "breath" or "swear," for example in *deth* ("death") and *bred* ("bread"). If closed, long "e" was pronounced like the "a" in Modern English "mate" or "hay," for example in *deme* ("deem," which sounded Modern English "dame") and *be* ("be," which sounded like Modern English "bay"). It is not always easy to distinguish between open "e" and closed "e" in reading without knowing the history of the word in question; however, as a rule of thumb, if the word is spelled with "ea" in Modern English, like "breath," it most often has an open "e"; if it is spelled "ee" in Modern English, as in "see" or "speed," it most often has a closed "e." Word-final "e" in this manuscript can represent either a short "e," which is sometimes silent and sometimes pronounced as an indeterminate vowel sound or "schwa," or the long closed vowel, as in *charyte,* "charity," or *cortayse,* "courtesy," both words of three syllables.

Long "i" or "y" was pronounced like the vowel sound in "meet" or "peek" in Modern English, for example in *wyf* ("wife") and *bryd* ("bride," which sounded like Modern English "breed").

Long "o" if closed was pronounced like the "o" in Modern English "globe" or "note," for example in *god* ("good," which sounded like Modern English "goad") and *do* ("do," which sounded like Modern English "doe"); if open, it was pronounced like the vowel sound in Modern English "brought" or "law," for example in *loke* ("look," rhyming with Modern English "hawk") and *glowed* ("glowed"). Again, it is not always easy to distinguish open and closed "o" without knowing the history of the word in question.

Long "u" was pronounced like the vowel sound in Modern English "boot," for example in *aboute* ("about") and *out* ("out").

The correct pronunciation of Middle English dipthongs is difficult, not only because vowels and diphthongs show more regional variation than consonants in pronunciation, but also because they can be spelled in many different ways; a detailed discussion of their spelling and pronunciation is beyond the scope of this essay. A good rule of thumb is first to pronounce the individual vowels separately, as above, and then elide them, which will result in an approximately correct pronunciation more often than not.

The best way of learning the correct pronunciation of Middle English is to listen extensively to recordings of scholars reading Middle English texts; it will soon become apparent, however, that there are numerous variations in the way scholars pronounce a given word in Middle English. For the novice, the best advice is still that given by William Strunk and E. B. White in *The Elements of Style*: "If you don't know how to pronounce a word, say it loud!" (12). This will at best lead people to believe you know what you are talking about, and at worst, allow them to hear what you are saying. Watch out for words that were accented differently in Middle English than they are in Modern English, especially words of French descent, such as *honour*, "honor," or *maner*, "manor," both accented on the last syllable, rather than on the first as in Modern English. Whatever else you do, do not become so focused on the pronunciation of individual words that you lose the sense of the rhythm and movement of the language, and above all, recite the poem with feeling, which, like love, covers a multitude of sins.

Works Cited

An Anglo-Saxon Dictionary, Based on the Manuscript Collections of Joseph Bosworth. T. Northcote Toller, ed. Oxford: Oxford UP, 1898; rpt. 1976. Print.

An Anglo-Saxon Dictionary, Based on the Manuscript Collections of Joseph Bosworth. Supplement. T. Northcote Toller, ed. With Revised and Enlarged Addenda by Alistair Campbell. Oxford: Oxford UP, 1921; rpt. 1973. Print.

Arnold, Matthew. "On Translating Homer." London: Longman, 1861. E-Texts for Victorianists. Electronic version 1.0. Ed. Alfred J. Drake. 17 July 2002. Web. 15 June 2011.

Borroff, Marie, trans. *Pearl.* New York: Norton, 1977. Print.

British Library MS Cotton Nero A.x, Series 3. British Library, 2008-2009. (High-resolution digital facsimile, available in the Manuscripts Reading Room of the British Library). DVD.

Capelli, Adriano. *Lexicon Abbreviaturarum: Dizionario di Abbreviature Latine ed Italiane Usate Nelle Carte e Codici Specialmente del Medio-Evo.* 6th ed. Milan: Ulrico Hoepli, 1990; rpt. 2004. Print.

- - - . *The Elements of Abbreviation in Medieval Latin Paleography.* Trans. David Heimann and Richard Kay. University of Kansas Libraries, 1982. Web.

Clemens, Raymond, and Timothy Graham. *Introduction to Manuscript Studies.* Ithaca, New York: Cornell UP, 2007. Print.

The Cotton Nero A.x. Project. Ed. Murray McGillivray. Web.

Gaylord, Allen T. *Pearl: Occasional Readings 19.* The Chaucer Studio, 2009. CD.

Gollancz, Israel, ed. *Pearl: An English Poem of the XIV Century, Edited, with Modern Rendering, together with Boccacio's Olympia.* London: Chatto and Windus, 1921. Print.

Gordon, E. V., ed. *Pearl.* London: Oxford UP, 1953; rpt. 1958. Print.

Middle English Dictionary. Editor-in Chief, Robert E. Lewis. Ann Arbor: Michigan UP, 1954-. Web.

Morris, Richard, ed. *Early English Alliterative Poems in the West-Midland Dialet of the Fourteenth Century, Edited from the Unique Manuscript British Museum MS. Cotton Nero A. x.,* 2nd ed. EETS, OS, 1. London: Oxford UP, 1869; rpt. 1965. Print.

Oxford English Dictionary. Second Edition on CD-ROM (v. 4.0.0.3) London: Oxford UP, 2009. CD.

Pearl: An Edition with Verse Translation. Trans. William Vantuono. Notre Dame: U of Notre Dame P, 1995. Print.

Pearl, Cleanness, Patience, and Sir Gawain: Reproduced in Facsimile from the Unique MS. Cotton Nero A.x in the British Museum. With Introduction by I. Gollancz. EETS, OS, 162. London: Oxford UP, 1923. Print.

Roberts, Jane. *Guide to Scripts used in English Writings up to 1500*. London: British Library, 2008. Print.

Strunk, William, Jr. and E.B. White. *The Elements of Style*. 4th ed. New York: Longman, 1999. Print.

Tolkien, J.R.R., trans. *Sir Gawain and the Green Knight, Pearl, and Sir Orfeo*. Ed. Christopher Tolkien. London: Harper, 1995. Print.

www.ingramcontent.com/pod-product-compliance
Lightning Source LLC
Chambersburg PA
CBHW030623110726
47901CB00002B/290